Chaplaincy for a Plural World

I0095139

Chaplaincy for a Plural World provides a theoretical foundation for an inclusive understanding of chaplaincy and lays out key chaplaincy methods for providing spiritual care in a modern context. Inspired by recent humanist chaplaincy in the Netherlands and based on the interdisciplinary science of humanistic studies, the book explains chaplaincy as a multifaceted profession in which supporting people's search for meaning in life is intertwined with the pursuit of humanizing organizations and society.

The book offers a wide range of methods and practical tools for use by a diverse group of readers: chaplains, other professionals or volunteers, and students in higher education who prepare themselves for spiritual care work in secularizing and pluralizing societies. These methods include such key areas of work as individual counseling, group work, ritual, educational activities, supporting the moral development of individuals, teams, and organizations, conducting research, and doing sociopolitical work. The book fills the meaning gap that secularization has left in Western societies and offers a hopeful perspective for all who strive for a humane and meaningful world.

Carmen Schuhmann is associate professor of humanist chaplaincy studies at the University of Humanistic Studies in Utrecht, the Netherlands.

Annelieke Damen is assistant professor of humanist chaplaincy studies at the University of Humanistic Studies in Utrecht, the Netherlands.

Gaby Jacobs is full professor of humanist chaplaincy studies at the University of Humanistic Studies in Utrecht, the Netherlands.

Marishelle Lieberwerth is completing her master's degree at the University of Humanistic Studies in Utrecht, the Netherlands.

Joanna Wojtkowiak is assistant professor of psychological and spiritual aspects of existential care at the University of Humanistic Studies in Utrecht, the Netherlands.

"Carmen Schuhmann and her team have assembled a groundbreaking contribution to the study of chaplaincy. They strike a balance between the vital theoretical underpinning of spiritual care and practical tools that all chaplains can use immediately. Drawing on the deep history of humanistic spiritual care in the Netherlands, they pose a critical question: how can humanistic spiritual care inform a capacitive definition of 'a good life' for both individuals and societies? Far beyond the Dutch context from which it arises, this book must be studied closely by all who seek to advance the profession of spiritual care."

—**Michael Skaggs**, *PhD, director of programs at the Chaplaincy Innovation Lab*

"The developing field of humanist and non-religious chaplaincy is fast paced and rich, though under-studied. This excellent volume is essential reading for everyone, from practitioners to students to researchers."

—**Andrew Copson**, *chief executive of Humanists UK and president of Humanists International*

"This book meets a critical need for collaboratively developed models of spiritual care based on chaplain-specific competencies. I urge those who teach chaplaincy studies and education to read this comprehensive, worldview-inclusive perspective on spiritual care and chaplaincy based on norms and competencies in humanist chaplaincy and illustrated through compelling case studies."

—**Carrie Doehring**, *PhD, professor emerita of pastoral care and counseling, Iliff School of Theology, Colorado, USA*

Chaplaincy for a Plural World

Humanistic Perspectives

Carmen Schuhmann, Annelieke
Damen, Gaby Jacobs, Marishelle
Lieberwerth, and Joanna Wojtkowiak

Routledge
Taylor & Francis Group

NEW YORK AND LONDON

Designed cover image: ©Getty Images

First published 2026
by Routledge
605 Third Avenue, New York, NY 10158

and by Routledge
4 Park Square, Milton Park, Abingdon, Oxon, OX14 4RN

Routledge is an imprint of the Taylor & Francis Group, an informa business

© 2026 Carmen Schuhmann, Annelieke Damen, Gaby Jacobs, Marishelle Lieberwerth, and Joanna Wojtkowiak
With contributions from: Sylvie de Kubber, Eva Trapman, Emy Spekschoor, Annemieke Kuin, Niels den Toom, Vicky Hölsgens, Tessa Heethaar, and Marjo van Bergen

ISBN: 978-1-032-49246-9 (hbk)
ISBN: 978-1-032-49244-5 (pbk)
ISBN: 978-1-003-42863-3 (ebk)

DOI: 10.4324/9781003428633

Typeset in Optima
by SPi Technologies India Pvt Ltd (Straive)

Contents

Illustrations

Contributors

Marjo van Bergen has worked as a registered humanist chaplain in a broad range of innovative contexts since 2004. She holds a master's degree in Humanistic Studies (University of Humanistic Studies, Utrecht, the Netherlands, 2005) and in Cultural Anthropology (Utrecht University, 1991). Since 2011 she has been affiliated with the University of Humanistic Studies as a supervisor for internships and a lecturer on group counseling. During her career as a humanist chaplain she has regularly published about diverse chaplaincy topics.

Annelieke Damen is assistant professor of Chaplaincy Studies at the University of Humanistic Studies, Utrecht, the Netherlands. She lectures in the humanist chaplaincy master's program. Her research focuses on chaplaincy outcomes and on spiritual care in the outpatient context. She is also a trained chaplain, active in health care.

Tessa Heethaar holds a master's degree in Humanistic Studies, and in Care Ethics and Policy from the University of Humanistic Studies (Utrecht, the Netherlands). She works as a teacher of religious studies at a teacher training college. In addition, she works as a humanist chaplain in a penitentiary.

Vicky Hölsgens holds a PhD in Humanistic Studies (University of Humanistic Studies, Utrecht, the Netherlands) and has worked in several hospitals in the Netherlands as a chaplain. Currently she works at the University Medical Centre Utrecht as a chaplain to support (medical) professionals at the ER and ICU. These departments are (one of) the first to hire a chaplain solely for the support of staff.

Gaby Jacobs is professor of Chaplaincy Studies at the University of Humanistic Studies (UHS), Utrecht, the Netherlands. She holds a master's degree in psychology, and a PhD in Humanistic Studies. She chairs the research group 'Humanist Chaplaincy Studies for a Plural Society' at UHS and the Knowledge Workplace on Spiritual Care and Chaplaincy in the Netherlands. She lectures on the humanist chaplaincy master's program, supervises PhD students, and leads research projects in chaplaincy and spiritual care with a focus on topics such as meaning in life and health; professional identity development; moral learning; and empowerment.

Sylvie de Kubber holds a master's degree in humanistic studies (University of Humanistic Studies, Utrecht, the Netherlands) and currently works as a humanistic chaplain in psychiatry with a focus on addiction care ritual design and arts-based interventions. She is a teacher at the University of Humanistic Studies in the field of dialogue skills, ethics, and grief.

Annemieke Kuin has worked as a hospital chaplain since she graduated from the University of Humanistic Studies (Utrecht, the Netherlands) in 2004. At this university she works as a lecturer practitioner. She also holds a PhD in medical biology and has conducted research in oncology at the Netherlands Cancer Institute and in palliative care at the Free University of Amsterdam.

Marishelle Lieberwerth has a bachelor's degree in Humanistic Studies and is currently completing her master's degree in Humanistic Studies (University of Humanistic Studies, Utrecht, the Netherlands). She is pursuing a career in chaplaincy, following a recent chaplaincy internship at a hospital. She is involved as an organizer and trainer in projects centered around meaning in life, inclusion, diversity, decolonization, and polarization.

Carmen Schuhmann is associate professor of Chaplaincy Studies at the University of Humanistic Studies in Utrecht, the Netherlands, and the director of the Humanistic Studies Master Program. She holds a PhD in mathematics from the University of Leiden (the Netherlands) and has worked as a researcher in the field of algebraic geometry at the University of Essen (Germany). After switching to humanistic studies, she worked for several years as a humanist prison chaplain. Her current research interests include: the relational and socio-political dimensions of meaning in life and spiritual care, moral injury and moral resilience, and chaplaincy in the military.

Emy Spekschoor has a background in fine art and holds a master's degree in Humanistic Studies from the University of Humanistic Studies, Utrecht, the Netherlands. She worked for several years as a humanist chaplain in elderly care in Amsterdam and had a private practice as a celebrant and humanist spiritual caregiver. Currently, she works at the University of Humanistic Studies as a PhD student and as the coordinator of the Celebrant Training Program.

Niels den Toom is assistant professor in Spiritual Care and Chaplaincy Studies at the Tilburg School of Theology (Tilburg University), the Netherlands. He has served as a prison chaplain and university chaplain, and currently works as a chaplain in a nursing home in Breda. He has published on chaplaincy care, case studies and the role of chaplain–researcher. His research focuses on methods in chaplaincy care, public theology, and nonverbal elements in chaplaincy.

Eva Trapman obtained a master's degree in Humanistic Studies at the University of Humanistic Studies in Utrecht, the Netherlands. Since 2018, she has worked as a humanist chaplain in several Dutch (psychiatric) prisons. Since 2022, she has taught Care Ethics at the Bachelor of Nursing at Avans+.

Joanna Wojtkowiak works as assistant professor at the University of Humanistic Studies (Utrecht, The Netherlands). She obtained her PhD in Religious Studies and a Master in Cultural Psychology (both at Radboud University, Nijmegen, the Netherlands). Her research focuses on existential concerns in contemporary post-secular society, new and re-invented rituals, and spiritual care. She has studied questions of meaning and spirituality in various cases, such as death and grief, birth and pregnancy, collective disaster, abortion, and eating disorders. She co-developed the one-year educational Celebrant Training Program at the University Academy and is currently the Director of the Bachelor program at the University of Humanistic Studies.

Introduction

Carmen Schuhmann, Marishelle Lieberwerth, and Gaby Jacobs

Chaplains come into the picture when life loses its self-evidence. They support people when life is at its most intense, beautiful, devastating, or horrendous. This support is needed as much as ever: we live in troubled times. We do not have to look far to see people suffering, despairing, feeling dehumanized, or dehumanizing others amidst an ever-worsening ecological crisis, political polarization, widespread greed and corruption, wars and conflicts, and an increasing inequality in welfare both globally and within societies. At the same time, we see people resisting dehumanization, showing resilience, building hope for the future, taking action, and connecting with others in diversity – co-creating visions of a good life and collaboratively acting on these. Chaplains are able to endure the suffering and also to foster the strength to counter or resist these troubled times, thereby contributing to a humane society in a modest and meaningful way.

Historically, chaplains provided support from within the religious traditions that were taken for granted within society. These traditions offer ideas and practices for staying connected with goodness, even in the face of challenging events and circumstances. In contemporary Western societies, however, religions are no longer the obvious frameworks from which people draw on their journey through life. Taylor (2007) speaks about "a move from a society where belief in God is unchallenged and, indeed, unproblematic, to one in which it is understood to be one option among others" (p. 3). In a 'secular age' – the term that Taylor uses to characterize the current situation in Western societies – one may still have an unwavering belief in God, but it is impossible not to be aware that there are alternatives. The alternatives that are available to people in our globalizing world include a wide variety of worldview traditions, representing a plurality of visions of a good life. People's spiritual lives thus play out in a plural world where they need to navigate a multitude of different notions of how to live a good life, and they often draw from and combine different (religious and nonreligious) worldviews (Ammerman, 2010, Liefbroer, 2020; Wilkins-Laflamme, 2021).

Simultaneously, we see an impoverishment of shared language to talk about and imagine living a good life: "In everyday speech, the term 'the good life' does not have particularly rich connotations" (Lynch, 2002, p. 12). According to Rosa (2016), this has to do with the individualization of people's endeavors to live a good life: "everyone must know for themselves what they want to make of themselves and their lives" (p. 18). This has led to a shift in Western societies towards a quantitative understanding of 'a good life' in terms of the level of resources that, regardless of what vision of the good one aspires to, increase one's chances to achieve this good: "Money, health, and community (in the sense of stable and resilient social relationship), as the three keys to happiness, are seen as fundamental resources that constitute the preconditions of a good life – only to then quietly become hallmarks of the good life itself" (Rosa, 2016, p. 23). In a similar vein, Rijksen and van Heijst (1999) speak about 'worldview illiteracy' in Western societies: there is a lack of language reflecting notions of a good life that express what is of ultimate value, in particular in the face of challenging life events and circumstances. People often turn to individualized psychological language to express existential concerns and struggles – they speak, for instance, about being depressed, over-stimulated, or having experienced a trauma.

In this context, there is a "need for a discourse on chaplaincy which preserves its core value but speaks to people of all religions and none" (Kevern & McSherry, 2015, p. 49; see also Cadge & Rambo, 2022; Doehring, 2015; Grung, 2023). Any contemporary understanding of chaplaincy needs to both offer a critical perspective on the current dominant narrow and impoverished understandings of 'a good life' and accommodate all kinds of worldviews of chaplains and the people they care for. This volume aims to contribute to such an understanding of chaplaincy by drawing from decades of practicing, educating, and theorizing humanist chaplaincy in the Netherlands. The objective is to make insights from humanist chaplaincy productive for all people providing spiritual care, in particular chaplains, working in plural societies, regardless of their worldview.

Terminology

This volume is about humanistic perspectives on chaplaincy and draws from insights about humanist chaplaincy as it was developed in the Netherlands. The terms 'chaplaincy,' 'humanist,' and 'humanistic' require some clarification. As for 'chaplaincy,' there is discussion about the suitability of the term to describe care provided by or to people who identify as nonreligious. Savage (2019) argues that, as most people associate a 'chaplain' with religion, "to require non-religious pastoral carers to describe themselves as some form of 'chaplain' is surely inappropriate, unethical, and could be misleading to service users" (p. 129). Actually, in the Netherlands, the term 'pastoral care(r)' has a Christian connotation too. We have decided to stick with the terms 'chaplain' and 'chaplaincy.' First of all, these terms currently are commonly used, also in relation to spiritual care provision on the basis of humanism. Furthermore, by providing a theoretical underpinning of these terms which is worldview-inclusive, we hope to contribute to a change in perception in which 'chaplain(cy)' is no longer exclusively associated with religion.

As mentioned, both the terms 'humanist' and 'humanistic' are used in this volume. Both adjectives refer to humanism, but we do not use them as synonyms. We use the term 'humanist' to refer to humanism as a world-view: a meaning framework that people may draw from in their search for meaning in life. We therefore speak about a humanist worldview.[1] We also use the term 'humanist' to refer to phenomena and concepts which are intrinsically connected with humanism as a worldview: we speak, for instance, about humanist spirituality, humanist chaplains, and humanist chaplaincy. We use the term 'humanistic' – for instance, in the title of this volume – in relation to perspectives and approaches within academic fields which, on the one hand, are inspired by humanism, and, on the other hand, allow for critical reflection on humanism. In this volume, we draw in particular from humanistic studies, a transdisciplinary academic field in which theoretical reflection on humanist chaplaincy is a central issue and which is introduced below.

Humanist chaplaincy and humanistic studies in the Netherlands

The authors of this volume work in the Netherlands, a country with a unique decades-long history of humanist chaplaincy. This history is closely connected with the work of Jaap van Praag (1911–1981), who played a key role in giving substance to humanism as a worldview in the Netherlands. Derkx and Gasenbeek (1997) point out that van Praag's efforts to theorize humanism and to establish humanist institutions and practices are closely connected with his experiences during World War II. Coming from a Jewish family, van Praag went into hiding during the Dutch occupation by Nazi Germany, but not all of his Jewish friends and family members survived persecution. As he witnessed how easily many people relatively thoughtlessly went along with the Nazi regime, it became his life's mission to strengthen people's resilience against the nihilistic inclination to comply with prevailing and potentially dehumanizing ideas and practices. In van Praag's view, such 'moral resilience' requires personal engagement with a worldview in which human dignity and human solidarity are central values. He aimed to develop humanism as a counterweight against nihilism for people who were seeking reflection on life and inspiration for life outside of the churches.[2] A secondary aim of his work was to secure an equal societal position for nonreligious worldviews and people. With a view to these aims, he co-founded the Dutch Humanist League in 1946 and laid the groundwork for the entry of humanist chaplains in different work contexts (Derkx & Gasenbeek, 1997).

Establishing the profession of humanist chaplaincy in the Netherlands was not without challenges. At first, religious associations deemed humanist chaplains to be incapable of offering moral and spiritual guidance on the basis of their nonreligious worldview. Over time, however, humanist chaplaincy became firmly integrated in public institutions like the military, penitentiaries, and healthcare institutions. At present, chaplains with a variety of worldview backgrounds, including humanist and nondenominational chaplains, are united in one national professional association, and they work together with a view to providing spiritual care to all people, regardless of their worldview (Schuhmann et al., 2021).

In the 1950s, the first humanist chaplains were employed in the Netherlands. Their training was based on a course that van Praag had designed in 1953 for the then new profession of humanist chaplaincy. In 1963, the Humanist Educational Institution was founded, which institutionalized the higher vocational training of humanist chaplains. Over the next two decades, as one of the main professors of this institution, van Praag (1982) further elaborated on his ideas about humanist chaplaincy and humanistic studies (van Praag, 1965). He posited that humanist chaplains should center on the freedom and responsibility of people to develop their own view on what is a life worth living. It is not up to the humanist chaplain to provide people with answers to such life questions as, from a humanist perspective, no definitive answers can be formulated. The task of humanist chaplains is to support people's search for answers to life questions, in particular by engaging in dialogue with them. In doing so, humanist chaplains represent human solidarity (van Praag, 1982, p. 153). This understanding of humanist chaplaincy reflects a view of human beings as fundamentally connected.

In 1989, the Humanist Educational Institution evolved into the University of Humanistic Studies, which led to the exploration of new perspectives on humanist chaplaincy. Elly Hoogeveen (1991) stressed that humanist chaplains need to connect with the lived reality of people instead of focusing on abstract humanist ideals. She also drew attention to the strategic work of humanist chaplains at the level of organizations, which she regarded as an essential part of humanist chaplaincy. Ton Jorna (2008) elaborated on an understanding of humanist chaplaincy as spiritual work, emphasizing the importance of the inner spiritual development of humanist chaplains. Jan Hein Mooren (2013) contributed significantly to the development of the methodical and narrative aspect of humanist chaplaincy. He highlighted the relevance of systematically describing interventions by humanist chaplains for educational purposes and for the professionalization of chaplains. The transition of the training institute for humanist chaplains to an academic institute also involved a broadening of the professional profile of humanist chaplaincy (Halsema & van Houten, 2022). Humanistic studies evolved into a broad transdisciplinary study which centers on the question: How do we optimize opportunities for people to live a dignified and meaningful life in a just and caring society?[3] Here, humanism plays a central role both as a source of inspiration and as an object of study. The transdisciplinary character of humanistic studies pertains both to its interdisciplinarity – it integrates various disciplinary approaches, drawing from disciplines like philosophy, psychology, anthropology, sociology, and history – and to the involvement of societal partners in research – it integrates academic and practical knowledge in the search for answers and solutions to complex questions.

At present, humanist chaplains are educated at the University of Humanistic Studies through a three-year master's program 'Humanistic Studies.'[4] Here, they are trained to offer professional guidance regarding existential and moral questions at the micro-, meso-, and macrolevel. While the focus of the program is chaplaincy, it is not intended only for those pursuing chaplaincy but also for humanistic professionals more broadly. The master's program entails academic and professional development in the areas of chaplaincy, humanism, research, ethics, organization, and education. Students develop knowledge of meaning in life and (de)humanization from different disciplines, while also advancing their professional skills, application of knowledge to professional practices, and personal worldviewing competences (Jacobs et al., 2021, pp. 87–90). The program includes a mandatory internship of 630 hours (22.5 EC) in the program's second year (Jacobs et al., 2021, pp. 88–89). Furthermore, the master's program is one of the accredited programs that is included in the Dutch professional chaplaincy registry, which grants membership of the national professional association and safeguards "an adequate level of knowledge and skills through continuous further training" (VGVZ, 2023, p. 5). In line with humanist principles, the university "encourage[s] students to critically relate to humanism, as well as to other worldviewing traditions" (Jacobs et al., 2021, p. 93). Graduates can pursue an endorsement from the Dutch Humanist Association, or a mandate by the Council of Institutionally Non-Commissioned Spiritual Caregivers.

Overview of the chapters

This volume consists of two parts: a theoretical part and a part about chaplaincy methods. Theory and practice are, however, by no means seen as separate but as feeding into each other: the theoretical part provides the underpinning of the methodical chapters, and in the theoretical chapters, fragments of six vignettes of humanist chaplaincy are included to illustrate the theory. The complete vignettes can be found in Appendix 1.

Theoretical part

The first three chapters in the volume together provide a theoretical understanding of chaplaincy as a profession which focuses on existential processes of meaning making.[5] An important starting point is the idea that people are necessarily engaged in such processes, often without even thinking about it: people's lives and actions themselves constitute an embodied, pre-reflective response to the existential question 'how to live?' We view chaplains as the professionals responsible for supporting processes of existential meaning making and for advising organizations and communities on how to take on this task as well. This support is particularly salient in situations in which life is not self-evident, when people, communities, or organizations struggle with tragic events, tough choices, or injustice, so that questions like 'how to live, act, or work in this situation?' come to the fore.

In Chapter 1, we develop an interdisciplinary perspective on existential meaning making as a process of orientation in life. We argue that this allows for a holistic understanding of existential meaning making which highlights not only its spiritual character but also its physical, relational, and socio-cultural dimensions. Experiences where life loses its self-evidence can then be understood in terms of disorientation and attempts to regain a sense of meaning in life as attempts to (re)orient in life. We pay attention to the role of worldviews – religious or nonreligious – in processes of (re)orientation in life, indicating how worldviews feed into processes of existential meaning making.

Given this connection between worldviews and processes of existential meaning making, and the focus on these processes in chaplaincy, worldviews necessarily play a role in chaplaincy. In particular, both speaking about humanist chaplaincy and developing humanistic perspectives on chaplaincy requires an understanding of humanism as a worldview. In Chapter 2, we present such an understanding of contemporary humanism as a critical, entangled, and inclusive worldview. We critically discuss four principles which are central in this understanding – one epistemological principle and three normative principles – and which inform the humanistic perspectives from which we approach chaplaincy in this volume.

In Chapter 3, we draw from the previous two chapters when elaborating on the notion of chaplaincy as the profession which is concerned with processes of existential meaning making. We present an understanding of chaplaincy in contemporary Western secularizing and plural societies which means to do justice both to the historical religious roots of the profession and to the diverse, fluid, and individualized ways in which people in these societies search for meaning. Starting from the idea that chaplains are specialist spiritual care providers, we theorize spiritual care as care for processes of (re)orientation in life and characterize the profession of chaplaincy in terms of certain competencies, the role of worldviews in chaplains' professionalism, and the specific aim and goals of the profession. We also explain how humanistic views resonate in this theoretical understanding of chaplaincy.

Methodical part

The seven chapters in the methodical part of the volume reflect the wide variety of activities that chaplains engage in to support existential meaning making. In Chapter 3, we explain that chaplains aim for people to experience a (renewed) sense of orientation and that this involves working at the microlevel of individual and group support as well as at the mesolevel of organizations and institutions, and the macrolevel of communities and society. The different methodical chapters show how, in practice, chaplains may work towards characteristic chaplaincy goals by describing different chaplaincy methods on the micro-, meso-, and macrolevel. Each chapter contains an illustrative case from the practice of the chaplain who is the co-author, written in the first person. In Chapter 8, a vignette was constructed which is written in the third person.

Chapter 4 focuses on one-on-one encounters in chaplaincy and in particular on the question of how existing counseling methods can be used by chaplains in specific situations and contexts. The chapter offers a five-step reflection model to address this question and describes various counseling methods that are directed at goals which may also be pursued by chaplains.

Chapter 5 provides an overview of humanist chaplaincy support groups in the Netherlands. The chapter elaborates on rationales for organizing these groups, the chaplaincy goals involved, and the ways in which these goals may be realized by offering pointers for the facilitation of chaplaincy support groups.

In Chapter 6, the focus is on ritual work in chaplaincy, in particular on ritualizing and (re)designing new rituals from humanistic perspectives. The chapter addresses themes like how to identify ritual needs, the ways in which humanist chaplains may increase their ritual sensitivity and competence, and the challenges involved in ritual-making in contemporary plural societies.

Chapter 7 outlines the relationship between spiritual care and the healthcare professions, and the state of the art of spiritual care education in the healthcare context. The chapter discusses what chaplains need for preparing and conducting spiritual care education to health care professionals, aimed at fostering knowledge, attitudes, and skills needed by health care professionals (or volunteers) to provide spiritual care to patients.

In Chapter 8, chaplains are invited to participate in chaplaincy research as research-minded chaplains, active researchers, or leaders in research. Chaplains are introduced to the context of chaplaincy research – illustrating the internal and external motivations for doing research – and are given suggestions to start their own research journey. Finally, the chapter provides chaplains with pointers to reflect on their research assumptions.

Chapter 9 focuses on the moral dimension of chaplaincy work with professionals within organizations. The chapter outlines the meaning of 'the moral dimension' and the ways in which chaplains may enhance the moral competence of teams and individuals within organizations. It is pointed out that, to do moral work, chaplains need to develop their own moral competence.

Lastly, Chapter 10 elaborates on the socio-political dimension of chaplaincy. This refers to the task of publicly exposing and questioning the impact of macrosystems and -structures on people's attempts to orient in life. In particular, a chaplaincy method for providing spiritual care to communities which are affected by challenging events or circumstances is described, consisting of four elements: presence, sharing community narratives, forging structural partnerships, and spiritual counseling.

Acknowledgments

We thank the Routledge team, and Anna Moore in particular, for their support on the road from envisioning to realizing this volume. We also thank everyone who gave feedback on (parts of) the volume, in particular Carlo Leget and Christoph Henning, and the humanist chaplains who kept track of the practical content and usefulness of the volume. Finally, a big shout out to all our students for keeping us on our toes.

Notes

1 In this volume we primarily approach humanism as a worldview; see Chapter 1 for a description of worldviews and Chapter 2 for an elaboration on humanism as a worldview.
2 It is important to note that van Praag did not see humanism as a counterforce against religion but saw both religious and nonreligious worldviews as

potential sources of moral resilience (Schuhmann et al., 2021, p. 210); see also Chapter 2.

3 www.uvh.nl/english.

4 This is one of various master's programs that are offered at the University of Humanistic Studies, see www.uvh.nl/university-of-humanistic-studies/studying/programmes-and-courses.

5 The Dutch Professional Association of Chaplains describes chaplaincy as "professional support, guidance and consultancy regarding meaning and world views" (VGVZ, 2023).

References

Ammerman, N. T. (2010). The challenges of pluralism: Locating religion in a world of diversity. *Social Compass 57*(2), 154–167. https://doi.org/10.1177/00377686 10362406

Cadge, W., & Rambo, S. (Eds.). (2022). *Chaplaincy and spiritual care in the twenty-first century: An introduction*. The University of North Carolina Press.

Derkx, P. H. J. M., & Gasenbeek, A. (1997). *JP van Praag: Vader van het moderne Nederlandse humanisme* [JP van Praag: Father of modern Dutch humanism]. De Tijdstroom.

Doehring, C. (2015). *The practice of pastoral care: A postmodern approach*. Westminster John Knox Press.

Grung, A. H. (Ed.). (2023). *Complexities of spiritual care in plural societies: Education, praxis and concepts*. De Gruyter. https://doi.org/10.1515/9783110717365

Halsema, A., & van Houten, D. (2022). *Empowering humanity: State of the art in humanistics*. De Tijdstroom.

Hoogeveen, E. (1991). *Eenvoud en strategie: De praktijk van humanistisch geestelijk werk* [Simplicity and strategy: The practice of humanist chaplaincy]. Acco.

Jacobs, G., Damen, A., Suransky, C., & ten Kate, L. (2021). Reconsidering humanist chaplaincy for a plural society: The implications for higher professional education. *Health and Social Care Chaplaincy, 9*(1), 80–96. https://doi.org/10.1558/hscc.40604

Jorna, T. (2008). *Echte woorden. Authenticiteit in de geestelijke begeleiding* [Real words. Authenticity in chaplaincy]. SWP.

Kevern, P., & McSherry, W. (2015). The study of chaplaincy: Methods and materials. In C. Swift, M. Cobb, & A. Todd (Eds.), *A handbook of chaplaincy studies: Understanding spiritual care in public places* (pp. 47–62). Ashgate.

Liefbroer, A. (2020). *Interfaith Spiritual Care* [PhD thesis, Vrije Universiteit Amsterdam]. https://research.vu.nl/en/publications/interfaith-spiritual-care

Lynch, G. (2002). *Pastoral care & counseling*. Sage.

Mooren, J. H. (2013). *Bakens in de stroom: Naar een methodiek van het humanistisch geestelijk werk* [Beacons in the stream: Toward a methodology of humanist chaplaincy]. De Graaff.

Rijksen, H., & van Heijst, A. (1999). *Levensvragen in de hulpvraag* [Life questions in the request for help]. Damon.

Rosa, H. (2016). *Resonance*. Polity Press.

Savage, D. (2019). *Non-religious pastoral care: A practical guide*. Routledge.

Schuhmann, C. M., Wojtkowiak, J., van Lierop, R., & Pitstra, F. (2021). Humanist chaplaincy according to Northwestern European humanist chaplains: Towards a framework for understanding chaplaincy in secular societies. *Journal of Health Care Chaplaincy*, *27*(4), 207–221. https://doi.org/10.1080/08854726.2020.1723190

Taylor, C. (2007). *A secular age*. The Belknap Press.

van Praag, J. P. (1965). *Wat is humanistiek?* [What is humanistic studies?]. Wolters.

van Praag, J. P. (1982). *Foundations of humanism*. Prometheus Books.

VGVZ. (2023). *Professional standard spiritual caregiver 2015*. VGVZ. https://vgvz.nl/wp-content/uploads/2023/02/VGVZ_Professional_Standard_2015_Main_Text_EN_v03_WITH_APPENDICES.pdf

Wilkins-Laflamme, S. (2021). A tale of decline or change? Working toward a complementary understanding of secular transition and individual spiritualization theories. *Journal for the Scientific Study of Religion*, *60*(3), 516–539. https://doi.org/10.1111/jssr.12721

Part I

Theoretical considerations

Chapter 1

Meaning making as a process of orientation in life

Carmen Schuhmann, Gaby Jacobs, and Annelieke Damen

Introduction

Meaning is generally considered to be a central concern in human life. This central concern is understood in terms of fundamental 'needs for meaning' (Baumeister, 1991) or of a fundamental 'will to meaning' (Frankl, 1958). These understandings emphasize the process character of meaning: meaning is something we search for, consciously or unconsciously. Although meaning has become a widely studied research subject, the term is still surrounded by ambiguity: "Pinning down the definition of meaning is difficult" (Park, 2010, p. 257). From an existential perspective, meaning has to do with living a life worth living. The philosopher Wolf (2012) states that "meaning ... comes from active engagement in projects of worth, which links us to our world in a positive way" (p. 58), while the psychologist Schnell (2021) writes that "meaningfulness is the basic trust that life is worth living" (p. 7).

In this chapter, we develop an interdisciplinary perspective on existential meaning making as a process of orientation in life. We start our exploration by briefly introducing a few commonly used conceptualizations of meaning, in particular from the field of psychology, where there is an extensive body of literature centering on meaning. We then apply focus to this understanding of meaning by elaborating on the spatial metaphor of orientation that various authors use in relation to existential meaning and spirituality. Here we build on work by Taylor (1989), who provides a thorough philosophical underpinning of the orientation metaphor in relation to existential processes. We argue that conceptualizing meaning making in terms of orientation highlights the spiritual character of existential meaning making and also draws attention to the physical, relational, and sociocultural dimensions of human existence.

We then turn to the notion of disorientation. Disorienting experiences are an inherent part of processes of orientation in life, interrupting habitual modes of meaning making. Such interruptions may be experienced as a

DOI: 10.4324/9781003428633-2

threat to meaning making but also as an opening towards new meaning. This emphasizes that our understanding of orientation in life does not equate to aiming for full control over one's position or attempting to follow a single, clearly visible path but includes not knowing where to go, being open to the unexpected, and embracing the ambiguity of being simultaneously drawn to different places and the paradoxicality of experiencing losing one's way as meaningful. We distinguish six types of disorienting experiences: wonder, tragedy, ontological insecurity, empowerment, injustice, and moral tension. We present a comprehensive model of existential meaning making which explains how processes of orientation in life play out in the context of disorienting experiences. Here we also point to the specific role of worldviews in people's attempts to (re)orient in life, in particular in the context of (severely) disorienting experiences.

Orientation towards visions of a good life

Meaning is usually presented as a multi-stranded construct. Martela and Steger (2016) review different ways of and rationales for distinguishing facets of meaning presented by different authors. They conclude that there is wide agreement about three meanings of meaning in life: coherence, purpose, and significance. Coherence is usually seen as corresponding to the cognitive domain of human experience: "Life is coherent when one is able to discern understandable patterns in it to make the wholeness comprehensible" (Martela & Steger, 2016, p. 533). Purpose, corresponding to the motivational domain of human experience, has to do with "having direction and future-oriented goals in life" (Martela & Steger, 2016, p. 534). Significance corresponds to the evaluative domain of human experience and refers to having the sense that one's life as a whole is inherently valuable.

Park (2010), when discussing the role of meaning frameworks in processes of meaning making in the context of stressful events, makes a similar distinction between beliefs, goals, and a subjective sense of meaning. Schnell (2021), in her comprehensive psychological account of meaning in life, describes four dimensions of meaningfulness: coherence, significance, orientation, and belonging. She equates orientation with purpose and adds existential belonging, a facet of meaning corresponding to the affective domain of human experience, to the three facets distinguished by Martela and Steger (2016) and Park. Belonging refers to being part of something larger or having a place in this world. A crisis of meaning occurs when one judges one's life as lacking meaning: "It is accompanied by disorientation and disintegration of self-view and worldview" (Schnell, 2021, p. 8). She also uses the orientation metaphor when describing sources of meaning as "represent[ing] a variety of orientations that give meaning to life when being actively pursued" (Schnell, 2021, p. 8).

In this chapter, we build on these understandings of meaning in life; however, we expand the notion of orientation to include all four meaning facets. We also show that this metaphor draws attention to how coherence, purpose, significance, and belonging are intertwined with visions of a 'good life.' The longing for a 'good life' has not been elaborated upon extensively within the psychological literature on meaning, except by Baumeister (1991), who presented value (justification) as a need for meaning, next to purpose, efficacy, and self-worth. Let us now take a closer look at the orientation metaphor.

The orientation metaphor

In the vignettes in Appendix 1, the spatial metaphor of orientation appears both in statements of humanist chaplains about how they support people to make sense of their lives and in statements of these people. For instance, in Vignette 1, Noa explains the importance of their marriage ceremony in terms of "taking this step together" and "understanding where we are in our lives." In Vignette 4, Jonas, who is incurably ill, speaks about "the final leg of my journey." And in Vignette 5, climate activist Robert feels a "pull towards the natural surroundings" during a group walk in nature. In Vignette 2, humanist chaplain Nathan points out that people "need to feel rooted," while humanist chaplain Kimberly, in Vignette 3, explains that "people may lose their foundations, their steady ground." In Vignette 6, humanist chaplain Noor talks about her work in terms of supporting people "as they search for the right path," adding that "we are all humans trying to find our way."

Taylor (1989) provides a thorough philosophical underpinning of the spatial metaphor of orientation when elaborating on existential processes of meaning making.[1] Here, the space in which we attempt to orient ourselves is the metaphorical 'space of existential questions' in which we are necessarily immersed. Taylor stresses that these existential questions are not factual or neutral questions about life but questions about how to live a 'good' life. He therefore calls the space in which we search for orientation 'moral space,' i.e., "the space of questions about the good" (Taylor, 1989, p. 41). Responding to these questions can then be understood as a process of finding one's way in moral space. This entails both having a sense of what is a 'good' place to be and what is a 'good' direction to take in life. The orienting frameworks that provide us with a sense of place and direction in moral space are 'visions of a good life' that we are drawn to. These visions of the good are meaning frameworks; they form "the horizon within which we know ... what meanings things have for us" (Taylor, 1989, p. 29). Existential processes can thus be understood as processes of orientation in moral space. Taylor emphasizes that he takes a somewhat unconventional, broad view of the 'moral,' which is not only about what is right and just, but also about "what makes life meaningful or fulfilling" (p. 4). In order to avoid confusion, we choose to speak about 'orientation in life' rather than 'orientation in moral space' in relation to processes of existential meaning making.

The spiritual character of orientation in life

Processes of orientation in life have a spiritual character. Taylor (1989) uses the term 'spiritual' in relation to orientation in life in order to indicate that visions of a good life that function as orienting frameworks are not just any visions of the good but those by which we judge whether or not life is worth living. In other words, in relation to orientation in life, the 'good' refers to our sense of what is of 'ultimate' value to us. When we manage to orient towards such visions of the good, "we make sense of our lives spiritually" (Taylor, 1989, p. 18). Two remarks are important here. First, we want to emphasize that this understanding of 'spiritual' does not necessarily link spirituality with something extraordinary – people may find ultimate value in 'ordinary', everyday experiences and activities. Second, people may make sense of their lives spiritually in ways that are ethically questionable. Visions of a good life that represent what is of ultimate value to people may well involve self-centeredness or parochial views: "various forms of ... seemingly universal spiritual outlooks may also foster inequality and the suppression of supposedly lesser beings" (Taylor, 1989, p. 100).

Taylor (1989) develops rich alternative terminology to denote the spiritual character of visions of the good and of orientation processes towards such visions, probably because he is somewhat reluctant to use "the vague term 'spiritual'" (p. 4). He speaks, for instance, about 'strong evaluations,' in order to indicate goods that are "of crucial importance, or of fundamental value" (Taylor, 1989, p. 42) to people; these are goods "in relation to which they literally live and die" (Taylor, 1989, p. 21). Taylor (2007) also uses the term 'fullness' to designate the spiritual aspect of orientation processes: in our spiritual life, we "situate a place of fullness, to which we orient ourselves morally or spiritually" (p. 6).[2]

Understanding existential processes of meaning making in terms of orientation in life is thus in accordance with other perspectives on meaning which highlight the central role of spirituality in meaning in life. Park et al. (2016), for instance, write that "for many, spirituality serves as the foundation of their meaning systems throughout the life course" (p. 19). Furthermore, this understanding provides an integrated perspective on the four meaning facets that are distinguished in the literature and were mentioned before: coherence, purpose, significance, and belonging. Orienting towards a vision of a good life involves having a vision of reality and of why – both good and bad – things happen (coherence); having the motivation to move towards a vision of the good (purpose); seeing one's life as valuable as it is in line with a vision of the good (significance); and engaging with life, finding one's way in the world (belonging).

Physical, relational, and socio-cultural dimensions of orientation in life

After explaining orientation in life as a spiritual process, let us now elaborate on the physical, relational, and socio-cultural dimensions of this process.

Physical dimension

Orientation in life is, in the most literal sense, an embodied process of orienting in the material world. As Merleau-Ponty (1945/2012) explains, the location and positioning of the body, as the point of view upon the world, determines one's field of vision, within which a certain part of the world comes into view and another remains out of view, and things appear as within or out of reach. Furthermore, prior to reflection, bodily sensations of familiarity or strangeness, of being 'in place' or 'out of place,' or of desire for or aversion towards objects, others, or places, affect what we commit to and what direction our life takes. Such sensations are reflected in expressions people use to talk about their lives, for instance: feeling at home or coming home, feeling rooted or taking root, making a safe landing. In particular, in this view searching for meaning is a largely pre-reflective, intuitive process, which is also emphasized by Taylor (1989) when he speaks about 'moral intuitions' that usually make up the visions of the good that guide us through moral space.

Relational dimension

As we are not alone in the world, we necessarily affect and are affected by specific others with whom we come into contact; directly or indirectly, intendedly or unintendedly. People's orientation processes are therefore entangled in complex and unpredictable ways. Merleau-Ponty's (1960/1964) notion of intercorporeality stresses that "each one of us [is] pregnant with the others and confirmed by them in his body" (p. 181). This notion breaks the divide between persons with separate minds and bodies and makes it possible to think about orientation as a co-creation of meaning: "everything happens as if the other person's intention inhabited my body, or as if my intentions inhabited his body" (Merleau-Ponty, 1945/2012, p. 191). In particular, every encounter carries the potential of a changed sense of orientation for those involved. It is precisely because of this relational entanglement of orientation processes that we may not only hinder but also support each other in our search for meaning. As Ahmed (2006) phrases it: "accidental or chance encounters ... redirect us and open up new worlds" (p. 19).

Socio-cultural dimension

Taylor (1989) emphasizes that visions of a good life that function as orienting frameworks are rooted in culture. We do not make these visions up individually; they originate from and are supported by the communities in which we find ourselves. Gergen (2009) explains that goods are generated and consolidated within communities as "we establish and perpetuate what has become the 'good for us'" (p. 357). Therefore, goods are primarily rooted in convention and habit rather than in ethical deliberation.[3] As such, goods may also function as invisible norms which normalize certain ways of living. Ahmed (2006) explains how, on the one hand, there is "social pressure to follow a certain course, to live a certain kind of life" (p. 17). Deviating from certain paths, going in a different direction, is not obvious and may lead to exclusion. On the other hand, Ahmed speaks about 'lines of privilege' which represent ways of life that are difficult or even impossible to follow for certain groups, thus leading to or exacerbating marginalization or social exclusion. Given the fact that we are always immersed in various communities, orienting in moral space is a complex socio-cultural process which involves navigating multiple normativities.

Disorienting experiences

Orientation in moral space is not an optional extra in our lives, but an inescapable human aspiration: "we cannot do without an orientation to the good" (Taylor, 1989, p. 47). This does not imply that we always manage to orient. On the contrary, experiences of disorientation where life loses its self-evidence are common and manifold. For instance, the passage of time may in itself lead to disorientation as "our place relative to the good ... is constantly challenged by the new events of our lives" (Taylor, 1989, p. 47). Disorientation may also occur through unexpected events:

> When our familiar environment is suddenly disrupted we feel uprooted, we lose our footing, we are thrown, we collapse, we fall. Such falling ... is a shock and disorientation which occurs simultaneously in body and mind, and refers to a basic ontological structure of our being-in-the-world.
>
> (Jackson, 2012, p. 55)

Disorientation is not necessarily undesirable or unpleasant. Transitions in life, such as falling in love, becoming a parent, or embarking on a long journey, may be disorienting and simultaneously transformative in a positive way. They break through the everyday way of being and acting, which can bring a certain openness to change, a feeling of strength and of connection to oneself, others, and the world. Also, experiences of surprise or wonder that we can have in encountering art, music, or friendship may contribute to self-development or human flourishing. However, disorientation may also be experienced as upsetting, unsettling, or devastating, for instance when people lose a loved one, become victims of violence, or face climate change. In such situations, people may feel that they can no longer live in accordance with their habitual visions of a good life. These visions either lose their perceived value – they are no longer perceived as 'goods' – or their reachability – it seems impossible to be close to or move towards these goods, to integrate them in one's life. Harbin (2016) focuses on such 'difficult' disorientations, which she understands as "roughly, temporally extended, major life experiences that make it difficult for individuals to know how to go on. They often involve feeling deeply out of place, unfamiliar, or not at home" (p. 2). In this volume, we acknowledge that disorientation can be experienced both as positive and as negative, sometimes even simultaneously. For example, the terminal illness of a loved one can bring the experience of grief and loss, and at the same time a deep sense of connectedness never experienced before.

We make a distinction between six disorienting experiences, two of which may – but not necessarily do – lead to the experience of meaningfulness: wonder and empowerment. The remaining four are 'difficult' disorienting experiences which trigger questions or crises of meaning in life and unsettle the self: tragedy, ontological insecurity, injustice, and moral tension. The existential experiences that are involved here often evoke strong emotions, such as happiness, feelings of strength, sadness, fear, or anger. Positive emotions make orienting to the good much more easy than negative emotions, which may hinder the experience of belonging or seeing purpose in life. On the other hand, people in both situations may also flee into conventions, denial, or rigidity, thereby expressing a deep sense of alienation or displacement in life.

We can categorize these six disorienting experiences in roughly two types, although they occur in all sorts of mixed forms in life. The first type concerns the unavoidable experiences that occur because of the inherent nature of human life: it is uncontrollable, emerging, and also finite and vulnerable. This is the case with life experiences that 'happen to us' beyond our own influence, which we have called the experience of wonder, tragedy, and ontological uncertainty as a more enduring condition. The other type of experiences arises from human actions: the experience of transformation or empowerment through positive life transitions and events on the one hand; and the experience of injustice and moral tension on the other hand.

Wonder

> *In Vignette 1, humanist chaplain Chris supports Noa and Robin in designing a wedding ceremony that celebrates the experience of falling in love and the decision to get married. Noa literally calls taking the step to build a life together something "wonderful," describing it as follows: "It is amazing to be in love and make this commitment. It is also a lot to wrap my head around. We really found each other and are taking this step together, wow." The disorientation Noa experiences is reflected in the difficulty to cognitively grasp being in love and making a commitment. Noa also explains how the ceremony is meant to express some of the new layers of meaning emerging from this disorienting experience: "We are not getting married because of God or simply because of legal and economic reasons, so what exactly does it mean for us to have this ceremony? Although we are both certain this is what we want, and it is wonderful and feels right, it can feel like a big step to merge lives and promise to do life together. How will we go about that, how will we maintain and grow who we are as individuals and as a couple?"*

Wonder refers to a sudden experience of intensified awareness that affects us in several ways, cognitively, sensorily, and spiritually. For example, Schinkel (2017) defines (deep) wonder as "a mode of consciousness … which engages us on all levels – emotionally, intellectually, aesthetically, and strongly existentially" (p. 552). A characteristic of wonder is that it entails an element of surprise or mystery; the object of wonder is not comprehended, which means that there is a gap or breakdown of meaning, at least momentarily (Schinkel, 2021; Schinkel et al., 2023), like in Noa's experience in the vignette. Or as Pedersen (2019) argues: "It is typically an unsettling, yet delightful experience that makes one aware that there might be more to the perceived object than meets the eye" (p. 1). So, wonder affects us and makes us both epistemologically and existentially vulnerable, because of the strangeness we encounter and the experienced lack of meaning. Yet, there is also the suggestion of a "new, deeper or more encompassing meaning" (Schinkel, 2021, p. 29), which makes it different from other experiences of disorientation. In addition, wonder appeals to our imagination and is reflected in an open, receptive attitude: how to respond is not determined yet but open for decision (Schinkel, 2021).

Wonder can happen to us in such diverse circumstances as encountering art, listening to music, falling in love, in seeing the sun set, in meeting people that are different from us or in visiting unknown places. In these experiences, the strangeness both epistemologically and aesthetically can be felt as a spiritual experience (Fuller, 2006). We 'sense' something that evokes the experience of transcendence and it urges us to reflect on what gives life meaning. Wonder, in this sense, undermines the notion of 'striving' for the good to experience meaning. Letting go of this striving may release new opportunities to relate to oneself, others, and the world, i.e., for re-orientation in life.

Tragedy

> Vignette 2 describes how Mrs. Smith's lifeworld is colored by experiences of tragedy after moving into a care home. She experiences disorientation in the most literal sense: "she has a hard time recognizing her new surroundings and all these new faces." She feels out of place and uprooted as she cannot "find a path back to the way things were. Everything feels out of her grasp recently: her surroundings, her possessions, her thoughts, the people around her." When she talks about her life before moving into the care home, we can hear how deep her sense of irreversible loss is: "But that is in the past. I guess I am just an old granny stuck in this place now."

Tragedy includes contingent experiences such as falling ill, the passing away of a loved one, a car accident, a natural disaster, or the forced move to a care home. The self-evident character of life – having a home, a family, or a functioning body – disappears and the fragility of existence is experienced. Contingent experiences may be disorienting when these undermine the ability to orient towards habitual visions of the good, for instance visions of being healthy or keeping our loved ones safe. These are experiences that happen to us and that are unsettling because they take away what we experience as meaningful. However, tragedy is often associated with existential growth and development:

> A significant element in the positive change that individuals experience in the wake of trauma is a transformation of their understanding of themselves, of their understanding of the priorities of life, and of their place in the universe. These are areas that are viewed by some persons as religious, and more generally as existential issues.
> (Calhoun & Tedeschi, 1998, p. 219)

Calhoun and Tedeschi call this posttraumatic growth and acknowledge the spiritual and existential dimension in it. The experience of loss and being thrown back on oneself, as well as the intensity of emotions, can lead to a renewed or stronger sense of meaning in life.

However, we may also question the strong urge in our society to make something beautiful or take strength out of the fragility and impossibilities of life, and to dismiss or ignore suffering, despair, and unhappiness. Tragedy is a critique of the ideal of manufacturability of our individual lives and points towards the limitations of the adage of making meaning, as some things in life just happen. In particular, tragedy undermines the notion that we may at all times orient towards visions of the good which deny or ignore fragility and vulnerability – visions which are dominant in Western society.

Ontological insecurity

Vignette 3 is about a 'fateful moment' in Anna's life: the moment she decided to end a pregnancy when she was 20. The vignette shows how this decision keeps resonating in her life: "Though Anna feels that she understood what she chose at the time, there was no way of knowing the full meaning of this decision. With time, her abortion experience changed with her. However, Anna would not speak much about the abortion after it happened, her experience remaining this unclear ball of feelings and thoughts she carried." Anna expresses the difficulty of grasping the impact of her abortion on her life now, when, in a group meeting for people who had an abortion, led by a humanist chaplain, she shares a song that is meaningful to her: "It covers all the confusing things I felt at the time. I still listen to it sometimes, to allow myself to feel it again because sometimes I feel so simultaneously distant from it and affected by it."

The third category of disorienting experiences concerns the profound uncertainty that life brings – uncertainty about our place in life or about where paths in life will take us. The sociologist Giddens (1991) uses the term 'fateful moments' to point out the situations that arise in people's life in which they become aware of that uncertainty. These are crossroads in a person's life, again a spatial metaphor, where a choice must be made about which way to turn, for example in accepting a new job. Whatever choice is made, it determines the fate of life:

Fateful moments are those when individuals are called on to take decisions that are particularly consequential for their ambitions, or more generally for their future lives. Fateful moments are highly consequential for a person's destiny.

(Giddens, 1991, p. 112)

And also:

Fateful moments are times when events come together in such a way that an individual stands, as it were, at a crossroads in his existence; or when a person learns of information with fateful consequences.

(Giddens, 1991, p. 113)

Literally, 'fateful' means fatal or disastrous. Fateful moments threaten the protective cocoon that gives people their ontological security. There is a lot at stake, because every choice or step one takes brings uncertainty, and one cannot go back to the 'old state.' Ontological insecurity undermines the idea that we can always know what a good way is to act or how we may move closer to living a good life. An infinite number of possible roads ahead may be felt as freedom but may be experienced as paralyzing too. When people grow older, they may feel trapped on a certain pathway, with fewer new roads in sight. The approaching end is the most drastic fateful moment because it ends any control over one's own life: "Death is unintelligible exactly because it is the point zero at which control lapses" (Giddens, 1991, p. 203). Psychiatrist Yalom (1980) also points to death as the ultimate experience of disorientation, because of the fear of nothingness, of desolation.

Empowerment

In Vignette 4, Jonas, who is incurably ill, has had his euthanasia request approved. He explains how requesting for euthanasia and obtaining approval has been an experience of empowerment as this countered the complete powerlessness he felt while getting more and more ill: "I was used to having control over my life. And then I worked on accepting that I do not have control over my illness. Now I want some control again. I do not have the duty to stay alive, right? Knowing there is a foreseeable end to this, on my terms, gives me new space and strength to look at what I want in these last weeks." Jonas recognizes that his sense of empowerment is still mixed with experiencing disorientation: "It is all a bit muddled and that sometimes I feel a bit scared about dying." He also explains how having an end to his suffering in sight has given him new courage to be authentic in relationships with others. He does not want to keep things hidden from his loved ones: "I think I will tell them these things. To be known for who I am, both the good and the bad parts, is better than to not be known at all."

The fourth category of disorientation refers to those actions or transitions that not simply happen to us but are of our own choice and explicate our visions of the good – for example, becoming a parent, leaving a job to volunteer with Greenpeace, embarking on a long journey, participating in community activities, moving house, or starting a new education. Like all life events they are experiences of disorientation because they unsettle one's usual ways of living one's life. But it's more than that, because changing one's life also leads to a different spatial position in life, bringing along new perspectives on life, new relationships, a different sense of self and new competencies. In this way, life transitions are disorienting and simultaneously transformative or empowering. Empowerment is defined by Rappaport (1984) within the context of community psychology as: "a process: the mechanism by which people, organizations, and communities gain mastery over their lives" (p. 1). Empowerment is characterized by feelings of strength and authenticity on an intrapersonal level; recognition by others and participating in shared endeavors to make one's experiences known on the interpersonal level; and the ability to act (with others) in the world and contribute to change on a social and structural level. This can also add to the experience of being part of something larger than the self, something of a higher value, also called 'spiritual empowerment.'

However, we should be aware that empowerment should not be seen as a deliberately chosen process and that mastery over one's life does not exclude vulnerability; empowerment can only take place if vulnerability and uncontrollability are acknowledged as part of life (Jacobs, 2002). Related to disorientation, empowerment undermines the notion that striving towards visions of the good is a cognitive and individual process, undertaken deliberately to receive control over one's life. Empowerment involves the ability to live with disorientation and take this experience to support others and act in the situation.

Injustice

> *Vignette 5 touches upon experiences of injustice, even though somewhat indirectly. The vignette is about Robert, a climate activist, who often feels powerless in the face of the climate crisis: "it is so much bigger than me and I am doing everything I can now. Some big players are destroying the planet, lives, and livelihoods, and they are getting away with it – it is wrong!" This remark can be related to the unfair distribution of the consequences of the climate crisis: certain lives and livelihoods are much more at risk than others. In particular, the 'big players' have the privilege and power to ignore the experiences of people whose lives and livelihoods are destroyed.*

The fifth category of existential experiences is dictated by social circumstances that have a dehumanizing effect. The Brazilian critical educator Freire (2000/1970) argues that people exist in a dialectical relationship of freedom and boundaries. For Freire, limit-situations are situations that are characterized by objectification: people are not being recognized or not fully recognized in their humanity (p. 99). These are situations in which freedom and justice are at stake. People may be unaware of these socially constituted limits for a long time or may experience them as 'the best possible' way to live their lives: "Dehumanization, which marks not only those whose humanity has been stolen, but also (though in a different way) those who have stolen it, is a distortion of the vocation of becoming more fully human" (Freire, 2000/1970, p. 44). Examples are the exclusion of migrant or refugee groups from our society or the objectification of patients in the bureaucratic system of health care. Philosopher Fricker (2007) adds to this a distinctive type of injustice that she calls 'epistemic injustice.' Epistemic injustice is driven by social (often structural) power and prejudice and is based in withholding the other the capacity as a knower, thereby privileging the dominant groups. However, according to Freire, "dehumanization, although a concrete historical fact, is not a given destiny but the result of an unjust order that engenders violence in the oppressors, which in turn dehumanizes the oppressed" (p. 44). People then may respond with actions directed at negating and overcoming, rather than passively accepting, the 'given.'

In relation to injustice, we may experience disorientation when we are confronted with the ways in which we are entangled in social structures that limit the possibility to orient in life of ourselves or of others. We may then start to wonder whether we are actually leading a good life or whether there are other ways to orient, leading us to question our place or direction in life. Furthermore, when we do have a view of the injustice we are suffering and know what goods we are deprived from, we may experience disorientation in relation to our inability to orient towards these goods. Injustice undermines the notion that visions of the good that are powerful in society, that people tend to embrace, usually or necessarily affirm the humanity of all.

Moral tension

In Vignette 6, Wesley talks about his experiences in relation to the military mission he participated in. Not only does he feel ashamed about some of his own actions during the mission, but he also questions the morality of the mission itself: "Why was I on that mission, what was it for? I was a pawn in some game. At the same time, I said yes. I wanted

> *to make a difference and thought I could do that by doing as I was told. I did things and I do not know what they were for, ultimately. Even more so, I am ashamed because I was unable to do things I think I should have done. There were kids who needed my help, and I could not or did not help them. The question whether in fact I could not help them or did not help them haunts me sometimes."*

The last category of disorienting experiences consists of 'morally charged' situations that cause moral tensions or even 'injuries.' Margaret Urban Walker (2007) stresses that morality is part of the small acts and decisions of everyday life and work, and thereby deeply connected with personal identity, which is often expressed in the care work delivered by nurses or general practitioners. According to Rushton (2018), moral tension or moral distress arise when one is unable to act according to one's personal or professional values. It always involves a tension between the person and their context, in which political or administrative decisions put 'good work' at stake, although it may often be experienced as an inner conflict. An example is a nurse trying to give attention to the personal stories of the older people in the nursing home but being unable to do so because of staff shortages. There are many other expressions of moral distress, such as moral insecurity (not knowing how to act 'right') or moral dilemma (having to choose between two options that both do not live up to visions of the good). Moral injury is a concept used in the context of the armed forces and refers to feelings of guilt, shame, and anger about actions that are contrary to deep moral values. This may for example concern the morally ambiguous feeling of having failed to aid the local population or comrades during deployment, even when military orders have been obeyed and having contributed to ending war. Disorientation related to moral tensions involves feeling unable in the given context or circumstances to act in accordance with our visions of what is morally good or even to determine what is morally good. Moral tensions undermine the notion that individuals have complete freedom to act and that there is an unambiguous or a universal vision of the good.

The six types of disorienting experiences together paint a rich picture of the diversity of disorientations people may encounter in life (see Figure 1.1). All give substance to a contextual view of meaning-in-life, i.e., they are experienced as a process in relationship to others and the world. However, the unavoidability of life circumstances from an existential perspective throws a different light on disorientation, i.e., the contingency involved, than the dehumanizing factors that cause moral tension or injustice, which point to a political and more active perspective. Furthermore, as stated above,

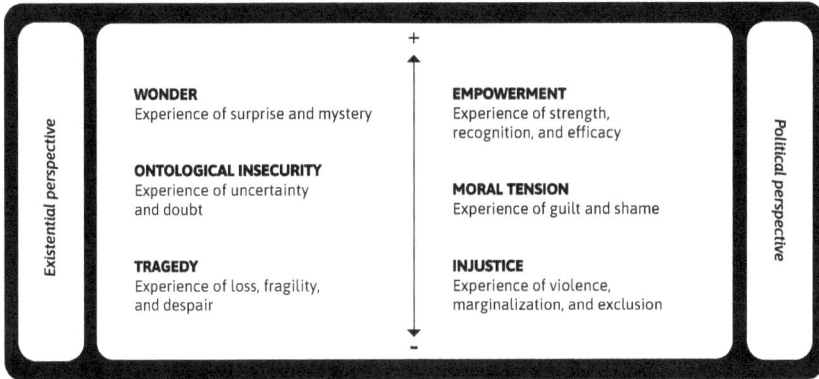

Figure 1.1 Six types of disorienting experiences.

experiences of disorientation are not necessarily experienced as either nega-tive or positive. For example, 'wonder' and 'empowerment' are predomi-nantly positive experiences of disorientation that may contribute to the experience of meaning in life, whereas 'tragedy' and 'injustice' could be seen as mostly negative. However, the categories do not exclude each other but may overlap or move into each other. For example, empowerment and injustice often go hand in hand; and wonder may be part of empowerment or be connected with insecurity. Lastly, it is important to stress that the active striving for reorientation in life not necessarily contributes to the finding of a new vision of a good life; and that as human beings we have part in the dehumanizing processes we reject, because of the inevitable limitations of our visions of the good.

An existential meaning-making model

As remarked earlier, existential meaning making generally is a pre-reflec-tive, intuitive process playing out at the background of our lives. It is often only in the context of disorientation, when meaning making is under pres-sure, that an urge for meaning is felt and attempts to (re)orient in life move to the foreground. Processes of existential meaning making are thus espe-cially salient in the context of disorientation. In order to get a better grasp on the kinds of changes involved in these processes, we present an existen-tial meaning-making model (see Figure 1.2) that is inspired by the inte-grated model of meaning making by Park (2010) (see also Schuhmann & van der Geugten, 2017). In her model, Park focuses on meaning making in the context of stressful events. She distinguishes between global meaning and appraised meaning of an event. From an existential perspective, appraised meaning refers to one's sense of place and direction in life in

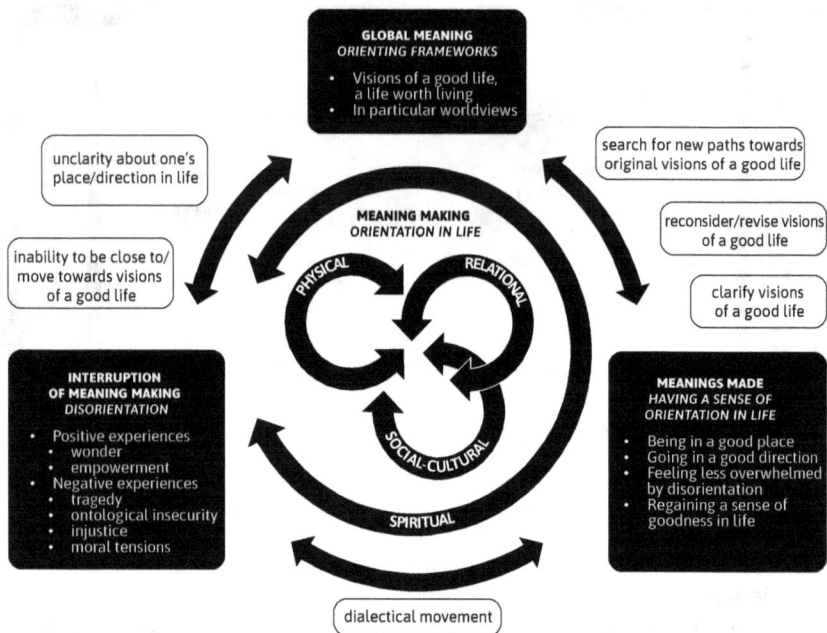

Figure 1.2 The existential meaning-making model.

one's current situation and circumstances, and global meaning refers to orienting systems consisting of visions of a good life. Like in Park's model, global meaning comprises beliefs, goals, and subjective feelings: beliefs about life, life goals we commit to, and a subjective sense of living a good life.

When people experience disorientation, their sense of where they are (going) in life in their current situation or circumstances is at odds with their visions of a good life, which therefore do not serve as orienting frameworks. This is not only the case in 'difficult' disorienting experiences but also in those that are experienced as positive. For example, the surprise that is experienced in wonder expresses that the current global meaning system falls short in capturing the experience. Following Taylor (1989, pp. 41–42), we may broadly distinguish two modes of disorientation which lead to different modes of reorientation. First, an event or our current situation may lead us to question where we are (going) in life and how to find out. This leads to a process of reorientation in which we clarify what are visions of a good life by which we may assess our place and direction in life. Second, an event or our current situation may undermine our ability to be close to or move towards the visions of the good we orient towards, closing off the possibility to live or act in accordance with them. This leads to a process of reorientation which involves either searching for new paths towards original visions of the good (assimilation) or searching for new visions of the good that we can be close to or move towards (accommodation).[4] Worldviews, whether religious or nonreligious, have a specific role in reorientation processes. In our model, we understand them as collective orienting frameworks that accommodate disorienting experiences, including those severely unsettling ones where all good seems lost. They provide visions of a good life which indicate that some good remains.[5]

From an existential perspective, meanings made, the changes resulting from attempts to reorient in life, can globally be understood in terms of having regained a sense of orientation in life. This may involve regaining a sense of being oriented in life – being in a good place or going in a good direction. However, if disorientation persists, processes of reorientation may also result in being less overwhelmed by disorientation, even if only temporarily, thus regaining a sense of goodness in life, involving, for instance, a sense of hope, strength, peace, or consolation. This underscores that disorientation and having a sense of orientation are not diametrically opposed but rather related in a dialectical way. In particular, having a sense of orientation in life should not be confused with knowing exactly where we are and aspire to go. Life, with its physical, relational, socio-cultural, and spiritual dimensions, is never completely within our view and grasp. Being 'fully oriented' would only be possible in an imaginary private space in which I am fully in control. In particular, attempting to be 'fully oriented' would close us off from the goodness that may be felt in the unexpected, and from experiencing wonder or awe. Having a sense of orientation in life therefore also comprises, to some extent, embracing experiences of disorientation. In particular, in the midst of severe disorientation, having a sense of orientation may entail just having a sense that the disorientation is livable or 'survivable' (Harbin, 2016, p. 166). Also, for example in the case of ontological insecurity, experiencing disorientation may become a way of life if one learns to live without feeling secure about one's future. This means that living a 'good life' can be understood as including disorientations (Harbin, 2016, p. 25).

While Park's (2010) psychological model focuses on meaning making as a cognitive process, the existential meaning-making model is more comprehensive. It includes embodiment – for instance, by understanding disorientation such as wonder, violence, or loss of a loved one as something which is first of all a bodily felt sense; socio-cultural aspects – for instance, by recognizing how social-structural power dimensions affect visions of the good; and relationality – for instance, by understanding processes of reorientation as relational processes that require care and recognition by others. Given the spiritual character of orientation processes, this model also highlights the role of spirituality in existential meaning making. When we experience disorientation, the spiritual character of meaning making comes to the fore, as we may start wondering what 'really' matters in life, what makes life worth living.

Conclusion

Conceptualizing existential meaning making in terms of orientation in life highlights that meaning making is a complex, messy, nonlinear process. Embodiment, relationships, material surroundings, and socio-cultural contexts all play into the process. Disorientation is an inherent part of existential meaning making; over time our position in relation to habitual visions of the good may change gradually or abruptly. Meaning making is especially salient in the context of disorientation, whether experienced positively, negatively, or both simultaneously, since disorienting experiences foreground the question of what 'ultimately' matters to us and how to orient towards corresponding visions of the good. Worldviews offer spiritual resources for regaining a sense of orientation, even in the context of severe disorientation. There is no end point to processes of meaning making: 'having a sense of orientation in life,' which we propose as an outcome of such processes, does not imply that disorientation is no longer experienced.

Notes

1 Speaking about the notion of orientation, Taylor states: "I feel myself drawn here to use a spatial metaphor; but I believe this to be more than a personal predilection. There are signs that the link with spatial orientation lies very deep in the human psyche" (1989, p. 28). Similarly, Lakoff and Johnson (1980) write that the conceptual metaphors we use are not arbitrary but that "they are shaped to a significant extent by the common nature of our bodies and the shared ways that we all function in the everyday world" (p. 245).

2 See Chapter 3, where we elaborate on the connection between Taylor's (1989) notion of the spiritual character of orientation processes and the consensus definition by Puchalski et al. (2009), which is widely used in the context of spiritual care.

3 As Gergen (2009) points out, this reflects the Latin origin of the term morality: mores, customs.

4 Here we follow terminology by Park (2010) who speaks about assimilation when a process of meaning making involves changing appraised meaning and about accommodation when meaning making involves changing global meaning.

5 Here we draw from the definition by Geertz (1973) of religions as systems of symbols that provide an image of a general order of existence in which even severely disorienting experiences are accounted for, generalizing this definition to worldviews in general.

References

Ahmed, S. (2006). *Queer phenomenology: Orientations, objects, others*. Duke University Press.

Baumeister, R. F. (1991). *Meanings of life*. Guilford Press.

Calhoun, L.G., & Tedeschi, R.G. (1998). Posttraumatic growth: Future directions. In R. G. Tedeschi, C. L. Park, & L. G. Calhoun (Eds.), *Posttraumatic growth: Positive change in the aftermath of crisis* (pp. 215–238). Erlbaum.

Frankl, V. E. (1958). On logotherapy and existential analysis. *American Journal of Psychoanalysis, 18*(1), 28.

Freire, P. (2000/1970). *Pedagogy of the oppressed*. Continuum.

Fricker, M. (2007). *Epistemic injustice: Power and the ethics of knowing*. Oxford University Press.

Fuller, R. (2006). *Wonder: From emotion to spirituality*. University of North Carolina Press.

Geertz, C. (1973). *The interpretation of cultures*. Basic Books.

Gergen, K. J. (2009). *Relational being: Beyond self and community*. Oxford University Press.

Giddens, A. (1991). *Modernity and self-identity*. Polity Press.

Harbin, A. (2016). *Disorientation and moral life*. Oxford University Press.

Jackson, M. (2012). *Lifeworlds: Essays in existential anthropology*. University of Chicago Press.

Jacobs, G. (2002). Reflection and action in the transitional space of the political and the existential. In A. Halsema & D. Van Houten (Eds.), *Empowering humanity. State of the art of Humanistics* (pp. 243–256). De Tijdstroom.

Lakoff, G., & Johnson, M. (1980). *Metaphors we live by*. The University of Chicago Press.

Martela, F., & Steger, M. F. (2016). The three meanings of meaning in life: Distinguishing coherence, purpose, and significance. *The Journal of Positive Psychology, 11*(5), 531–545. https://doi.org/10.1080/17439760.2015.1137623

Merleau-Ponty, M. (1964). The philosopher and his shadow. In R. C. McLeary(Trans.), *Signs* (pp. 159–181). Northwestern University Press. (Original work published 1960)

Merleau-Ponty, M. (2012). *Phenomenology of perception* (D. A. Landes, Trans.). Routledge. (Original work published 1945)

Park, C. L. (2010). Making sense of the meaning literature: an integrative review of meaning making and its effects on adjustment to stressful life events. *Psychological bulletin, 136*(2), 257. https://doi.org/10.1037/a0018301

Park, C. L., Currier, J. M., Harris, J. I. & Slattery, J. M. (2016). *Trauma, meaning, and spirituality: Translating research into clinical practice*. American Psychological Association.

Pedersen, J. B. (2019). *Balanced wonder: Experiential sources of imagination, virtue, and human flourishing*. Rowman & Littlefield.

Puchalski, C., Ferrell, B., Virani, R., Otis-Green, S., Baird, P., Bull, J., Chochinov, H., Handzo, G., Nelson-Becker, H., Prince-Paul, M., Pugliese, K., & Sulmasy, D. (2009). Improving the quality of spiritual care as a dimension of palliative care: the report of the Consensus Conference. *Journal of Palliative Medicine, 12*(10), 885–904. https://doi.org/10.1089/jpm.2009.0142

Rappaport, J. (1984). Studies in empowerment: Introduction to the issue. *Prevention in Human Services, 3*(2–3), 1–7.

Rushton, C. H. (2018). *Moral resilience: Transforming moral suffering in healthcare.* Oxford University Press.

Schinkel, A. (2017). The educational importance of deep wonder. *Journal of Philosophy of Education 51*(2), 538–553. https://doi.org/10.1111/1467-9752.12233

Schinkel, A. (2021). *Wonder and education: On the educational importance of contemplative wonder.* Bloomsbury.

Schinkel, A., Wolbert, L., Pedersen, J. B., & de Ruyter, D. J. (2023). Human Flourishing, Wonder, and Education. *Studies in Philosophy and Education, 42*(2), 143–162. https://doi.org/10.1007/s11217-022-09851-7

Schnell, T. (2021). *The psychology of meaning in life.* Routledge.

Schuhmann, C., & van der Geugten, W. (2017). Believable visions of the good: An exploration of the role of pastoral counselors in promoting resilience. *Pastoral Psychology, 66*(4), 523–536. https://doi.org/10.1007/s11089-017-0759-z

Taylor, C. (1989). *Sources of the self.* Harvard University Press.

Taylor, C. (2007). *A secular age.* The Belknap Press.

Walker, M. U. (2007). *Moral understandings. A feminist study in ethics.* Oxford University Press.

Wolf, S. (2012). *Meaning in life and why it matters.* Princeton University Press.

Yalom, I. (1980). *Existential psychotherapy.* Basic Books.

Chapter 2

Humanism as a critical, entangled, and inclusive worldview

Carmen Schuhmann, Joanna Wojtkowiak, and Gaby Jacobs

Introduction

Humanism is a term with many different, sometimes conflicting, meanings. In fact, the term did not emerge until the eighteenth century and is often used post hoc to describe historical phenomena which, when they occurred, were labeled differently (Derkx, 2011). The question of what kind of phenomena the term humanism refers to is in itself a topic of discussion:

> Humanism appears as an ideology, a theology, an anthropology, a philosophy, a psychology, a politics … a noun, an adjective, a verb. In short, it is many things and no single thing. There seems no definitive reply to the question: What is humanism?
>
> (Radest, 2014, p. 7)

These days, humanism is often understood as a worldview: "Humanism has been variously termed a 'worldview,' an 'approach to life,' a 'lifestance,' a 'way of life,' and a 'meaning frame'" (Copson, 2015, p. 5). Pinn (2014) refers to humanism as a "life orientation" (p. 33) which "like those things we recognize easily as religious traditions, seeks to provide a systematic approach to life" (p. 33). Derkx (1993) distinguishes three main features of Western European humanism which point to different facets of humanism as a worldview:

1. Humanism as formation to higher humanity. This refers to the tradition of _Bildung_ and the belief in the potential of human beings for development, resilience, and flourishing.
2. Humanism as a moral and political aspiration, directed at a caring and just society that is characterized by supporting human flourishing for all, freedom, peace, and recognition of human dignity.

DOI: 10.4324/9781003428633-3

3. Humanism as an 'art of living' in which the focus is on the desire to enjoy and share things of beauty, and esthetic experiences are seen as important entry points to living a good life.

In this chapter, we develop a view of contemporary humanism as a world-view in the sense of a framework that may provide people with orientation in life, in particular in disorienting situations and circumstances (see also Chapter 1). Worldviews accommodate experiences of severe disorientation by providing some kind of transcendence: a sense of goodness 'beyond' the severely disorienting situations and circumstances people may find them-selves in.[1] Worldviews also function as sources of faith – faith that some good remains, even in the face of extreme adversity (Tillich, 1957). Any worldview may thus be seen as comprising an understanding of spirituality: an understanding of what is ultimate goodness – goodness that involves transcendence and inspires faith –and how to connect with it.[2] Following Smart (1999), we may distinguish seven dimensions of worldviews: (1) practices which support or express people's connection with the good (*ritual/practical*); (2) formal ideas about reality that underlie the visions of a good life making up a worldview (*doctrinal/philosophical*); 3. (meta)narra-tives or myths expressing these visions (*mythic/narrative*); (4) a sense of how the good is experienced and what emotional states are involved (*experiential/emotional*); (5) ethical notions that prescribe good (versus bad) behavior and action (*ethical/legal*); (6) institutions and communities in which visions of the good making up a worldview are upheld, consoli-dated, practiced and discussed (*organizational/social*); and (7) material objects like buildings or works of art that are seen as symbolizations or manifestations of the good (*material/artistic*). So, worldviews offer a variety of modes of meaning making in the context of negative or positive experi-ences of disorientation, for instance by means of rituals, core texts, or meaningful objects.

When outlining a view of humanism as a worldview, we draw in par-ticular from humanistic studies, a transdisciplinary academic field in which humanism is both a source of inspiration and an object of study (see Introduction to the volume). In humanistic studies, critically looking at humanism goes hand in hand with developing and renewing views of humanism. From this perspective, critiquing humanism does therefore not imply that humanism needs to be discarded. In contrast, over the last decades humanism has sometimes been declared outdated, dead, or dan-gerous on the basis of claims that it promotes a Westernized notion of 'the human' and an anthropocentric view of human life, contributing to many of the problems we struggle with today, like colonialism, racism, and the ecological crisis.[3] Still, when using humanistic perspectives – for instance, as we do in this book, to better understand contemporary chaplaincy – we need to acknowledge that these perspectives are contested. In our explorations of contemporary humanism, we therefore draw from the following three recent developments in humanist thought, all of which address critical notes on humanism: (1) *critical humanism*, which addresses the criticism of universalism and essentialism in humanism; (2) *entangled humanism*, which addresses the criticism of seeing human beings as decontextualized individuals, separate from each other and 'masters over nature'; and (3) *inclusive humanism*, which addresses the criticism of humanism as anti-religious and as complicit in the disenchantment of the modern world. We start the chapter by briefly introducing each of these humanisms.

While developing an understanding of humanism as a (multi-stranded) worldview, we build on the pioneering work of van Praag (1982), a key figure in Dutch humanism (see Introduction to the volume). He emphasized that, as a worldview, humanism needs to be more than a set of abstract beliefs and values: it needs to provide motivation and inspiration to actual people in their actual situations, in particular supporting them to contribute to society.[4] We also elaborate on the question of how to understand humanist spirituality. In particular, we explore what notion of transcendence can be found in humanism, and what inspires humanist faith in the face of severely disorienting experiences.

Humanisms: critical, entangled, inclusive

A starting point for identifying a common core in the various appearances of humanism is to consider related terms like 'humaneness,' 'humanity,' and 'humanization,' which are evaluative words, indicating an aspiration or a task that human beings should pursue in this world. "The human so understood is of and in the world" (Pinn, 2014, p. 34), and any appearance of humanism comprises a value-laden project of engaging with the world in an attempt to promote humanization and to counter dehumanization. Such projects acknowledge on, the one hand, the creative and moral potential of human beings, which allows them to strive for humanization, and, on the other hand, the fallibility of human beings which, time and again, results in dehumanizing behavior and societal or institutional structures.

It is precisely because of human fallibility that appearances of humanism, as human-made ideas, projects, and practices, need to be critically assessed as to the question of what notion of 'being human' underpins striving for humaneness and humanization. The three developments described below, towards critical, entangled, and inclusive humanism, each of which address a certain element of existing criticism on humanism, allow us to critically assess appearances of humanism throughout this chapter.

Critical humanism

A main point of criticism that humanism nowadays faces is that it propagates an essentialist view of human nature that is rooted in Western Enlightenment and reflects a Western-centric view of being human. Humanism thus confirms existing power structures and contributes to marginalization and oppression. Addressing this criticism requires a contextualized and multiple understanding of humanism, in which Western Enlightenment humanism is just one form of humanism. The fact that humanism is so often identified with this form of humanism in itself reflects how power operates in relation to establishing what humanism 'is' and what it 'is not.' Plummer (2021) elaborates on the notion of 'critical humanism' to allow a variety of humanisms into the picture and counter parochial understandings of humanism:

> Different humanisms bring contested claims about what it means to be human. These change over history as different (usually powerful) groups make different claims. Critical humanism engages with (and tells the stories of) the perpetual narrative reconstructions and conflicts over what it means to be human.
>
> (p. 5)

Critical humanism thus comprises nonessentialist views of humans living in relation to dynamic socio-political, cultural factors, and power structures. Examples of critical humanism are Frantz Fanon's (1952/2008) "new humanism" (p. vii), Mahatma Ghandi's nonviolent humanism (van Goelst Meijer, 2015), and African American humanism (Pinn, 2012). Critical humanism is never 'finished' as "it is an ever-changing endeavor to rethink and remake a narrative of world humanity" (Plummer, 2021, p. 12). Always again, the critical question of which voices are not heard in this narrative and which lives do not fit within it needs to be posed. A similar move away from essentialist humanism is proposed by Wentzer and Mattingly (2018) when they advocate for a 'new humanism': "Such a humanism highlights the ambition to approach the human through its complex and multifocal variations. It takes its point of departure in real people living real and messy lives in their sociocultural and natural ecologies" (p. 146).

Entangled humanism

A second, often-repeated critique of humanism concerns its individualism and anthropocentrism, which is rooted in a view of human beings as separate from other life forms and nature in general. The conception of human domination over nature plays a key role in major problems like climate change, environmental pollution, and loss of biodiversity. Connolly (2017) proposes entangled humanism, a form of humanism with a different view on the world and human beings:

> Today it is perhaps wise to try to *transfigure* the old humanisms that have played important roles in Euro-American states into multiple affirmations of entangled humanism in a fragile world. … One such transfiguration of humanism acknowledges a world composed of innumerable entanglements.
>
> (p. 168)

This links in with critical humanism; as Connolly points out, outside of the Western world we can find various traditions which have embraced an entangled view of the world for centuries. In entangled humanism, human beings are no longer seen as having a special place in, or rather above, nature, but as entangled with other life forms and with planetary forces and processes. Even though the focus here is on the entanglement of human beings with the nonhuman, entanglement also applies to the interpersonal domain, leading to a radically relational perspective on human beings instead of an individualistic one.

Vignette 5 introduces humanist chaplain Lilian who leads group meetings for climate activists. Her humanist worldview strongly resonates with entangled humanism: "In her work, Lilian is inspired by an eco-humanist perspective on life on this planet: she sees the value of all life forms, and sees human beings as a humble part of and connected to all life on earth. She also draws from indigenous views on land and water." Lilian underscores the importance of these indigenous views as follows: "There is acknowledgment of what nature has to teach us and what it has done for us, showing a reciprocal and interdependent relationship with nature."

Furthermore, in an entangled perspective, humanism should not be equated with secularism or an antireligious stance: "Some variants of entangled humanism may embrace a god or gods of entanglement; some may be nontheistic; some may pursue an immanent divine, and some the theme of an immanent naturalism" (Connolly, 2017, p. 170). Entangled humanism is therefore linked to inclusive humanism, which we introduce next.

Inclusive humanism

A third point of critique that contemporary humanism needs to address is the reproach that it opposes religion. There certainly is a link between secularization and humanism: according to Taylor (2007), the change in the West after the late Middle Ages from a world in which it is almost impossible not to believe in God to a world in which belief in God is optional is intimately linked with the rise of 'exclusive humanism.' Exclusive humanism refers to "a humanism accepting no final goals beyond human flourishing, nor any allegiance to anything beyond this flourishing" (Taylor, 2007, p. 18). While in the pre-modern, enchanted world, people generally had a 'porous' sense of self, open and vulnerable to forces beyond the human realm, the modern disenchanted world is linked with a 'buffered' sense of self which is central in exclusive humanism: "This self can see itself as invulnerable, as master of the meaning of things for it" (Taylor, 2007, p. 38).

Derkx (2015) emphasizes that what is crucial in humanism is not 'exclusivity' but openness, dialogue, and tolerance. Embracing humanism should never lead to intolerance towards others, including religious people. Derkx proposes to "speak of 'inclusive humanism' by means of which humanism is conceived as an open, dialogical, and tolerant meaning frame found not only outside churches, mosques, and the like, but also inside them" (p. 429). Inclusive humanism acknowledges that values which are central in humanism may also be found in other worldviews, and vice versa. It also acknowledges that there are ethical limits to the perspective of the buffered self, and thus to exclusive humanism, as this may entail closing oneself off from dialogue in order to hold on to a sense of invulnerability.

Humanism as a worldview

In the Netherlands, since the middle of the twentieth century, there have been efforts to systematically develop humanism as a worldview. The main initiator of these efforts was the Dutch humanist van Praag (1982), who played a key role both in providing a theoretical underpinning of humanism as a worldview and in founding humanist organizations aimed at providing people, interested in humanism, with inspiration, and supporting them to put humanism into practice (see Introduction to the volume). It is mainly due to his tireless efforts that the first humanist chaplains were employed in the Netherlands in the 1950s (see Schuhmann et al., 2021). We outline a view of humanism as a contemporary worldview by first presenting key ideas by van Praag. We then describe ideas about humanism by Derkx (2014) and by Alma and Anbeek (2013), all of whom build on the foundational work of van Praag. In our discussion of these ideas, we apply the perspectives of critical, entangled, and inclusive humanism that were introduced earlier.

Humanist postulates

When elaborating on humanism as a worldview, van Praag (1982) used a method of phenomenological reduction to figure out the core ideas that lie at the root of all appearances of humanism. He calls these core ideas 'humanist postulates,' formulating both anthropological postulates, which are core ideas about human beings, and ontological postulates, core ideas about the world. Humanist postulates underpin "a humanist orientation pattern from which humanist views unfold themselves, as it were, of their own accord" (van Praag, 1982, p. 58). The postulates thus capture the view of reality that underpins humanist orienting frameworks. Two examples of the anthropological humanist postulates are the postulate of equality – despite their differences, all human beings are equal in dignity; and the postulate of rationality – even though much in life and the world cannot be grasped rationally, human beings have the ability to use reason, in particular in relation to moral evaluations.[5]

If we look at van Praag's (1982) work from the perspective of critical humanism, we see that he does understand humanism as a worldview which may appear in a variety of ways. He also emphasizes that his humanist postulates are not set in stone; they provide a theoretical model that always again needs to be reviewed and revised on the basis of real experiences of real people. Furthermore, van Praag has an eye for the limited scope of his historical explorations of humanism, stating that he restricts himself to Western humanist traditions only and, because of his lack of expertise on the matter, excludes non-Western traditions that might also deserve a place in the story of humanism. However, he does not elaborate on the questions of what it means that non-Western voices are left out of his account of humanism, and how humanist ideas and practices are entangled in power structures that have contributed to or are contributing to marginalization and oppression.

Furthermore, the perspective of critical humanism leads us to question the focus on equality and reason in van Praag's (1982) postulates. These can easily lead to exclusion and marginalization of those who cannot take part equally in society because the 'right to be different' and make autonomous decisions is attributed to individuals who are first equated as rational, independently judging, masculine beings. This still does not allow the other to name their own experiences and desires and to articulate their uniqueness (see also Kunneman, 1993).

Taking the perspective of entangled humanism also leads to questions about the postulate of reason. Even though the postulate does leave space for that which cannot be understood rationally, it does take the rational as the dominant view. From the perspective of entangled humanism, humans are entangled in a material and social world. They have a body and they are embodied in a natural and material world with others. Drawing from the work of the French feminist philosopher Irigaray (1990), this embodiment can itself be seen as an essential source of freedom for making choices, and for an open and equal communicative relationality. Moreover, while humans have the strength or capacity to reason, questions of meaning are strongly guided by emotions. Emotions tell us when something 'doesn't feel right' or when we are immensely happy. Emotions, while often being underrepresented in research on or the conceptualization of processes of meaning, are significant in the search for meaning (Nussbaum, 2014; Martela & Steger, 2016; Park, 2010) and in moral life (Haidt, 2001). Anthropologist Rosaldo (1984) frames it as follows: "Feeling is forever given shape through thought and ... thought is laden with emotional meaning ... Emotions are thoughts somehow 'felt' in flushes, pulses, 'movements' in our livers, minds, hearts, stomachs, skin. They are *embodied* thoughts" (p. 143). The relation between emotion and cognition is established here through embodiment: feelings contain thoughts and thoughts contain feelings.

In Vignette 2, humanist chaplain Nathan, who works in a care home for elderly people, expresses how, in his view on life, the senses are an important pathway to meaning making. Working with people who sometimes struggle to tell coherent stories, he follows this pathway to connect with clients and to create space for embodied meaningful experiences, for instance, by listening to music together: "Music contains slices of life that we can feel and recognize together. Listening together, sometimes holding hands, I see our shared human vulnerability. I might not know exactly what they feel or think then. But I know there is something known to both of us, intuitively, in that moment."

From the perspective of inclusive humanism, we see that van Praag sometimes seems to set humanism and religion against each other in order to clarify humanist positions, for instance when he states that "as opposed to the traditional forms of the major religions, humanism does not provide definitive answers to fundamental questions" (van Praag, 1982, p. 12). However, he also writes about religious humanism, and describes the affinity between religion and humanism when it comes to certain experiences:

This idea of being related to the whole of existence leads us to consider a religious feeling that also occurs in humanist expression ... One should think of one of the original meanings of the word *religere*, in the sense of being awed. What it means is that people can stand in awe of the world and realize that they don't have it in their pocket.

(van Praag, 1982, p. 128)

Characterizing contemporary humanism

Building, amongst others, on the work by van Praag, Derkx (2014) proposes a concise characterization of humanism as a category of meaning frames that fulfill four criteria – or 'tenets,' as Derkx usually calls them. Derkx describes meaning frames as follow: "A meaning frame provides you with a sense of direction, stability, identity, continuity, and with criteria to evaluate situations and one's life course" (Derkx, 2014, p. 49). They are what we call orienting frameworks, as explained in Chapter 1.[6]

The first tenet that Derkx (2014) proposes is epistemological in nature. It states that *any ontological or normative view, in particular any meaning frame, any view of reality, any vision of the good, any worldview, is a context-dependent human construct* (see Derkx, 2014, p. 49). In particular, meaning frames – religions included – are historically and socio-culturally situated. They do not express final, eternal, unchanging, supra-historical ideas, and are open to doubt, questioning, and revision:

> Embedded in this tenet is recognition of historical consciousness, human fallibility, and experience of doubt. It also draws from a critical and dialogical attitude and requires a willingness to account for one's views and actions with openness, tolerance, and an appreciation of diversity.
>
> (Derkx, 2014, p. 49)

Looking from the perspective of critical humanism, we find that this criterion counters essentialist accounts of human nature in humanism, as there is no final such account. We also see that meaning frames cannot be considered in isolation from questions of power and social justice, questions of how power structures prevent people and groups to orient towards certain visions of the good that are available and reachable for others.[7]

The three remaining criteria are normative in nature. The second humanist criterion mentions human dignity, one of the central values in humanism: "*all human beings ought to regard and treat each other as equals, with human dignity*" (emphasis in original, Derkx, 2014, p. 51). This implies that "humanism conflicts in principle with all forms of discrimination—racism, sexism, ageism, and discrimination based on sexual orientation" (Derkx, 2014, p. 51). From the perspective of critical humanism, however, we see that any notion of human dignity already entails a view of what it means to be human which may leave out easily overheard voices, thus increasing marginalization, as we already remarked in relation to the anthropological humanist postulate of equality formulated by van Praag. We therefore add that regarding and treating each other as equals involves constant critical questioning of how privilege and power operate in the specific situation at hand, and, more generally, in the story of humanism.

This tenet also points to another important humanist value, that of self-determination. This means "that each person is best positioned to assess and determine how he/she should live" (Derkx, 2014, p. 51). The perspective of entangled humanism provides a caveat here. Self-determination should not be understood in terms of striving to cut oneself off from the influence of others or from one's environment – which is impossible in light of entanglement – but in terms of acknowledging that, for all human beings, at all times, living their life starts from their unique, embodied position in the world, a position that no one can take for them.

> *Vignette 6 shows how humanist chaplain Noor, who works in the military, takes the idea of self-determination as the starting point in her work: "I help the person in front of me figure out what they do, feel, choose, think as they search for the right path. I do not claim to know what path they should take. We are all humans trying to find our way, and instead of seeing a uniform, I ask about the person in the uniform that I encounter and try to offer a landing spot for them to rest and reroute. Humanist institutions, doctrines, and so on are of less interest to me than the very practice of humans showing genuine interest in each other: 'who are you, what matters to you, how can I help you along?'" This statement also seems to reflect a relational view of self-determination: we find out who we are and what matters to us by speaking with someone who shows genuine interest.*

The third humanist criterion that Derkx (2014) proposes is the one that is probably most often associated with humanism, as it is related to autonomy and to the capacity of thought. Derkx calls this the principle of *self-fulfillment* and formulates it as follows: "*one should consciously create the form and content of life, choose purposes and seriously try to achieve them, and one should use one's freedom to develop one's personal capacities and talents*" (emphasis in original, Derkx, 2014, p. 52). In light of the perspective of entangled humanism, we propose an 'entangled' interpretation of this tenet, where the self is seen as entangled with others and the environment. This also leads to an entangled view of autonomy, a view which we already find in van Praag's work, when he connects autonomy with people's shared responsibility (see Derkx, 2009, pp. 70–71). Furthermore, embracing an entangled perspective has ethical implications concerning the purposes or goods that one should try to achieve. These should involve attempts to engage with others or otherness in as wide a sense as possible. In a similar vein, van Praag writes that true self-realization requires engaging with the 'not-self,' and that humanism can be understood as anti-egoism (see Derkx, 2009, p. 69). We go deeper into this ethical understanding of self-fulfillment when writing about humanist spirituality below.

> In Vignette 4, humanist chaplain Lucas, when talking about supporting Jonas, who is severely ill and has had his request for physician-assisted dying approved, expresses how the principle of entangled autonomy is the basis of his humanist worldview and his work: "As a humanist, I support people's autonomy and thus the possibility of dying with dignity. I believe everyone has the right to choose for themselves how to live and die, and I believe that there are no ready-made answers to questions about life and death, only the answers we formulate and reformulate for ourselves. Human relationality is of immeasurable value, so when meeting with others I focus on the connection between us and ask about meaningful connections to other humans and nonhumans in their life."

The fourth and final humanist tenet is that *human beings should nurture a love of specific, vulnerable, and irreplaceable persons* (see Derkx, 2014, p. 54). This counters the idea that human beings may be grasped and approached in terms of a generalized notion of 'the human being,' which connects this tenet to critical humanism. There is also a link with entangled humanism, as this principle emphasizes that human beings are vulnerable instead of always 'in control.' However, the perspective of entangled humanism also shows that this tenet has a narrow focus on people and suggests that people should nurture love in a wider sense, for all kinds of beings and for our fragile world in its entirety.

If we think about worldviews in terms of the seven dimensions distinguished by Smart (1999) which were outlined in the introduction to this chapter, the postulates by van Praag (1982) can be seen as a proposal for characterizing the doctrinal dimension of humanism. Furthermore, Derkx's (2014) tenets can be seen as a proposal for characterizing both the doctrinal and the ethical dimension of humanism. Alma and Anbeek (2013) come up with a proposal for all seven dimensions of humanism. They conclude that humanism "manifests itself, particularly in the narrative, philosophical, ethical and experiential dimensions" (Alma & Anbeek, 2013, p. 14). They point to the poverty of humanism when it comes to the ritual, organizational, and material dimensions. As the different worldview dimensions offer various spiritual pathways towards meaning making, this suggests that there might be a certain poverty when it comes to spiritual resources in humanism. If we take a closer look, however, we see how humanism also manifests in the ritual, organizational, and material dimensions – although in somewhat nontraditional ways. For instance, even though there are no ancient, shared rituals in humanism that people may fall back on in hard times or when celebrating life events, we see a development towards more openness to and appreciation of humanist rituality while in some European countries (e.g. Belgium, UK, and Norway), there are already more established humanist rituals and celebrations.

Vignette 3 shows how humanist chaplain Kimberly uses embodiment, symbols, and small rituals as pathways towards meaning making, in this case in an abortion support group. For instance, "Kimberly has asked participants to bring something meaningful to them regarding their abortion, for instance an object, a song, or a poem." These symbols allow participants to share feelings and experiences which cannot be grasped by rational logic and are difficult to put into words. Kimberly also stresses the embodied dimension of meaning making, as she asks participants where in the body these feelings and experiences are felt. Another ritual element Kimberly uses is her invitation "to write a letter to themselves and/or the imagined child." According to Kimberly, working in this way expresses her humanist values, as "she believes in and strives to nourish the power, potential, connectedness, dignity, and freedom of humans." Kimberly herself symbolized her abortion by getting a tattoo a few months afterwards: "It symbolizes my loss and transformation. Getting an abortion changed me. This tattoo makes that visible. That is something I missed: some visible mark that this happened to me."

Humanist spirituality

In Chapter 1, we explained that worldviews comprise an understanding of spirituality: an understanding of what is ultimate goodness – goodness that inspires faith and involves transcendence – and how to connect with it. So, when exploring humanism as a worldview, we need to address the question of how humanism involves an understanding of goodness that we may orient towards, even in situations of severe disorientation. How can humanism provide a sense of orientation in situations which cannot be grasped or understood by reason or logic – in the context of severe suffering, tragic events, or interpersonal and structural violence, or when people experience awe and wonder? What notion of transcendence, of goodness 'beyond' severely disorienting experiences can be found in humanism? And what inspires humanist faith in the face of extreme adversity?

In Vignette 1, humanist chaplain and celebrant Chris explicitly states how spirituality is part of his humanist worldview and resonates in the marriage celebrations he holds: "Feelings and spirituality are important to my humanism and I understand spirituality as a broad term. Spirituality can be anything that makes someone feel connected in a transcendent way, to something bigger, while still down-to-earth – or not. For example: if a couple wants to honor their ancestors during the ceremony and either they feel like their ancestors are watching over them or they feel this connection in the sense of gratitude for what their ancestors have done to make their current lives possible ... both can be examples of spirituality, if you ask me. I adjust my ceremonies to be as spiritual or down-to-earth as the couple wants. But there is also down-to-earth spirituality – connecting with each other. That is important to my humanism." Chris elaborates further on this relational quality of spirituality: "Humanist values play a role in how I go about guiding couples. Most importantly, reverence for humans as equal individuals but not just individuals. We are social creatures, we need each other. Community is everything. People want these ceremonies because they want to share their story, they want to involve people in their story, they need others to help them with their story."

An early text about humanist spirituality is by Elkins et al. (1988), who write: "The concept of humanist spirituality is not new, but it may be an idea whose time has come" (p. 15). They build on work by authors like Abraham Maslow and John Dewey when describing spirituality as a human phenomenon that may be expressed through religious traditions but also in nonreligious ways. Even earlier, van Praag, without actually using the term spirituality (which was not current at the time), provided us with a wealth of ideas that we would now see as describing humanist spirituality. For instance, he paints a picture of the world that has 'enchanted' aspects when he speaks about "the mystery of life" (van Praag, 1982, p. 163) or about how "miracles" (van Praag, 1982, p. 163) may happen when people really listen to one another. Also, in van Praag 's humanism there is room for experiences of awe (as mentioned earlier), and for experiencing "ecstasy: a sense of standing outside the normal reality of day-to-day living" (van Praag, 1982, p. 129).

Starting from these early ideas, we elaborate on humanist spirituality along three lines. First, we explain how Iris Murdoch, on the basis of assumptions that are in line with the view of humanism presented in this chapter, develops notions of spirituality and transcendence in terms of attentively and lovingly looking beyond the self. Second, we present Emmanuel Levinas' notion of 'small goodness' as a central element of humanist spirituality. Third, we explore how Hannah Arendt's notion of natality informs a worldly view of faith which fits within humanism.

Humanist spirituality as cultivating courageous love

Like Taylor (1989), Murdoch (1970) understands people's spiritual life in terms of orientation towards visions of the good that have a certain weight.[8] While in Taylor's account of spirituality visions of the good have spiritual weight when they represent what is of ultimate value to people, Murdoch offers a more substantial and explicitly ethical account.[9] Her account is rooted in two assumptions: "I assume that human beings are naturally self-ish, and that human life has no external point or τέλος" (Murdoch, 1970, p. 76). In this view, when we orient to visions of the good that represent what is of crucial importance to us, we might well be engaging in rather egocentric projects. Murdoch reserves the designation 'spiritual' for orientation processes in which we are not driven by selfishness but cultivate love and compassion for others and otherness. She uses the term 'the Good' to denote the focal point of such orientation processes: "We are spiritual creatures, attracted by excellence and made for the Good" (p. 100).[10]

According to Murdoch (1970), the Good is indefinable, unreachable and remains forever mysterious: "it lies always beyond, and it is from this beyond that it exercises its *authority*" (p. 61). So, there is no prescribed endpoint to our spiritual journey – orienting to the Good involves some form of transcendence, of always moving 'beyond.' Murdoch pays extensive attention to the notion of transcendence, pointing out that the term is often used to refer to a move away from the world – a 'vertical, upward' move – and thus away from seeing and loving what is 'here.' She proposes a view of transcendence which involves a move *towards* the world, which may be understood as a 'horizontal' or 'downward' move.[11] What is transcended here is not the world and its fragility and imperfection but the human tendency to look at the world in terms of personal interests and wishes. This tendency prevents us from "seeing what there is outside one" (Murdoch, 1970, p. 57). It often leads us to remain in our personal fantasy world, to overlook, to look away, or to judge. In Murdoch's view, 'seeing what there is outside one' requires, on the contrary, an attentive, loving, and compassionate gaze. A loving gaze shows us what is 'really there' instead of the reflections of our own fantasies.

According to Murdoch (1970), transcendence can therefore be seen as a form of realism. Orienting to the Good is a spiritual journey towards 'what is.' It involves a sustained effort to engage with the world by "really *looking"* (Murdoch, 1970, p. 89). This explains why, in Murdoch's eyes, spiritual journeys are hard, and require devotion and discipline: on many occasions, we find looking at reality difficult, and we are inclined to over-look or look away. Murdoch mentions severely disorienting situations like confrontation with evil and suffering as examples of such occasions. Orienting to the Good in such situations is possible; learning to do so is a task: "It is a *task* to see the world as it is" (Murdoch, 1970, p. 89). This spiri-tual task of cultivating attention, love, and compassion requires courage and is never finished. Furthermore, Murdoch emphasizes that this task can-not be achieved by will. It is a matter of 'willingness' and discipline to always again turn our attention away from our own fantasies, thus inducing a "reorientation of an energy which is naturally selfish" (Murdoch, 1970, p. 53). Sometimes, this reorientation just 'happens to us,' in what we may call spiritual moments: when something 'catches our attention' we are drawn to it, and our sense of ego dissolves.

The centrality of small goodness in humanist spirituality

Murdoch's (1970) emphasis on the crucial role of love and compassion in our spiritual life relates to the work of Levinas (1988/1994), who positions 'goodness' in the love and compassion that people bear in their hearts for everything that is alive. According to Levinas, goodness is a small act, stem-ming from an insatiable desire that is aroused in the encounter with the other, manifesting as an unplanned, coincidental, fleeting, humble, largely invisible kindness. This goodness, like the orientation to the Good accord-ing to Murdoch, cannot be produced by will or plan, it cannot be orga-nized, and there is no certainty about the outcome either. Small goodness exists without a guarantee that it will survive or have an effect. It is fragile because it can easily be transformed and misused. Levinas explains the notion of small goodness using, among others, the following quote from Vasily Grossman's novel *Life and Fate*:

> There exists, side by side with this so terrible greater good, human kind-ness in everyday life. It is the kindness of an old lady who gives a piece of bread to a convict along the roadside. It is the kindness of a soldier who holds his canteen out to a wounded enemy. The kindness of youth taking pity on old age, the kindness of a peasant who hides an old Jew in his barn. It is the kindness of those prison guards who risk their own freedom, smuggle the letters of prisoners out to wives and mothers. That private goodness of an individual for another individual is a goodness without witnesses, a little goodness without ideology. It could be called goodness without thought. The goodness of men outside the religious or social good.
>
> (cited in 1988/1994, p. 91)

Even when we face evil and, as a consequence, experience severe disorientation, small goodness has the potential to make a slight difference. Levinas (1988/1994) speaks about "the sovereignty of that primordial goodness or mercy that evil cannot overcome" (p. 90).[12] At the same time, Levinas warns us that often small, casual, and thoughtless forms of indolence, laziness, indifference, and absent-mindedness, push back or inhibit goodness (Burggraeve, 2020). Therefore, the essence of goodness is 'nonindifference,' which allows for a selfless and caring attitude towards the other.

Natality as inspiring humanist faith

Levinas' (1988/1994) emphasis on human encounters as the place where goodness manifests resonates with the focus on relationality in Arendt's (1958) work. Natality is an important concept here. Arendt originally framed natality as the human condition that emerges from our birth, our literal beginning. Our birth stresses that we come from someone and are not born from no one. Moreover, we are born into a world that already exists, which acknowledges that, from the beginning, we are relational beings who are entangled with the world and others. We are, as Arendt phrases it, born into a "web of human relationships" (p. 183). Moreover, we originate from the body of another human, which means that our entanglement with others is necessarily embodied. This makes us somewhat mysterious creatures as we cannot be captured by any description of 'who we are': "The moment we want to say who somebody is, our very vocabulary leads us astray into saying what he is ... his specific uniqueness escapes us" (Arendt, 1958, p. 181). According to Arendt, it is only when we speak and act in the context of the web of relationships that our uniqueness and humanness can be revealed. This disclosure of who we are requires an atmosphere "where people are *with* others and neither for nor against them" (Arendt, 1958, p. 180). In such an atmosphere the human condition of natality is actualized: something new, completely unexpected, may happen. Arendt speaks about this emergence of something new in terms of a miracle: "the new therefore always appears in the guise of a miracle" (p. 178).[13]

While spirituality is often linked to mortality, humanist spirituality may also be linked to natality (Wojtkowiak & Schuhmann, 2022). From a natality perspective, goodness may be understood as involving the nurturing of an attitude of being *with* others, thus encouraging them to appear in their uniqueness through speech and action. Nurturing this attitude may be seen as a humanist spiritual practice that supports life, countering the objectification of human beings. Echoing Arendt (1958), we may say that where people come together, a potential space is opened up where 'miracles' may happen. In particular, the perspective of natality allows for a worldly understanding of faith which also nurtures hope: "Only the full experience of this capacity [to act] can bestow upon human affairs faith and hope" (Arendt, 1958, p. 247). Even when all hope seems lost, for instance when people face tragedy and suffering, we may have faith in the possibility that something new and unexpected may happen when people show interest in each other.[14]

Conclusion

Understanding humanism as a worldview starts from the notion that visions of the good do not represent pre-given, supra-historical ideas but are dynamic, contextualized human constructs. In particular, any set of normative postulates, principles, or tenets that is proposed as characterizing humanism requires a continuing process of critical reflection. Such reflection needs to address both the more global question of how these principles are entangled in power structures and involved in dehumanizing tendencies and major current problems humanity struggles with, and the more local question of how they relate to the lived reality of actual people and their actual desires and struggles. Our reflections on these questions in this chapter have led us to highlight that humanism as a lived worldview needs to accommodate the ways in which people orient in life as embodied and relational creatures in a material and entangled world. In particular, we have proposed a view of humanist spirituality as arising in the encounter with the other or otherness. Paradoxically, in humanist spirituality, what is called the 'sacred' or the 'highest' is at the same time earthly, messy, and modest, since it emerges from our embodied relationships with others and the world.

Notes

1   In religions, such transcendence often involves a move beyond worldly affairs toward a supernatural, eternal world.
2   This notion of spirituality is grounded in the understanding of the 'spiritual' as described in Chapter 1. In Chapter 3, we show how this understanding of the 'spiritual' character of orientation processes connects (and is in line) with the consensus definition of spirituality by Puchalski et al. (2009) which is usually used in relation to spiritual care.
3   For instance, Levinas (1972/2003) speaks about "the crisis of humanism" in view of the atrocities and cruelty that people time and again prove to be capable of (p. 127); or we may think of radical feminist thought which criticizes the idea of 'the human' implicated in Western humanism, where the sovereign notion of 'reason' – a masculine, white and Western ideal – is seen as the standard for what counts as human and as the motor for human development. As a response, feminist and anti-racist movements developed their own forms of anti- or neo-humanism (Braidotti, 2017).

4 For van Praag, understanding humanism as a worldview was especially important with a view to his efforts to establish humanist chaplaincy (see Introduction to the volume).

5 The remaining anthropological postulates state that human beings are natural (they are part of the world); related (they are interconnected and independent), and free (free – even when possibilities are limited in the given circumstances, they (need to) make choices among these possibilities). The ontological postulates state that the world (1) can be experienced through the senses; (2) exists, not as something 'out there' but as something that is inseparable from human experience; (3) is complete, in the sense that it does not refer to something outside or beyond it; (4) is accidental (it has no pre-given purpose); (5) is dynamic. See van Praag (1982) for further explanation of these postulates.

6 These four criteria – clarified and slightly reworked – form the heart of the 'humanistic perspectives' that we adopt throughout this book.

7 See also Chapter 1, where we describe the socio-cultural dimension of orientation processes.

8 In Chapter 1, we elaborate on Taylor's understanding of the spiritual aspect of orientation in life.

9 In Chapter 1, we mentioned that Taylor's view of the spiritual character of orientation processes includes the possibility that people make sense of their lives spiritually in ways that are ethically questionable.

10 In the chapter 'On God and Good,' Murdoch explains the similarities between the way in which the Good functions as the central object of attention in people's moral-spiritual life and the way in which God is the focus in people's religious life.

11 See Wojtkowiak and Schuhmann (2022) for an explanation of the concept of horizontal transcendence and its background.

12 Interestingly, Murdoch (1970) uses a similar phrasing in the title of her book: *The sovereignty of Good.*

13 Arendt emphasizes that our actions, precisely because they take place in the web of relationships, have unpredictable consequences, which may also be negative. The consequences of our actions transcend our intentions: "Since actions act upon beings who are capable of their own actions, reaction, apart from being a response, is always a new action that strikes out on its own and affects others" (Arendt, 1958, p. 190). Arendt speaks about the 'boundlessness' of human action; as relational beings, we are not in control of how our actions eventually play out. We become, as Arendt points out, 'guilty' of unintended and unforeseen consequences of our actions. As remedies to the irreversibility and the unpredictability of action, Arendt points to the human capacities to keep promises and to forgive.

14 Similarly, van Praag often used the phrase "Expecting nothing, hoping for everything," which illustrates his humanist faith.

References

Alma, H., & Anbeek, C. (2013). Worldviewing competence for narrative interreligious dialogue. In D. Schipani (Ed.), *Multifaith views in spiritual care* (pp. 131–147). Pandora Press.

Arendt, H. (1958). *The human condition.* University of Chicago Press.

Braidotti, R. (2017). Four theses on posthuman feminism. In R. Grusin (Ed.), *Anthropocene Feminism* (pp. 21–48). University of Minnesota Press.

Burggraeve, R. (2020). *Geen toekomst zonder kleine goedheid. Naar genereus samenleven in verantwoordelijkheid vanuit Emmanuel Levinas* [*No future without small goodness. Towards generous coexistence in responsibility on the basis of Emmanuel Levinas*]. Halewijn.

Connolly, W. E. (2017). *Facing the planetary: Entangled humanism and the politics of swarming*. Duke University Press.

Copson, A. (2015). What is humanism? In A. Copson & A. C. Grayling (Eds.), *The Wiley Blackwell handbook of humanism* (pp. 1–33). Wiley Blackwell.

Derkx, P. (1993). Wat is humanisme? [What is humanism?] In P. Cliteur & D. van Houten (Eds.), *Humanisme. Theorie en praktijk* (pp. 99–114). De Tijdstroom.

Derkx, P. (Ed.). (2009). *J. P. van Praag. Om de geestelijke weerbaarheid van humanisten* [*J. P. van Praag. About the existential resilience of humanists*]. Papieren Tijger.

Derkx, P. (2011). *Humanisme, zinvol leven en nooit meer 'ouder' worden'* [Humanism, a meaningful life, and no longer ageing]. VUBPRESS.

Derkx, P. (2014). Humanism as a meaning frame. In A. B. Pinn (Ed.), *What is humanism, and why does it matter?* (pp. 42–57). Routledge.

Derkx, P. (2015). The future of humanism. In A. Copson & A. C. Grayling (Eds.), *The Wiley Blackwell handbook of humanism* (pp. 426–439). Wiley Blackwell.

Elkins, D. N., Hedstrom, L. J., Hughes, L. L., Leaf, J. A., & Saunders, C. (1988). Toward a humanistic-phenomenological spirituality: Definition, description, and measurement. *Journal of Humanistic Psychology, 28*(4), 5–18. https://doi.org/10.1177/0022167888284002

Fanon, F. (2008). *Black skin, white masks* (R. Philcox, Trans.). Penguin Books. (Original work published 1952)

Haidt, J. (2001). The emotional dog and its rational tail: A social intuitionist approach to moral judgment. *Psychological Review, 108*(4), 814–834. https://doi.org/10.1037/0033-295X.108.4.814

Irigaray, L. (1990). *Je, tu, nous: Towards a culture of difference* (A. Martin, Trans.). Routledge.

Kunneman, H. (1993). Humanisme en postmodernisme [Humanism and postmodernism]. In P. Cliteur & D. van Houten (Eds.), *Humanisme. Theorie en praktijk* (pp. 65–77). De Tijdstroom.

Levinas, E. (1994). *In the time of the nations* (M. B. Smith, Trans.). Indiana University Press. (Original work published 1988)

Levinas, E. (2003). *Humanism of the Other* (N. Poller, Trans.). University of Illinois Press. (Original work published 1972)

Martela, F., & Steger, M. F. (2016). The three meanings of meaning in life: Distinguishing coherence, purpose, and significance. *The Journal of Positive Psychology, 11*(5), 531–545. https://doi.org/10.1080/17439760.2015.1137623

Murdoch, I. (1970). *The sovereignty of good*. Routledge.

Nussbaum, M. (2014). *Political emotions. Why love matters for justice*. The Belknap Press.

Park, C. L. (2010). Making sense of the meaning literature: An integrative review of meaning making and its effects on adjustment to stressful life events. *Psychological bulletin, 136*(2), 257. https://doi.org/10.1037/a0018301

Pinn, A. B. (2012). *The end of God-talk. An African American humanist theology*. Oxford University Press.

Pinn, A. B. (2014). Humanism as guide to life meaning. In A. B. Pinn (Ed.), *What is humanism, and why does it matter?* (pp. 28–41). Routledge.

Plummer, K. (2021). *Critical humanism: A manifesto for the 21st century*. Polity Press.

Puchalski, C., Ferrell, B., Virani, R., Otis-Green, S., Baird, P., Bull, J., Chochinov, H., Handzo, G., Nelson-Becker, H., Prince-Paul, M., Pugliese, K., & Sulmasy, D. (2009). Improving the quality of spiritual care as a dimension of palliative care: The report of the Consensus Conference. *Journal of Palliative Medicine, 12*(10), 885–904. https://doi.org/10.1089/jpm.2009.0142

Radest, H. B. (2014). Humanism as experience. In A. B. Pinn (Ed.), *What is humanism, and why does it matter?* (pp. 2–27). Routledge.

Rosaldo, M. Z. (1984). Toward an anthropology of self and feeling. In R. A. Skewder & R. A. Levine (Eds.), *Culture theory. Essays on mind, self and emotion* (pp. 137–157). Cambridge University Press.

Schuhmann, C. M., Wojtkowiak, J., van Lierop, R., & Pitstra, F. (2021). Humanist chaplaincy according to Northwestern European chaplains: Towards a framework for understanding chaplaincy in secular societies. *Journal of Health Care Chaplaincy, 27*(4), 207–221. https://doi.org/10.1080/08854726.2020.1723190

Smart, N. (1999). *Dimensions of the sacred: An anatomy of the world's beliefs*. University of California Press.

Taylor, C. (1989). *Sources of the self. The making of the modern identity*. The Belknap Press.

Taylor, C. (2007). *A secular age*. The Belknap Press.

Tillich, P. (1957). *Dynamics of faith*. HarperOne.

van Goelst Meijer, S. L. E. (2015). *Profound revolution: Towards an integrated understanding of contemporary nonviolence*. [Doctoral dissertation, University of Humanistic Studies]. www.researchgate.net/publication/282357103

van Praag, J. P. (1982). *Foundations of humanism*. Prometheus Books.

Wentzer, T. S., & Mattingly, C. (2018). Toward a new humanism: An approach from philosophical anthropology. *Journal of Ethnographic Theory, 8*(1/2), 144–157. https://doi.org/10.1086/698361

Wojtkowiak, J., & Schuhmann, C. M. (2022). Natality and relational transcendence in humanist chaplaincy. *Religions, 13*(4), 271. https://doi.org/10.3390/rel13040271

Chapter 3

Chaplaincy in secularizing, plural societies

Carmen Schuhmann, Gaby Jacobs,
and Annelieke Damen

Introduction

In this chapter, we turn our attention to the central matter of this volume: chaplaincy in contemporary Western secularizing and plural societies. Traditionally, the authority of chaplains was rooted in their link with religious traditions and institutions. In plural societies, however, the view of chaplains as representing and embodying a specific religious tradition no longer serves as the generally accepted foundation for the legitimacy and credibility of chaplaincy (Schuhmann & Damen, 2018). These days, chaplains need to be able to support people whose orienting frameworks are diverse, dynamic and individualized (Cadge & Rambo, 2022; Doehring, 2015; Grung, 2023). This has, among other things, led to a development towards legitimizing chaplaincy in terms of professional accountability, in particular through research. Nowadays, chaplaincy is usually presented as a particular profession, implicating that it involves a specific body of knowledge and a set of specialized skills (Swift, 2004; Swinton, 2003). The transition towards professional accountability, however, is by no means complete (Glasner et al., 2023; Jacobs et al., 2023). Chaplaincy still seems to be in need of a new conceptualization that provides a convincing response to the question: "What are the specific aims, methods, and key images of the profession?" (Zock, 2008, p. 139).

In this chapter, we develop an inclusive view of chaplaincy in secularizing and plural societies which aims to do justice both to the historical religious roots of the profession and to the diverse ways in which people in these societies search for meaning (see Introduction to the volume). A starting point of our explorations is the idea that chaplains still, like they have always done, support people's search for meaning in life, in particular when life is not self-evident (Grefe et al., 2022). We develop our view of chaplaincy along three lines. First, we argue that the specific domain of chaplaincy consists of processes of orientation in life and present a view of what are the specific competencies of chaplains that make them specialists in providing

DOI: 10.4324/9781003428633-4

spiritual care. Second, we explore the role of chaplains' orienting frameworks, in particular their worldviews, in their professionalism. We argue that chaplains can be characterized as 'normative professionals' who 'represent faith in goodness.' Third, we develop an understanding of the distinctive aim of chaplaincy as 'having a sense of orientation in life' and specify this aim by distinguishing goals at the micro-, meso-, and macrolevel of chaplaincy.

The domain of chaplaincy: supporting processes of (re)orientation in life

In Chapter 1 we explained existential meaning making in terms of orientation in life. We followed Taylor's (1989) understanding of the spiritual character of orientation processes in terms of 'ultimate' value: we orient towards visions of the good that represent what is, to us, a life worth living. Furthermore, in Chapter 1 and 2 we explained that, in this view, worldviews play a specific role in existential meaning making, as these provide spiritual resources for reorientation, in particular in the context of severely disorienting events and circumstances. In line with these ideas, we understand chaplaincy as care for processes of orientation in life. This involves supporting people as they look for, figure out, or express what, to them, is of ultimate value, and to experience connectedness with ultimately valuable objects, people, communities, entities, views, etc. Chaplaincy is especially relevant when people experience disorientation, when their habitual modes of orientation are interrupted.

In relation to spiritual care, the most common definition of spirituality that is used is the consensus definition by Puchalski et al. (2009):

> Spirituality is the aspect of humanity that refers to the way individuals seek and express meaning and purpose and the way they experience their connectedness to the moment, to self, to others, to nature, and to the significant or sacred.
>
> (p. 887)

This definition expresses the view that spirituality is something that concerns all people, whether they identify as religious or not. It can be linked to understanding orientation processes as having a spiritual character, as explained in Chapter 1: orientation in life may involve *seeking* and *expressing* what we see as of ultimate value, and *experiencing* a sense of orientation – i.e., experiencing *connectedness* with what is of ultimate value to us. Understanding chaplaincy in terms of care for processes of orientation in life thus fits in with the notion that chaplains are spiritual care providers.

These days, spiritual care is often seen as a shared task of the various professionals (and volunteers) who, in a specific context, are involved in caring for and supporting people (Puchalski et al., 2014).[1] While for most of these professionals, spiritual care is not their main focus, this is the case for chaplains, who may thus be characterized as spiritual care professionals par excellence or as specialists in providing spiritual care. In terms of competencies, what makes chaplains specialist spiritual caregivers is, first, their ability to provide care to people in the context of (severe) disorientation – both in situations where people feel that hope is lost and in the context of joyful life events. Second, chaplains are attentive to the role of worldviews in processes of (re)orientation in life, which may be something other professionals or volunteers are not comfortable doing. Third, chaplains recognize and know how to navigate the multiplicity of potentially conflicting visions of the good involved in (caring for) processes of (re)orientation in life.

Vignette 4 illustrates all three characteristics of chaplaincy as specialist spiritual care. In the vignette, Jonas describes the severely disorientating experience of being so seriously ill that he sees no path towards a good life anymore, which leads to his request for physician-assisted dying. First, humanist chaplain Lucas points out that staying with such severe disorientation is characteristic for his approach: "People who request physician-assisted dying often encounter people who want to fix the situation and encourage them to stay – through medication, treatment plans, peptalks, prayers, practical help. That is not what I do. I join them in that difficult place, I listen and ask." Second, Lucas makes space for discussing the ways in which views on physician-assisted dying of both Jonas and his family members are informed by their worldview backgrounds. "Jonas grew up Catholic and he sometimes worries that maybe he is doing something wrong. He thought he did not believe in God anymore and he did not think about afterlife much – until faced with death. His mother and extended family are all Catholic, and while they try to be as supportive as they can, they do struggle to fully understand his decision. All of this he discusses with Lucas." Third, not only does Lucas make room for discussing how Jonas' view on death and physician-assisted dying differs from that of his family members; he also offers a space where Lucas may explore the ambivalence and complexity of his own views. While Jonas does not wish to burden his family members with his doubts and fears which exist alongside the relief and strength he feels, he does discuss all of this with Lucas.

The role of chaplains' worldviews in their professionalism

Understanding chaplains as professionals who are specialists in caring for processes of (re)orientation in life raises the question of how their own orienting frameworks, i.e. their worldviews, come into play in their professional practice. This question has become especially salient in plural societies, as chaplains have to relate to people with a variety of worldview orientations so that they cannot provide care from within a certain worldview which serves as a self-evident, shared normative framework. Chaplains are cautious not to impose their own worldview on others. This may incite them to aim for a 'neutral' approach, attempting to disentangle their practice from their orienting frameworks, in particular their worldviews (Lynch, 2002; van Houten & Mooren, 2002).

In order to characterize the professionalism of chaplains in a 'secular age,' we first elaborate on the notion of 'normative professionalism': a view on professionalism which addresses the role of professionals' normative frameworks in their practice. We then propose the notion of 'representing faith in goodness' as a way to characterize the role of worldviews in the normative professionalism of chaplains in plural societies.

Normative professionalism

The concept of normative professionalism was coined in the 1990s in the Netherlands (Kunneman, 2002) to acknowledge the normative components of orienting frameworks in caring professions, a normativity that often stays hidden in the objectifying approaches common in health and social care. Chaplaincy can be seen as a 'normative profession' *pur sang*, for two reasons. First, it expresses the idea that disorientations in life cannot be treated according to a biomedical model as solvable problems, but that they are complex, unsettling, and multidimensional. This requires an approach of searching, learning, and trying, in which the chaplains' orienting frameworks matter, as well as their relational skills and moral sensitivity. It also expresses the idea, put forward in Chapter 1, that existential questions always already have a social-structural dimension (see also Jacobs, 2008): "But the *professionals* ... are also confronted with moral and existential dilemmas – and thus with sub-political questions – as an integral part of their professional activities" (Kunneman, 2002, p. 35). This means that the chaplain reflects on the normative orienting frameworks that may foster or hinder the striving towards visions of the good on a personal, interpersonal, organizational, and societal level. This reflexive ability thus also includes the normativity in the professional relationship: the orienting frameworks of the chaplain and how these may interact with those of the client, the power hierarchies that may be disrupted or sustained through the use of language,[2] and the visions of the good that are co-created in the interaction. From a normative perspective, chaplaincy is always practiced within a context in which different values and norms collide and strive for priority, meaning that choices and acts are not value-free, including those made by the chaplain. Therefore, it is necessary for chaplains to continue questioning their frameworks and practices to strive for the good in their institutions. Processes of globalization and pluralization of orienting frameworks (see also Chapter 1), and of democratization in society, stress the importance of dialogue about the values and normativity underlying orienting frameworks and practices.

This brings us to a second reason for emphasizing normative professionalism in chaplaincy. This concept proposes a relational and dialogical attitude to others and the world. This means that the orienting frameworks and practices – the visions of the good – are not fixed but open and emerging. The chaplain does not know beforehand where a conversation with a client or a colleague will take them. This is expressed well by a quote from the philosopher Heidegger (1968, cited in Dall'Alba, 2009, p. 67):

> His learning is not mere practice, to gain facility in the use of tools. Nor does he merely gather knowledge about the customary forms of the things he is to build. If he is to become a true cabinetmaker, he makes himself answer and respond above all to the different kinds of wood and to the shapes slumbering within wood – to wood as it enters into man's dwelling with all the hidden riches of its nature. In fact, this relatedness to wood is what maintains the whole craft. Without that relatedness, the craft will never be anything but empty busywork.
>
> (pp. 14–15)

As chaplains' professionalism is the guidance in processes of orientation in life; this often involves searching for answers to difficult questions and moral dilemmas through dialogue with those directly involved: clients, spouses, colleagues, management, and other stakeholders. Cooperation with other disciplines and policymakers is part of this, proceeding from a shared commitment to create a vision of the good. Normative professionalism in chaplaincy then is characterized by the development of dynamic cultures of cooperation, instead of chaplains operating autonomously and in an enclosed environment. This means that the chaplain has a responsibility to interfere with dehumanizing practices and to be a change agent in organizations and society. This dialogical attitude and competence does not mean, however, that chaplains' expertise, experience, and discretionary judgment – the competence to form judgments within their own area of expertise – is less important. What it does mean is that this is seen as part of a process of dialogue in which clients' experience-based knowledge and expertise, as well as expertise from other disciplines, have a place. This 'democratic professionalism' then is characterized by a self-critical attitude and openness to other orienting frameworks:

> Though they [professionals] retain the authority and at least somewhat privileged voice of people with experience and specialized training, they recognize that they may know only part of what is important in taking a decision about a treatment plan, a service, a public policy that relates to their domain. Above all, they seek to open their professional domain to other voices, other experiences.
>
> (Dzur, 2003, p. 25)

In spiritual care as a collaborative endeavor of chaplains and other health care professionals, this democratic attitude is an important addition to chaplains' normative professionalism.

Representing faith in goodness

Understanding chaplaincy as a normative profession implies that chaplains' own orienting frameworks, and, in particular, their worldviews, matter in their practices. In Chapter 1 we characterized worldviews as collective orienting frameworks that accommodate disorientation – even severely disorientating experiences, where all good seems lost. While different worldviews offer different spiritual resources for meaning making in the face of disorientation, all worldviews comprise a profound belief – or faith – that not all good is lost forever, that some notion of the good remains believable against the odds (see Chapter 2).[3] Schuhmann and Damen (2018) argue that it is this faith, shared by different worldviews, rather than the specific worldview traditions from which a chaplain draws their faith, that characterizes chaplaincy in a 'secular age': chaplains, "independent of their tradition, do not promote a fixed vision of the good but rather represent the possibility of somehow, eventually, connecting to some good that is not rendered utterly meaningless by suffering and evil" (p. 410).

We denote this faith that can be found in all worldviews, and that all chaplains represent, as faith in goodness, a goodness that people may experience, even in desperate situations, sometimes in fleeting moments.[4] Such an experience of goodness may be related to God or the divine, or it may be about experiencing connectedness with others, animals, beauty, or nature. Following Murdoch's (1970) view of the Good as transcendent and mysterious, and Levinas' (1988/1994) notion of 'small goodness' which cannot be controlled or planned (see Chapter 2), goodness is associated with human vulnerability, suffering, and imperfection. Goodness is fragile (Nussbaum, 2001) and may easily disappear in the hassle of everyday life or as a consequence of hierarchic power relationships. Representing faith in goodness therefore not only points to the hope and consolation that chaplains offer to individuals and groups but also to the critical role chaplains may play in organizations and society when dominant visions of the good leave no room for human vulnerability and fallibility. Furthermore, representing faith in goodness "involves addressing the political question of which visions of the good are available to whom" (Schuhmann & Damen, 2018, p. 415), thus countering marginalization and dehumanization, which is in line with how we described the chaplain's role as a normative professional.

In Vignette 2, we see how humanist chaplain Nathan represents faith in goodness in the context of a care home. Nathan describes the care home as a place where it is far from obvious to experience goodness: "It is not always a pleasant place to be. Many of my clients miss home. They do not feel at home here, or struggle to still feel at home anywhere. They do not get to decide much and they cannot do much for themselves – permanently or temporarily. That is a difficult way to live: they are fragile, perhaps close to death, and at the same time they lack rooting." In a care home, faith in goodness might easily erode. Nathan says the following about his faith in goodness: "Our shared human vulnerability and strength is a source of inspiration to me. From that place, I approach the person in front of me and I am reminded that there is a lot I can share with them."

The sanctuary function of chaplaincy

A particular way in which chaplains can exercise their normative professionalism is through their sanctuary function. Originally a sanctuary[5] was a place of asylum that shied away from the authority of the area in which that sanctuary was located, often offered by the churches. Nowadays, the sanctuary of chaplaincy is still a place where the institutional rules and regulations do not hold, e.g., the sharing of information about patients by medical staff or the need for therapy compliance. The sanctuary is connected with being an office-holder and having a mission from a worldview or religious organization, and with the duty of confidentiality. In this sense, it is a safe space for vulnerable people to share their utmost concerns with the chaplain, to ponder over issues without any need to make a decision, or to be simply silent. The sanctuary function enables the chaplain to do their work independently and disinterestedly at all times, regardless of hierarchy. It is precisely in hierarchical institutions such as the police or armed forces, hospitals or mental health care institutes, as well as penitentiaries, that being outside that hierarchy is of vital importance. From the perspective of normative professionalism, the sanctuary can be seen as a critical space to address disorientations in life, such as suffering, tragedy, social injustice, and indignity within organizations and society (Jacobs, 2001). It is not so much a place separate from the organization or society, without having a connection. Instead, it is a space in-between, connecting society or the organization with a higher good. Chaplains then have both an insider's and an outsider's position (a 'double position') with regard to the institutions in which they work: they are an inside-outsider or outside-insider. The chaplain as 'representing faith in goodness' then becomes a boundary crosser, having a connecting and at the same time critical function (Jacobs et al., 2023). When theorizing this space in-between as a sanctuary and relating this to the core task of chaplaincy as 'representing faith in goodness,' it becomes clear that humanist values are practiced in this space. Therefore, working from the border area allows the sanctuary not only to be a relatively 'safe haven' for people (clients, professionals) to share their stories but also to be a place from which empowerment and humanization take shape (Jacobs, 2001).

'Having a sense of orientation in life' as the central goal in chaplaincy

The idea of normative professionalism put forward in the previous sections puts the focus on visions of the good that chaplaincy strives for. Professions characteristically involve "devotion to a transcendent value which infuses its specialization with a larger and putatively higher goal … Each body of professional knowledge and skill is attached to such a value" (Freidson, 2001, p. 122). Similarly, MacIntyre (2007) speaks about practices as forms of socially established activity that are aimed at realizing specific 'internal goods' or central goals that determine what counts as 'change for the better' in the practice. He emphasizes the historical dimension of practices and their goals: "Practices never have a goal or goals fixed for all times … but the goals themselves are transmuted by the history of the activity" (MacIntyre, 2007, p. 225). For chaplaincy, this raises the question of how the internal good or central goal[6] of the profession has changed, given the historical evolution of chaplaincy from religious care to spiritual care.

Understanding the domain of present-day chaplaincy in terms of processes of (re)orientation in life, implies that *having a sense of orientation in life* may be seen as the overarching central goal or aim of chaplaincy.[7] Two remarks are in place here. First, this does not imply that, in chaplaincy, disorientations are seen as purely negative phenomena that need to be overcome as quickly as possible through reorientation. We already argued in Chapter 1 that people may experience disorientation in relation to joyful events, and that disorientation and orientation are not diametrically opposed but rather related in a dialectical way. Second, this internal chaplaincy good is inherently unstable over time. Having a sense of orientation is not something we arrive at once and for all. Minor and major disorientations are part of life and may at all times affect our sense of orientation. The 'changes for the better' that chaplains aim to realize in their practices are therefore not necessarily lasting and may be temporary. People may have a sense of orientation just by experiencing some goodness in the moment. Also, having a sense of orientation may be less about being oriented in the present moment but rather about having faith or hope that we may, at some point, maybe in unexpected ways, orient towards some vision of the good.

Chaplaincy goals at the micro-, meso-, and macrolevel

As orientation in life is not only a spiritual process but also a relational, socio-cultural, and political process (see Chapter 1), the central chaplaincy goal of having a sense of orientation in life should not just be considered and fostered by chaplains at the level of individuals (microlevel) but also at the level of groups (microlevel), organizations (mesolevel), and society (macrolevel). Our embodiment and physical surroundings, our spiritual orientation or worldview, our relational networks, and the socio-cultural and political structures we find ourselves in, all affect our sense of (dis)orientation in life. Let us therefore explore how the aim of 'having a sense of orientation in life' can be specified to goals at the micro-, meso-, and macrolevel of chaplaincy. An overview of these goals is listed in Table 3.1.

Table 3.1 Goals of chaplaincy on a micro-, meso-, and macrolevel

Overarching goal:
Having a sense of orientation in life

Microlevel – individuals, groups:

1. Express and explore experiences of disorientation.
2. Explicate and potentially reconsider visions of a good life.
3. Explore how to actually be close to or move towards renewed visions of a good life.
4. Experience relational affirmation and empowerment.

Mesolevel – organizations, institutions:

1. Recognize and articulate disorientations.
2. Provide (collaboration in) spiritual care in order to enhance the conditions for having a sense of orientation.
3. The inclusion of visions of a good life in ethics and policy.

Macrolevel – communities, society:

1. Hold visions of a good life in which people are seen as disorientable and that allow for vulnerability and fallibility.
2. Have or create spaces for critical dialogue about collective visions of living a good life that include all – in particular marginalized – voices.
3. Conduct experiments with 'disorientation sanctuaries' that develop new practices of living a good life.

Goals at the microlevel of chaplaincy

People can get disoriented in a variety of ways: "Disorientations are a spectrum of widely varying experiences that in all cases disrupt everyday ways of acting and being … The effects of disorientations are very different in different cases" (Harbin, 2016, p. 154).[8] In Chapter 1 we distinguished four types of 'difficult' disorienting experiences: tragedy, ontological insecurity, injustice, and moral tension; and two types of 'uplifting' disorienting experiences: wonder and empowerment. Taylor (1989) broadly distinguishes two movements that may be involved in people's attempts to reorient when facing disorientation.[9] The first one is a movement of gaining insight into visions of a good life that are of ultimate value to us. The second one is a movement of exploring how to actually be close to or move towards such visions of a good life. The two reorienting movements thus are connected with different aspects of 'having a sense of orientation in life' that can be seen as two goals of chaplaincy at the microlevel (the second and third microlevel goals in Table 3.1). It is important to note that this distinction between chaplaincy goals is by no means sharp: even though, in processes of reorientation, the emphasis may be on one of the reorienting movements, these will usually go hand in hand and intermingle in complex and unpredictable ways.

Vignette 1 provides an example of how chaplains may support people to both gain insight in their visions of a good life and move towards those visions. In the vignette, humanist chaplain and celebrant Chris supports Noa and Robin to articulate the meaning of the experience of falling in love and deciding to get married. Chris invites them to tell "about who they are as individuals and as a couple, how they met, and what they find important." Noa explains that this has helped them to gain a clearer vision of what a good life together means to them: "Throughout the process, Chris asked thoughtful questions that helped us think about what our relationship means to us and what kind of life we want to build together." As the marriage ceremony that Chris co-creates with Noa and Robin is designed on the basis of this vision of a good life together, the ceremony also helps the couple to experience what it means to 'live' this vision, to move towards it. This experience is deepened by including the loved ones of the couple as participants in the ceremony. In Chris' words: "At the end of the ceremony, I ask if the couple's loved ones promise to support the couple, and the guests say 'we do.'" In this way, the couple's commitment to move towards their vision of a good life together is affirmed by a community of loved ones.

The previous two chaplaincy goals are derived from theoretical considerations about the different ways in which people may (re)orient in life, and do not take into account the specific context in which chaplaincy takes place in plural societies. If we do so, two more chaplaincy goals on the microlevel can be identified. First, if we look at the relational context in which chaplaincy takes place at the microlevel, either individually or in groups, we see how people may obtain a sense of orientation that originates from the relationship. Goodness may be experienced in the relationship with the chaplain or with members of a chaplain-led group, so that experiencing relational affirmation and empowerment is a chaplaincy goal. We might even say that this is the most fundamental way in which having a sense of orientation may be achieved in chaplaincy, as chaplaincy starts with the encounter between the chaplain and the other.

Second, in secularizing Western societies, the dominant normative vision about disorientation is that "disorientations are inevitably bad and orientedness inevitably good" (Harbin, 2016, p. 161). This does not leave much space for expressing and exploring disorientation, let alone for exploring whether some good may somehow be found in disorienting experiences. In chaplaincy, people may express and explore disorientation without pressure to reorient as quickly as possible. As this approach counters the view that being disoriented equals being in a bad place, expressing and exploring disorientation may, somewhat paradoxically, help people to regain some sense of orientation.

Vignette 3 shows how chaplains may support people to express and explore experiences of disorientation. Humanist chaplain Kimberly offers group meetings where disorientation in relation to abortion may be explored. According to Kimberly, abortion experiences often remain unarticulated: "I offer my clients space to feel and say what they might be holding back, in fear of offending, hurting, or scaring off others, or in fear of being misunderstood and judged." Anna, one of the participants, confirms that it is difficult to speak about abortion – her abortion experience had been "cloaked in isolation, shame, and guilt." Kimberly encourages participants to explore their abortion experience in all its complexity. For Anna, it was helpful to hear Kimberly stress "that abortion did not just have to make her stronger – it could make her stronger and simultaneously bring her more in touch with her fragility, pain, sadness, and uncertainty." The group meeting "helped her look at her abortion experience with more clarity, recognizing more of the layers in her feelings and thoughts."

Taken together, this yields four goals at the microlevel of chaplaincy which may be in play simultaneously or consecutively in specific chaplaincy situations. In Chapters 4 and 5, we further elaborate on how chaplains may work towards these goals by means of individual counseling and group work. In Chapter 6, we indicate how chaplains may design and perform rituals with a view to these goals (and also with a view to the goals at the meso- and macrolevels, described below). Furthermore, in Chapter 8, we explain how chaplains may also contribute to these microlevel goals by taking up the role of a researcher (and also, how doing research may contribute to chaplaincy goals at the meso- and macrolevels).

Goals at the mesolevel of chaplaincy

Within organizations and institutions, explicit and implicit norms, sometimes laid down in rules, allow, promote, and legitimize certain orientations and obstruct and delegitimize other ones. This may even literally be the case, for instance in penitentiaries where movement of inmates is strictly regulated and confined. Organizational and institutional norms have an impact on the possibilities that people, working or staying there, have to orient, and therefore on whether or not they have a sense of orientation in life. On the mesolevel, the goal then is to have institutional and organizational conditions hospitable to those who are disoriented, both to their experiences of disorientation and to their attempts to (re)orient. Here, we follow Harbin's (2016) explanation of hospitable conditions as "the kind of conditions that are accepting and supportive of people who are disoriented" (p. 161). Creating hospitable conditions in institutions and organizations can be broken down into three goals.

The first goal is to recognize and articulate disorientations. As we stated above, in current Western societies, suffering, violence, and exclusion in general are all unwelcome truths, that are easily ignored or hidden behind less disturbing truths (Burggraeve, 2020). The violence that takes place within health care organizations, the military, or penitentiaries – taking different forms such as humiliation, indifference, or rigidity – will not be easily acknowledged. In this chapter we wrote about the sanctuary function of chaplaincy as a critical space to allow these experiences to be discussed, for example among health care personnel or in the military. Chaplains as boundary crossers within the organization also are the 'eye and ear' that can make marginalized experiences heard within the organization. They may bring in these voices with the board, or find creative means (e.g., theater, storytelling, arts) to create awareness of disorientation within the organization. Also, chaplains can guide moral deliberation sessions, in which normative questions and moral tensions as forms of disorientation can be discussed and possibly new ways can be found to deal with these issues. More examples can be found in Chapter 9.

In Vignette 6, Noor works with veterans who often have had disturbing experiences that raise moral questions. "I ask what happened on their missions and I ask what got them through, the meaning of camaraderie, their values, and beliefs. It is not something they are all always immediately open about, but usually they warm up to me and welcome me as an insider. And I see the complexity: soldiers are an instrument of the state, the military world contains levels and layers that make everything a single soldier does so much more complex than individual choices." According to Noor, the significance of her work lies in being a neutral insider party who does not serve anyone but the soldiers themselves and does so unconditionally: "I am not focused on getting people back to work, I do not represent politics or superiors, I am not thinking about treatment steps, timelines and success rates. This is also a humanist principle – I have no end point in mind when I work with these soldiers and veterans. Dealing with the effects of military missions is not linear, it can be messy and tangled and circular. When veterans like Wesley feel like they are out of options, I want them to feel that I am still here to listen and support."

A second goal is that organizations provide spiritual care, e.g., by taking care that professional caregivers follow guidelines and standards and collaborate with each other in this area. Since chaplains are specialists in spiritual care, but their representation in numbers is low, one of the goals is to educate other professionals within the organization. This can take different forms as well: clinical lessons within hospitals, e.g., on the topic of grief or spirituality; moral education of military personnel to prepare them for deployment; or having lunch consultations with colleagues (psychologists, social workers, doctors) about characteristics of disorientations in life and how to contribute to orientation processes. In Chapter 7 we outline the educational goal of chaplaincy, aiming at enhancing the conditions for orientation in life within institutions.

Third, organizations need an (organizational) ethics and policy concerning spiritual care in order to create the conditions for orienting in life. This is still a wasteland, especially in organizations outside the health care sector. There is still a lack of knowledge about disorientations, and the secular nature of organizations prevents the discussion of worldviews or visions of the good. The presence of chaplains is not enough to contribute to spiritual care in policy: they also need to actively participate in, e.g., multi-disciplinary meetings, an ethics board, project groups responsible for quality of care, mediation; and need to host spaces within the organization for retreat, meditation, and prayer. See also Chapter 9 where we elaborate on these goals and chaplains' activities to achieve them.

Goals at the macrolevel of chaplaincy

Chaplaincy is often seen as involved with disorientations only on an individual level. However, as we have argued in Chapter 1, disorientations are multilevel processes that also include the social-cultural dimension of living one's life. When society or communities regard disorientations as individual problems, the social and structural factors that are involved will not be addressed. It may lead to a 'blaming the victim' approach, i.e., blaming individual persons for not being able to cope with tragedy or injustice in life. On the macrolevel, the goal then is to arrive at societal visions of the good which are inclusive in the sense that they do not rule out disorientation, support social justice efforts, and address pressing social problems and issues. This is a threefold goal for communities and society.

First, a goal is to hold visions of a good life in which people are seen as disorientable and which allow for vulnerability and fallibility. Chaplains may feel that as individuals they are not capable of changing the circumstances that influence disorientations, nor of changing the way society views disorientations and the concurrent fragility and vulnerability of human existence. However, we want to restore the possibility of 'small acts of goodness' (see Chapter 2) by chaplains in society which is a way of expressing visions of a good life that may spread to other people and environments. Also, chaplains can voice these visions in social media, in newspapers, or in interviews, thereby engaging with a wider audience.

The second macrolevel goal is that communities and society have or create spaces for critical dialogue about collective visions of living a good life that include all – in particular marginalized – voices. The good is not universal, nor static, as we discussed in previous chapters. Visions of the good proposed by dominant groups in society can easily overlook that these will not produce a 'good life' for (specific) vulnerable or marginalized groups, or worse, are prescriptive, oppressive, and dehumanizing (Schuhmann & Damen, 2018; hooks, 2009). Therefore, it is essential that there are public spaces to discuss these visions. Chaplains can contribute to this by helping to find or create these spaces, e.g., in community centers or health care centers, and to support the inclusion of marginalized people, or alternatively, bring the absence of marginalized voices into discussion. In this way they are promoters of social justice (Lee & Gibson, 2021). An example is the work of chaplains in the earthquake area in the Netherlands, where they create awareness of the different interests of government, industry, and inhabitants, and the diverse disorientations that are at stake (see Chapter 10).

Third, a goal is to conduct experiments with 'disorientation sanctuaries' in communities and societies that develop new practices of living a good life. As new social problems and issues emerge, new challenges arise for orientation in life and there is a need for developing new practices of living a good life. For example, living with climate change, war, or multiple gender identities raises existential questions that require reorientation in life. Chaplains are well positioned to develop projects to address these issues, together with other professionals, volunteers, policymakers,, and those affected by the issue; for example, a learning community for young people who feel anxious about climate change, or a LGBTQIA+ support group. By creating these 'safe and brave' spaces, participants may become empowered to change their own contexts, by developing trust, connections, and the spirit to act in the world.

In Vignette 5, humanist chaplain Lilian, who leads a series of group meetings for climate activists, explains how these meetings not only have the goal of supporting the individual participants to deal with their worries about climate change but also have a goal at the macrolevel: "This is about the participants entering into empathetic dialogue with each other, finding moments of rest, and getting their bearings for their continued coping and activism." This illustrates how chaplaincy

> *goals at different levels may be entangled: feeling less overwhelmed by the climate crisis may go hand in hand with gathering new energy for climate activism, leading to public action for a better world. Robert, one of the participants, points out how "through sharing both despair and hope, sadness and joy, anger and humor with others" in the group meetings, he "feels strengthened."*

In Chapter 10 we elaborate further on these macrolevel goals and chaplains' activities to achieve them.

Conclusion and introduction to the next chapters

In Chapter 1 and 2, we have delineated the core concepts of this volume: the notion of existential meaning making as a process of orientation in life, and humanism as a critical, entangled, and inclusive worldview. In this third chapter, we brought these concepts together in the description of chaplaincy as the profession that supports people in processes of (re)orienting in life towards a (renewed) sense of orientation in life. Chaplains' worldview orientations are important in their professionalism, as well as their normative-reflexive ability to relate to the worldviews of others and the orientations within their organizations, communities, and society. In the next chapters we show how, in practice, chaplains may work towards characteristic chaplaincy goals, describing different chaplaincy methods on the micro-, meso-, and macrolevel.

Notes

1 While this is the prevailing view on spiritual care provision in many contexts, in particular in many health care organizations, there are also contexts where this is not (yet) the case.
2 Burggraeve (2020) argues that especially in spiritual care, the use of rhetoric, such as metaphors, is common to talk about disorientation in life. The eloquence and beauty of this rhetoric may enthrall people: it is a form of 'linguistic magic.' However, the downside is that it may turn into violence, if it outvoices the experiences of clients and forces clients to surrender to the 'truth' encapsulated in the words spoken by the spiritual caregiver.
3 Such spiritual notions of goodness involved in worldviews are embedded in an ethical framework as worldviews have an ethical dimension (see Chapter 2). In general, spiritual visions of a good life which represent what is of 'ultimate' value to people are not necessarily connected to an explicated ethics, as we pointed out in Chapter 1. These might, for instance, involve a glorification of violence or the idea that some people are less worthy than others.
4 Schuhmann and Damen (2018) speak about 'representing the Good,' referring to the notion of the Good as theorized by Murdoch (1970). They point out that,

without a firm understanding of Murdoch's ideas, 'representing the Good' may easily be misunderstood in terms of imposing a vision of the good. We therefore choose a different designation here.

5 The Dutch Constitution guarantees freedom of religion and worldview and the access to chaplaincy (art. 6) for every person who resides in an institution (e.g., a prison, a hospital, or in the army) for more than 24 hours. This access does not need an indication or approval by a third party because it is related to the so-called sanctuary function of chaplaincy.

6 From now on we will use the term 'aim' or 'central goal' instead of 'internal good' to avoid confusion with the term 'visions of the good' which are associated with processes of orientation in life, making up the domain of chaplaincy.

7 See the existential meaning-making model in Chapter 1: here meanings made are understood in terms of having regained a sense of orientation in life.

8 Harbin (2016) suggests to understand 'disorientation' as a family resemblance concept in a Wittgensteinean sense.

9 See the two modes of disorientation distinguished by Taylor (1989) that we mentioned in Chapter 1 in relation to the existential meaning-making model.

References

Burggraeve, R. (2020). *Geen toekomst zonder kleine goedheid. Naar genereus samenleven in verantwoordelijkheid vanuit Emmanuel Levinas* [*No future without small goodness. Toward generous coexistence in responsibility on the basis of Emmanuel Levinas*]. Halewijn.

Cadge, W., & Rambo, S. (Eds.). (2022). *Chaplaincy and spiritual care in the twenty-first century. An introduction*. The University of North Carolina Press.

Dall'Alba, G. (2009). *The learning of professionals*. Springer.

Doehring, C. (2015). *The practice of pastoral care: A postmodern approach*. Westminster John Knox Press.

Dzur, A. W. (2003). Democratic professionalism: Sharing authority in civic life. *The Good Society, 13*(1), 6–14.

Freidson, E. (2001). *Professionalism. The third logic*. Polity.

Glasner, T., Schuhmann, C., & Kruizinga, R. (2023). The future of chaplaincy in a secularized society: A mixed-methods survey from the Netherlands. *Journal of Health Care Chaplaincy, 29*(1), 132–144. https://doi.org/10.1080/08854726.2022.2040894

Grefe, D., McCarroll, P., & Ansari, B. (2022). Meaning making in chaplaincy practice: Presence, assessment, and interventions. In W. Cadge & S. Rambo (Eds.), *Chaplaincy and spiritual care in the twenty-first century* (pp. 66–89). The University of North Carolina Press.

Grung, A. H. (Ed.). (2023). *Complexities of spiritual care in plural societies: Education, praxis and concepts*. De Gruyter. https://doi.org/10.1515/9783110717365

Harbin, A. (2016). *Disorientation and moral life*. Oxford University Press.

Hooks, B. (2009). *Belonging: A culture of place*. Routledge.

Jacobs, G. (2001). *De paradox van kracht en kwetsbaarheid. Empowerment in feministische hulpverlening en humanistisch raadswerk* [*The paradox of strength and vulnerability. Empowerment in feminist counselling and humanist chaplaincy*]. SWP.

Jacobs, G. (2008). The development of critical being? Reflection and reflexivity in an action learning programme for health promotion practitioners in the Netherlands. *Action Learning: Research and Practice, 5*(3), 221–235. https://doi.org/10.1080/14767330802461306

Jacobs, G., Schuhmann, C., & Wierstra, I. (2023). Healthcare chaplains' conflicting and ambivalent positions regarding meaning in life and worldview. *Journal of Health Care Chaplaincy, 30*(2), 107–121. https://doi.org/10.1080/08854726.2023.2210026

Kunneman, H. (2002). Humanistics and the future of the human sciences. In A. Halsema & D. van Houten (Eds.), *Empowering humanity. State of the art in humanistics* (pp. 13–36). De Tijdstroom.

Lee, K. S., & Gibson, D. (2021). Justice matters: Spiritual care and pastoral theological imaginations in times of the COVID-19 pandemic. *Journal of Pastoral Theology, 31*(2–3), 81–88. https://doi.org/10.1080/10649867.2021.2010993

Levinas, E. (1988/1994). *In the time of the nations* (M. B. Smith, Trans.). Indiana University Press.

Lynch, G. (2002). *Pastoral care & counselling*. Sage.

MacIntyre, A. (2007). *After virtue: A study in moral theory* (3rd ed.). Bloomsbury.

Murdoch, I. (1970). *The sovereignty of good*. Routledge.

Nussbaum, M. C. (2001). *The fragility of goodness: Luck and ethics in Greek tragedy and philosophy* (Rev. ed.). Cambridge University Press.

Puchalski, C., Ferrell, B., Virani, R., Otis-Green, S., Baird, P., Bull, J., Chochinov, H., Handzo, G., Nelson-Becker, H., Prince-Paul, M., Pugliese, K., & Sulmasy, D. (2009). Improving the quality of spiritual care as a dimension of palliative care: The report of the Consensus Conference. *Journal of Palliative Medicine, 12*(10), 885–904. https://doi.org/10.1089/jpm.2009.0142

Puchalski, C. M., Vitillo, R., Hull, S. K., & Reller, N. (2014). Improving the spiritual dimension of whole person care: reaching national and international consensus. *Journal of Palliative Medicine, 17*(6), 642–656. https://doi.org/10.1089/jpm.2014.9427

Schuhmann, C., & Damen, A. (2018). Representing the Good: Pastoral care in a secular age. *Pastoral Psychology, 67,* 405–417. https://doi.org/10.1007/s11089-018-0826-0

Swift, C. (2004). How should health care chaplaincy negotiate its professional identity? *Contact, 144*(1), 4–13. https://doi.org/10.1080/13520806.2004.11758985

Swinton, J. (2003). A question of identity. What does it mean for chaplains to become healthcare professionals? *Scottish Journal of Healthcare Chaplaincy, 6*(2), 2–8. https://doi.org/10.1558/hscc.v6i2.2

Taylor, C. (1989). *Sources of the Self*. Harvard University Press.

van Houten, D., & Mooren, J. H. (2002). Humanist counselling in the Netherlands. In A. Halsema & D. van Houten (Eds.), *Empowering humanity: State of the art in humanistics* (pp. 105–120). De Tijdstroom.

Zock, T. H. (2008). The split professional identity of the chaplain as a spiritual caregiver in contemporary Dutch health care. *Journal of Pastoral Care & Counseling, 62*(1–2), 137–139. https://doi.org/10.1177/154230500806200113

Part II

Methods

Chapter 4

Using counseling methods in chaplaincy

Carmen Schuhmann and Sylvie de Kubber

Introduction

> *I get out of my car. I am in a desolate area and there is garbage on the street. I work as a humanist chaplain for a psychiatric hospital, visiting people in different places: in their homes, in institutions and clinics. Today I visit Mrs. Miju for the third time in the care flat where she is staying. During the first two sessions, we talked about her childhood and about the voices she hears in her head. I ring the doorbell of her department. A nurse lets me in.*[1]

Providing spiritual care to individuals is a core task of chaplains. In the taxonomy of chaplaincy activities developed by Hughes et al. (2019), the vast majority of items refer to one-on-one encounters. The focus on one-on-one encounters is also reflected in the scope and emphasis of current research into the profession. An overview of chaplaincy-related research in the context of health care by Fitchett (2017), for instance, shows that the existing research usually focuses on spiritual care provided to individual patients. Also, in the recent call for doing more outcome research into chaplaincy, chaplaincy outcomes are generally situated at the level of individuals receiving chaplaincy (Damen et al., 2020; Handzo et al., 2014).

In the context of secularization and pluralization of worldviews, chaplains increasingly use methods from the domains of psychotherapy and counseling when providing individual care.[2] This development goes back to the 'therapeutic turn' in pastoral care in the second half of the previous century (Stollberg, 1969; Clinebell, 1984). Here the role of pastoral caregivers shifted from primarily acting as religious experts to primarily supporting others by engaging in a helping relationship with them. As chaplains these days usually provide care to people with a variety of worldview

DOI: 10.4324/9781003428633-6

backgrounds, the therapeutic approach has become more widely embraced. Factors common to most psychotherapeutic approaches like building rapport, empathy, active listening, and unconditional positive regard have been adopted as central elements of chaplaincy (Nolan, 2019; Woldemichael et al., 2013). In humanist chaplaincy, there has always been a focus on counseling methods when it comes to supporting individuals (Schuhmann, 2015). This is not surprising since "the foundation of counseling is solidly humanistic" (Dollarhide & Oliver, 2014, p. 207).[3] In the education of Dutch humanist chaplains, methods from person-centered, existential, and narrative counseling figure prominently (Mooren, 2013).

The boundaries of the disciplines of chaplaincy and counseling have therefore become more fluid, and in the case of humanist chaplaincy, always have been. This is not a one-way development: not only are counseling methods increasingly embraced as relevant for chaplaincy but religion and spirituality are also increasingly taken into account as relevant phenomena in the domains of psychotherapy and counseling (Woldemichael et al., 2013; Pargament, 2007). Several chaplains fear that this "has a negative impact on chaplaincy as chaplains become less clearly distinguishable from other helping professionals such as psychologists, counsellors and social workers" (Glasner et al., 2023, p. 139). Nolan and MacLaren (2021), for instance, warn that "what began as a Christian ministry is visibly morphing into a secularized form of therapeutic service, at least within the context of healthcare" (pp. 1–2). Woldemichael et al. (2013) argue that leaning too heavily on the disciplines of psychotherapy and counseling might result in reductionist chaplaincy practice as "the pastoral care understanding of the human being [is] different from the secular psychotherapeutic understanding of man that is viewed as mainly a biological, psychosocial being" (p. 9).

In this chapter, inspired by insights from humanist chaplaincy as it is theorized and practiced in the Netherlands, we explore how chaplains may draw from existing counseling methods when providing spiritual care in one-on-one encounters. Rather than going along with the fear that using such methods leads to a further blurring of boundaries between the disciplines of chaplaincy and counseling, we take the position that carefully reflecting on what counseling methods to use in what situations, to what ends, and in what way, supports chaplains to articulate what is characteristic about the one-on-one care they provide. First, we describe a model that guides this reflection. We then take a look at the various characteristic chaplaincy goals at the microlevel that were distinguished in Chapter 3 and elaborate on counseling methods that help chaplains to work towards these goals. Our aim here is by no means to give an exhaustive overview of the methods chaplains may use when providing individual care. This would be impossible anyway, given the "wide diversity in counselling practice" (McLeod, 2003, p. 10), and the variety of methods for supporting individuals which have been described and developed specifically for chaplains without explicit reference to the domains of counseling or psychotherapy. The aim is to show how 'secular' counseling methods can be used in one-on-one encounters by chaplains from all worldview backgrounds in a way that is in line with the spiritual character of chaplaincy practice.

Using counseling methods in chaplaincy – a reflection model

What do we mean when we talk about methods in chaplaincy? Smit (2015) points out that, from an etymological perspective, the term 'method' indicates 'the road along which.' In relation to a practice, he characterizes methods as ways of acting which are (1) purposeful – they are directed at a certain goal (related to the central good of the practice)[4]; (2) systematic – they are not a matter of trial and error but consist of elements which are connected according to a logic; (3) process-oriented – the ways of acting are directed at processes of change which take place over time; and (4) reflective – they involve reflection on whether the way one is acting is attuned to the situation at hand. Methods connect a 'practice perspective' – in which the question is how to realize the central good of the practice – with an 'actor perspective' – in which the question is what, in a concrete situation, would be a good outcome and how to work towards this outcome. Acting methodically as a practitioner means acting with a view to the question of how one's actions contribute to the central good of the practice (Smit, 2015).

In the context of chaplaincy, this implies that acting methodically as a chaplain in one-on-one encounters means acting with a view to the question of how to contribute to the other's sense of orientation in life.[5] This is the basis of the model we propose to guide chaplains' reflection on the question of what (counseling) methods to use as a chaplain in specific situations (see Figure 4.1). The model takes the form of a reflection cycle which starts with the question 'how to act?' arising in a concrete one-on-one chaplaincy encounter. Here we are in the actor perspective, in which methodical action by a practitioner is directed at a 'good outcome.' The first step in the cycle is therefore to ask oneself what would be a good outcome of chaplaincy in this encounter. The second step connects the actor perspective with the practice perspective: here the chaplain reflects on the question of how a good outcome in this concrete encounter is connected with the central good of chaplaincy. Here, the chaplain may, in particular, look at the various different characteristic chaplaincy goals at the microlevel that were distinguished in Chapter 3. Staying within the practice perspective, the question in step 3 is what (counseling) methods are aimed at the goal(s) at hand. These first three reflection steps pertain to the

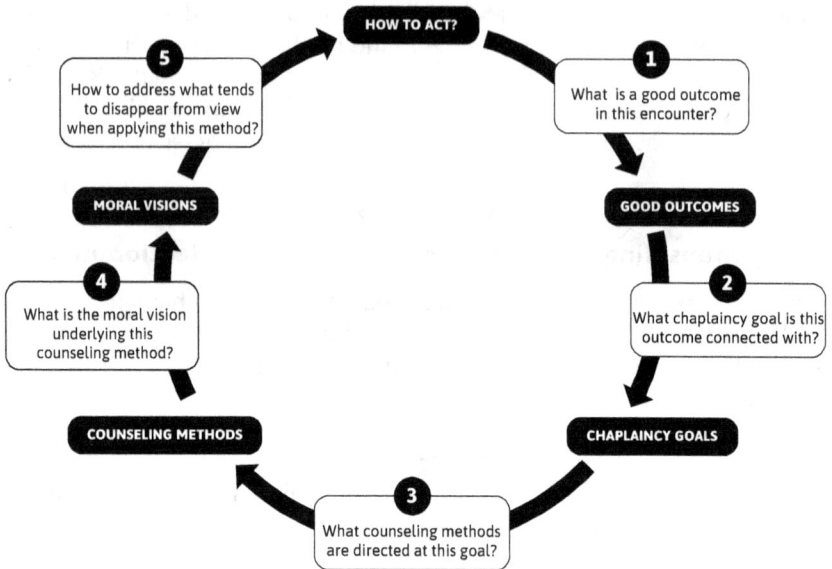

Figure 4.1 Reflection model for using counseling methods in chaplaincy.

purposeful character of methodical action, guaranteeing that it is the central good of chaplaincy which the chaplain's actions are aimed at.

The final two steps in the reflection cycle pertain to the process-oriented character of methodical action, addressing the question of how to apply the chosen counseling method in a concrete one-on-one encounter 'in the spirit of chaplaincy.' Chaplains typically work on the basis of a spiritual vision of human beings as ultimately mysterious: "They realize that their attempts to see the reality of their clients are never exhaustive, that there is always more to see, to hear, and to know about them" (Schuhmann & Damen, 2018, p. 412). Christopher (1996) argues that counseling approaches are also informed by certain 'moral visions' – normative notions of what human beings are and should become – which decide what comes into view as 'the problem' in counseling practice and what kind of change is seen as desirable. This counters the idea that "counselors … can interact with clients in an objective and neutral manner" (Christopher, 1996, p. 19). For instance, counseling approaches often reflect individualistic moral visions dominant in Western culture (Christopher, 1996) – visions which do not necessarily or obviously have a spiritual character. For chaplains, it therefore seems crucial that they clarify what moral visions inform the counseling methods that they use instead of perceiving these as neutral interventions.

This clarification constitutes the fourth reflection step. Here the question is what view of human beings is foregrounded by the counseling method that is used, and what tends to disappear from view. For instance, individualistic moral visions may foreground personal aspects of existential struggles and processes, while relational or socio-cultural aspects of these struggles and processes may seem less relevant. In the final reflection step, we return to the specific one-on-one encounter. Here the question is how to address not only what is foregrounded by the method in the encounter but also what might easily disappear from view, thus honoring the chaplaincy view that 'there is always more to see, to hear, and to know about the other.' This may lead to starting a new round of following the reflection cycle.

Counseling methods in relation to chaplaincy goals

In Chapter 3, chaplaincy is characterized as the profession of caring for processes of orientation in life, aimed at the central chaplaincy goal of 'having a sense of orientation in life.' At the level of individual (and group) support, this overarching goal is broken down into four characteristic chaplaincy goals (see Chapter 3). For each of these four goals, we present a counseling method that is directed at that specific goal. Before doing so, however, we look at how one-on-one encounters are embedded in a specific chaplaincy mode of approaching others.

Approaching others: Presence and critical self-reflection

The term 'presence' is often used by chaplains to explain what is unique about their work (Adams, 2019). In the context of humanistic approaches to therapy, presence is associated with attentiveness, openness, and attunement to others; it "involves being available to oneself and the other in a complex way that is centered on the bodily" (Malet et al., 2022, p. 2). In the context of chaplaincy, the term presence is extended to a mode of approaching people in all kinds of encounters, and more generally to the way in which chaplains move through the spaces in which these encounters may take place (Baart, 2004). The presence of chaplains has a spiritual dimension: chaplains are a 'hopeful presence' (Nolan, 2015) as they 're-present' "the faith that some good remains believable in ultimate situations" (Schuhmann & Damen, 2018, p. 412).[6]

The centrality of presence in chaplaincy stresses the crucial importance of critical self-reflection in one-on-one spiritual care provision. In order to be and remain attentive, open, and attuned to others, chaplains need to reflect on how their visions of the good may hinder or nourish attentiveness and openness. Moral visions of chaplains have an impact on how they interpret stories of others, on what themes they tend to respond to or ignore in these stories, and on what (counseling) methods they are (un)comfortable with. Lynch (2002) points out that chaplains should not aim to neutralize this impact: "Pastoral practice uninfluenced by some form of vision of the good life is simply not possible" (p. 16). One-on-one counseling by chaplains may rather be understood as a hermeneutic dialogue, involving "a kind of continuing dialectic between openness and critical application" (Christopher, 1996, p. 22).[7] Here openness refers to taking seriously the viewpoints of others, also when these viewpoints challenge one's own moral visions. Critical application refers to offering one's moral visions to others as potentially helpful for making sense of their situation. Critical self-reflection of chaplains should therefore be aimed at clarifying and questioning their moral visions, so that they are accountable about how these feed into the care they provide. This is an ongoing process as visions of the good life may contain contradictory and inconsistent elements and may change over time. Furthermore, critical self-reflection also involves examining how personal problems and needs play a role in encounters with others. According to van Praag (1982), critical self-reflection entails learning "to understand and handle one's own personality" (p. 155). In his view, it is the chaplain's personality, rather than knowledge and skills, which is key in one-on-one encounters. This stresses the importance of practicing self-care – "care of self, emotionally, physically, and spiritually" (White et al., 2019, p. 30) – in chaplaincy.[8]

I am in the apartment of Mrs. Miju, in a spacious room overlooking the garden. In the corner there is a single bed with a pink bedspread and pink pillows. Everything is in beige and pastel colors, and there are fake flowers here and there. It smells strongly of smoke. I hesitate for a moment, but, knowing that the strong smell of smoke would prevent me from being fully present, I ask Mrs. Miju whether a window may be opened [presence]. She moves slowly to the other side of the room to open the window; she seems to have very stiff legs and back pain. She makes her way back and sits down at the small table, in front of me. She leans with her elbows on the table, folding her hands before her chest. I deliberately sit up straight, neither leaning towards her, which would bring her too close, nor leaning backwards, which would seem disinterested. She looks at me with slightly raised eyebrows. I am not sure whether she remembers me or our previous conversations. I therefore introduce myself again and say: "I am here for you. You can talk about anything that is on your mind or whatever feels important to you at this moment in your life." Before I can say anything else, she starts talking about the black magic controlling her life. She tells me about voices of evil spirits that tell her that she must use a pink scarf to hang herself. Her eyes wander to a pink scarf that lies on a chair in a corner. I follow her gaze and take a deep breath, realizing the heaviness of this situation. I say: "That must be heavy for you." "The voices never stop," she replies.

Offering relational affirmation and empowerment: Person-centered counseling

'Experiencing relational affirmation and empowerment' is the goal of one-on-one chaplaincy that is situated in the relationship with the chaplain (see Chapter 3). As processes of orientation in life have a relational dimension, 'good' relationships may provide a sense of orientation (see Chapter 1). Even when people are severely disoriented and feel that all good is lost, they may still experience goodness in relationships with others. It is therefore the chaplain's task to build relationships in which others feel affirmed and empowered, thus providing them with a sense of orientation. In order to promote relational affirmation, chaplains may draw from the person-centered approach to counseling which was developed halfway through the last century in the United States by Carl Rogers.[9] What was revolutionary about the approach at the time was the idea that it is the client, not the counselor, who is the expert about what is the problem at hand and what kind of change is desirable – hence the term 'nondirective counseling' that is often used for this approach (McLeod, 2003).

The person-centered approach reflects a basic trust in human beings as naturally striving towards growth and self-development. This natural process may, however, get stuck due to negative relational experiences, for instance neglect or disapproval. The task of the counselor then is to create a helping relationship in which others feel safe and accepted, so that they dare to get into contact with and express their experiences, and the process of growth may be set in motion again (Mearns & Thorne, 2007). Rogers describes 'core conditions' that are necessary and sufficient for creating such a helping relationship: empathy, unconditional positive regard, and congruence (Schuhmann, 2015). Congruence – "the state of being of the counsellor when her outward responses to her client consistently match her inner experiencing of the client" (Mearns & Thorne, 2007, p. 121) – is, in Roger's view, the most important of these core conditions.

> Mrs. Miju starts to cry, saying: "It is a struggle – I pray all day." The spirits keep telling her that she is not a good person, that she is worthless, that she will die. She breathes heavier and heavier and utters: "This is no life; I can hardly walk." I look at her folded hands with the long nails and chipped red nail polish. I notice her arched neck, and how her back is bent forward, as if there is a weight pressing on her. In my own body I feel the urge to bend forward with her, but, in reaction, also the urge to breathe deeply and straighten my back. I decide to ask her: "Can you feel the evil spirits somewhere in your body; are they in a specific part of your body?" She is silent for a moment, and then replies that they are somewhere near her lungs, putting pressure on her chest

and back. She gasps for breath. She tells me that she smokes constantly because the spirits tell her to. I reply that I do not find it surprising at all that she smokes a lot, given the severe stress she experiences, but that I also feel that it would do her a lot of good to quit smoking [congruence]. She replies that she very much wants to stop smoking.

In the moral vision underlying person-centered counseling, it is assumed that living a 'good' life requires trusting relationships. The emphasis is, however, still on the individual; eventually, building trusting relationships is seen as a means to the goal of individual growth rather than as a goal in itself. In order to take a more thoroughly relational approach, chaplains may, for instance, draw from relational-cultural therapy, an approach influenced by feminist thought (Jordan, 2017). In this approach, there is criticism of the emphasis on autonomy and self-sufficiency in Western societies, which are seen as standards of psychological maturity in most therapeutic approaches. In relational-cultural therapy, building trusting relationships, in particular between therapist and client, is seen as a form of empowerment and a goal in itself.

Mrs. Miju starts to talk about her ex-husband, about how he spent her father's inheritance on his motorbike and fun outings for himself, locking her up for 20 years. She was not allowed to leave the house, not even to go to the hairdresser – she saw no one during that time, losing contact with family and friends. Only when she became very ill did he allow her to go to the family doctor. The doctor listened to her and urged her to get a divorce. Hearing this story, I nod my head, and I frown. I feel shocked by the horrible situation this woman was in for so long. In my worldview and in my work, feminist perspectives are crucial and male violence against women makes me very angry. My anger is especially intense because I have until recently been in an abusive relationship myself. I do not want to draw attention to my own experiences, but I do want to acknowledge the injustice Mrs. Miju has suffered. I look straight in her eyes, saying: "It is horrible what this man did to you – he should never have done that. I am so impressed by the power you showed getting out of there." She reacts: "Well, it was the doctor who told me to do that." "Yes," I respond, "but you are the one who got out." [empowerment]. "That is true," she says pensively. She describes how she found a caravan on a campsite where she lived alone for some years. Now she lives here in the psychiatric hospital and the evil spirits try to control her every day. I think to myself that she managed to escape the control of her husband, and now there is another force taking control: the spirits.

Supporting explication and/or revision of visions of a good life: Existential counseling

The chaplaincy goal of 'explicating and potentially reconsidering visions of a good life' is about helping people to find out what, to them, are visions of the good that may guide them through life (see Chapter 3). This involves questioning what worldviews or spiritual traditions offer them direction, strength, and hope. With a view to this goal, chaplains may draw from the existential approach to counseling. This approach is rooted in existential-ism, a strand of philosophy associated with Western European thinkers like Søren Kierkegaard, Martin Heidegger, Jean-Paul Sartre, and Albert Camus. Existentialism emphasizes the tragic dimension of existence, which is con-nected with the inevitability of our confrontation with existential givens. Yalom (1980), a founding father of existential psychotherapy, distinguishes four such givens of existence, which he refers to as 'ultimate concerns': death, freedom, isolation, and meaninglessness. The goal of existential psy-chotherapy is to help people learn how to live in the face of ultimate con-cerns without being overcome by anxiety. The notion of (in)authenticity is crucial here. Referring to Heidegger, Yalom (1998) argues that the confron-tation with ultimate concerns is an opportunity to move to an authentic mode of being, that is, a state in which we are "mindful of being, not only mindful of the fragility of being but mindful, too, of one's responsibility for one's own being" (p. 186).

Earlier in the week, at home, I had been thinking about Mrs. Miju, about her precarious situation and her sense of being controlled by evil spirits; but also about her strength which I can time and again see shining through, and her courage to tell me about her uphill struggle. Standing in front of my bookcase, I found a poem titled 'My life is mine,' which is about resisting the pressure to conform to expecta-tions and conventions, about refusing to be controlled by others, and about taking the risk to live authentically.[10] I felt that sharing this poem with Mrs. Miju might convey to her that I see not only her vul-nerability but also her strength and might express what I wish for her. I wrote the poem down on a postcard picturing a four-leaf clover and brought it to this session. Taking the postcard out of my bag, I tell her that I brought her a poem which reminds me of her and ask whether she would like me to read it. She nods in agreement. When I have finished reading, she looks at me, tells me that she really likes the poem, and slowly repeats: "My life is mine" [authenticity]. After a while, she gets up and puts the postcard on the chimney in the mid-dle of the room.

Existential counselors support people to move to an authentic mode of living by helping them to clarify their personal worldview (van Deurzen, 2002) – that is, their visions of the good. This entails "working with clients towards their understanding of what it is that has ultimate value for them" (van Deurzen, 2002, p. 109), and about assisting clients in finding "the ultimate direction one wants one's life to take" (van Deurzen, 2002, p. 109). The role of the existential counselor is to gently question basic assumptions underlying statements of clients instead of falling in with these assumptions. This allows clients to examine whether or not the assumptions that function as the foundation of their lives have ultimate value for them. Moving towards authenticity is crucial here, as the idea is "to determine what matters to the clients, not what ought to matter to them" (van Deurzen, 2002, p. 106). In order to take such a questioning role, existential counselors need to refrain from making value judgements about assumptions of clients. Assumptions are not seen as wrong or right in themselves but are examined with a view to the question of whether they have ultimate value for the client.

The moral vision underlying the existential approach to counseling reflects a certain timelessness when it comes to people's ultimate values. What is not addressed in this approach is the way in which people's visions of the good are formed and change throughout their lives. Biographical methods like those used in life review therapy (Westerhof & Slatman, 2019) seem an important addition to existential counseling when it comes to supporting people to explicate and/or reconsider their visions of the good.

Supporting movement towards visions of a good life: A narrative therapy approach of counseling

Chaplains not only support people to clarify their visions of the good, but also to integrate these in their lives. This chaplaincy goal is about 'exploring how to actually be close to or move towards renewed visions of a good life' (see Chapter 3). This is especially important when people feel that the path towards their visions of a good life is blocked or impassable. The role that chaplains may play here depends on the kind of blockage in the situation at hand. For instance, when physical, psychological, social, or material issues play a role in disorientation, chaplains need to refer to professionals specialized in these areas, like social workers or psychologists. When visions of a good life are irrevocably out of sight and reach, for instance, when people face tragedy,[11] the chaplains' role is to support them to somehow come to terms with this (see the next section). When, however, the impossibility of moving towards certain goods has to do with socio-political circumstances – for instance, with discrimination or marginalization – chaplains need to address these circumstances. This humanizing role goes beyond the one-on-one encounter and may involve providing education, initiating moral deliberation, or doing political work (see Chapters 7, 9, and 10). Still, in individual spiritual care provision too, chaplains need to be able to address the role of socio-political contexts in orientation processes. In order to do so, chaplains may draw from narrative therapy, a therapeutic approach originated by Michael White and David Epston (therapists from Australia and New Zealand, respectively) on the basis of poststructuralist philosophy, in particular work by Michel Foucault. The underlying moral vision reflects this philosophy: "narrative therapists view identity as relational, distributed, performed, and fluid" (Combs & Freedman, 2012).

Narrative therapy derives its name from the central idea that people make sense of their experiences and who they are through telling and retelling stories.[12] These stories are not individual constructions: people make use of existing discourses while telling stories. Here certain discourses are more likely to be used – in particular dominant discourses that are seen as truths representing expert knowledge. This is not a conscious choice as "we don't usually notice the powerful influence of these discourses" (Combs & Freedman, 2012, p. 1038). According to White and Epston (1990), the power of dominant discourses leads to 'thin stories' in which people are not able to express themselves well.[13] The task of narrative therapists is to assist people to identify and generate alternative stories which are richer in the sense that these better represent their lived experience and open up new, more helpful meanings and ways of acting. Here narrative therapists take the position that clients are the privileged authors of their own stories. Narrative therapy may thus be seen as a practice of resisting the interpretive power of dominant discourses in people's lives. This implies that narrative therapists also need to recognize and keep critically examining the ways in which they themselves are entangled in dominant discourses and tend to reproduce these in therapy.

A central method in narrative therapy consists of 'externalizing the problem.' This entails referring to the problem as something that affects the person rather than as an intrinsic characteristic of the person, so that the person may dis-identify from dominant stories about themselves and from problem-saturated stories. Another central method is that of listening for 'unique outcomes': "clues which may indicate a potential alternative storyline or sub-plot running alongside the story being told" (Payne, 2006, p. 65). Such clues which are not in line with or contradict the problem story may be verbal or nonverbal: a silence, a facial expression, a sigh. Such clues may then be explored for their potential to generate alternative stories.

> *Sometimes Mrs. Miju's whole body starts shaking and her head flips up – this is because of the black magic, she explains. It makes her afraid to engage in social contacts in the communal living room: "What would others think of me if that happens?" I respond that I understand this seems scary to her, but that I at least am not frightened by her uncontrolled movements. I suggest that the people here are used to quite a lot, and maybe she can just say something about the beautiful ceiling when her head flips up. We laugh together about this idea [unique outcome]. "When this is all over," she suddenly exclaims, "I will get one of those delicious fresh custard rolls for us at the bakery. Don't you like those fresh rolls filled with custard?" I respond that I am looking forward to it. I feel that we have put a ritual of celebration on the horizon together, an anchor of hope.*

Given the focus on resisting dominant labels and descriptions in narrative therapy, Combs and Freedman (2012) argue that this approach may help counselors to be attuned to social justice issues. However, narrative therapy has also been criticized for having "sneaky and subversive colonial roots" (Dumaresque et al., 2018, p. 112). More generally, "being historically and culturally situated, all counseling theories may reproduce North American and European colonist ideologies related to power, marginalization, and oppression" (Singh et al., 2020, pp. 261–262). Despite a growing emphasis on multicultural competences in counseling, multicultural counseling is often practiced in ways that reproduce colonialism instead of exposing and dismantling systems of oppression (Gorski & Goodman, 2015). Singh et al. (2020) argue that "as counselors, we can begin to decolonize our practice by unabashedly integrating social justice theories alongside traditional counseling theories" (p. 269). They present four key theories that are helpful for decolonizing counseling practice: relational-cultural theory (Miller, 1976), critical race theory (Bell, 1995), intersectionality theory (Crenshaw, 1991), and liberation psychology (Martín-Baró, 1994).[14] When chaplains make use of counseling methods in order to address the role of socio-political contexts in orientation processes, it is imperative that they 'unabashedly integrate' social justice theories in their spiritual care practices as well. One way to do so is by using these theories as a critical framework in the fourth step of the reflection cycle presented earlier (see Figure 4.1).

Supporting expression and exploration of experiences of disorientation: Focusing

When people come into contact with chaplains because of disorienting experiences, a chaplaincy goal that comes into view is that of supporting 'expression and exploration of experiences of disorientation' (see Chapter 3). Harbin (2016) argues that staying with disorientation instead of rushing towards reorientation counters the common way of dealing with disorientation in Western societies, where people who experience disorientation may feel pressure to reorient as quickly as possible. When, however, people are invited to explore their disorienting experiences without the demand that they put these in a positive light and without pressure to reorient, this may make disorientations more livable (Harbin, 2016). This is especially important in the face of tragic events.[15] Here, disorientation may lead to despair, as visions of the good are irrevocably out of sight and reach, and there is no obvious way out of disorientation.

A relevant notion in relation to staying with disorientation is the metaphor of 'inner space' which Leget (2012) introduces as a central element in his ideas about the art of dying. He describes inner space as a state that allows someone to freely and calmly relate to emotions and attitudes that are evoked by a situation. When people are, for instance, completely overwhelmed by anxiety or guilt, there is no space for other emotions or perceptions of the situation. Having inner space allows people to stay with difficult emotions and situations without feeling overwhelmed. Leget (2017) describes six paths towards inner space: humor, the body, emotions, virtues, spiritual traditions, and silence. Supporting people to find a path towards inner space fits in with the chaplaincy goal of expressing and exploring experiences of disorientation, as disorienting experiences are often overwhelming. A counseling method that chaplains may use to that end is experiential focusing, a method that was developed by Eugene Gendlin, an American philosopher and therapist, in the context of the person-centered approach to counseling. Later on, Gendlin (1981) also described focusing as a self-help method that people may practice outside of therapeutic settings. The method makes use of various paths towards inner space: the body, emotions, silence, and also imagery.

With several clients I have built a habit of being silent together for a few minutes at the end of each session. As a humanist chaplain, I don't say traditional prayers for people, but I value the intimacy, calmness, and spirituality of shared silence. At the end of our conversation, I ask Mrs. Miju whether she would like to be quiet together for a moment, and when she affirms, we sit together in silence with folded hands [silence]. I close my eyes. I feel how the atmosphere changes: I feel something heavy pressing on me and start to feel dizzy. I appeal to a faith in the 'good' in me and wish the best for Mrs. Miju with all my heart. I hear her heavy breathing, open my eyes, and say: "So there is a lot going on, you are struggling – I can see that. But I also see so much strength in you." She replies that she has the feeling that there is a small burning candle in her chest which always gives light. I thank her for her openness and for trusting me with her stories today. We shake hands. I wish her well and say: "See you next week."

Focusing starts with what Gendlin (1981) calls 'clearing a space.' Here, the counselor invites clients to ask themselves how they feel and listen inwardly to what happens in their body in response to this question. The metaphor of space here refers to inner space, as clearing a space involves "the inner act of *distancing* yourself from what is troubling you. You don't go into the problems. You stand back just a little way – far enough so that the problems no longer feel overwhelming, but close enough so that you can still feel them" (Gendlin, 1981, p. 82). After clearing a space, the counselor invites the client to focus on a specific issue that has come up and requires attention. This is where the notion of the 'felt sense' comes in: "The felt sense is an internal, physical sense of the situation. In this inner sense the person knows there is more to the situation than he or she is currently able to say" (McLeod, 2003, p. 179). By inviting clients to turn their attention towards a bodily felt sense of an issue, words, images, or phrases may come up which may symbolize certain meanings implicit in the felt sense. When the symbolization is accurate, this leads to a felt bodily shift.[16] The process of focusing may also be understood in spiritual terms, which emphasizes the potential of the method for chaplains. Leijssen (2007a), for instance, refers to focusing as a path towards spiritual growth: "The awareness of subtle but concrete bodily feelings can become a self-transcendent, spiritual way of knowing" (p. 269). In her view, the introspective discipline of focusing allows people to access the world of the soul (Leijssen, 2007b).

Conclusion

Even though counseling and chaplaincy are different disciplines, the boundaries between them are blurry. In particular, in both disciplines there is a focus on engaging in a helping relationship with others and supporting them to find their own way through life. This chapter shows how chaplains, in one-on-one encounters, may draw from the vast array of existing counseling methods in a way that is in line with their profession. A reflection model was presented that allows chaplains to carefully and critically reflect on the question of what counseling methods they may use in what situations and to what ends. The model reflects a spiritual vision of human beings as ultimately mysterious and supports chaplains to always again attune to *this* specific person in *this* specific context.

> *I leave Mrs. Miju's room and close the door behind me. I walk through the hallway, seeing several other people in their rooms. Leaving the building, I see someone in a wheelchair who smiles at me, and I smile back. I look at the trees and think back to the session. I notice that I am still a bit short of breath and shake my body loose to let go of the lingering feelings of heaviness and tightness [bodily feelings]. I wonder what the voices in Mrs. Miju's body are telling her, now that I have left the room. I feel grateful that we found moments of togetherness – sharing a poem, sharing a custard roll in the future, sharing silence – and that, a few times, she mentioned experiencing some relief.*

Take-home messages

- Providing spiritual care to individuals takes the form of a dialectical movement between openness towards their visions of the good and offering one's own visions of the good as potentially helpful.
- Providing spiritual care to individuals not only requires an attitude of presence in one-on-one encounters but also when moving through the spaces in which these encounters may take place.
- Keep critically reflecting on how your visions of the good – in particular your worldview – resonate in the care you provide in one-on-one encounters.
- Be prepared to have your visions of the good challenged in one-on-one encounters, and be open to the possibility of reconsidering them on the basis of these encounters.
- Include practices of self-care – emotionally, physically, and spiritually – into the continuing process of critical self-reflection.
- When using counseling methods in chaplaincy, reflect on the moral visions underlying these methods in relation to a spiritual view of human beings.
- In particular, critically reflect on the role of dominant normative views – for instance, individualistic moral visions dominant in Western culture which often feed into counseling approaches – in the methods you use.

Notes

1 This case description does not seamlessly fit into the structuring of the chapter. We have decided to not artificially alter the case in such a way that every fragment only illustrates the counseling method presented in the corresponding

section but to leave the case intact: it can be read as a whole by reading the fragments in order throughout the chapter. Still, in every fragment there are links with the counseling method described in the corresponding section; per fragment we give a hint for one such link by adding a term in square brackets that is used in the description of the counseling method. The fragment may, however, contain more links, and also describe modes of working that do not fit within or even contradict that specific counseling method. We think that this reflects the way in which we propose to use counseling methods in chaplaincy: in order to attune to the specific person in a specific context, counseling methods may or even need to be modified and combined.

2 Psychotherapy and counseling refer to a wide variety of practices in which a psychotherapist resp. counselor provides guidance to people who face a "problem in living" (McLeod, 2003, p. 15). These professions are "a product of late twentieth-century modernity" (McLeod, 2003, p. 15). Furthermore, there is no clear distinction between the two professions; it may depend on the context whether a certain practice is perceived as a psychotherapeutic or a counseling practice.

3 Here the term 'humanistic' refers to humanistic psychology and its theoretical assumptions, which is in line with how we use the term in this book (see Introduction).

4 See Chapter 3 for an explanation of a practices as aimed at a characteristic central good or goal.

5 See Chapter 3 where we designated the overarching goal of chaplaincy as 'having a sense of orientation in life.'.

6 See the notion of 'representing faith in goodness' as explained in Chapter 3.

7 Christopher refers here to work by Gadamer (1960/2004), a central figure in the development of hermeneutics.

8 Spiritual self-care can be understood as caring for one's 'faith in goodness,' a faith that chaplains represent – see Chapter 3.

9 McLeod (2003) argues that "the social and cultural background that shaped the work of Carl Rogers gives some indication of the extent to which his approach of counselling was rooted in the values of the American society" (p. 156).

10 The poem was written by Michael Kunze as the text for a song in the Dutch musical production *Elisabeth* by Joop van den Ende.

11 See Chapter 1 for a description of tragedy as a disorienting experience.

12 The emphasis on narrative reflects what is known as 'the interpretive turn' in social sciences. White and Epston (1990), in particular, draw from the work of Bruner (1986), founding father of narrative psychology. Important notions that they translate from his work to narrative therapy are the distinction between a logico-scientific and a narrative mode of constructing reality, and the notion of 'stories of literary merit.'.

13 White and Epston (1990) borrow the metaphor of 'thin' versus 'rich' description from Clifford Geertz (1973).

14 We introduced relational–cultural therapy, which is rooted in relational–cultural theory, as a critical perspective on person-centered counseling earlier in this chapter.

15 Obviously, when exploring disorientations, the question of privilege comes to the fore: "The relation of privilege to experiences of disorientation is complex" (Harbin, 2016, p. 155). We described ways to address privilege in the previous section; in this section we focus on the tragic aspects of disorientations.

16 According to Gendlin (1981), this bodily shift is at the heart of all successful therapeutic efforts, no matter what approach is used.

References

Adams, K. (2019). Defining and operationalizing chaplaincy presence: A review. *Journal of Religion and Health, 58*, 1246–1258. https://doi.org/10.1007/s10943-018-00746-x

Baart, A. (2004). *Een theorie van de presentie* [A theory of presence]. Lemma.

Bell, D. (1995). Who's afraid of critical race theory? *University of Illinois Law Review, 4*, 893–910.

Bruner, J. (1986). *Actual minds, possible worlds*. Harvard University Press.

Christopher, J. C. (1996). Counseling's inescapable moral visions. *Journal of Counseling and Development, 75*, 17–25. https://doi.org/10.1002/j.1556-6676.1996.tb02310.x

Clinebell, H. J. (1984). *Basic types of pastoral care and counseling: Resources for the ministry of healing and growth*. Abingdon.

Combs, G., & Freedman, J. (2012). Narrative, poststructuralism, and social justice: Current practices in narrative therapy. *The Counseling Psychologist, 40*(7), 1033–1060. https://doi.org/10.1177/0011000012460662

Crenshaw, K. (1991). Mapping the margins: Intersectionality, identity politics, and violence against women of color. *Stanford Law Review, 43*, 1241–1299. https://doi.org/10.2307/1229039

Damen, A., Schuhmann, C., Leget, C., & Fitchett, F. (2020). Can outcome research respect the integrity of chaplaincy? A review of outcome studies. *Journal of Health Care Chaplaincy, 26*(4), 131–158. https://doi.org/10.1080/08854726.2019.1599258

Dollarhide, C. T., & Oliver, K. (2014). Humanistic professional identity: The trans-theoretical tie that binds. *The Journal of Humanistic Counseling, 53*(3), 203–217. https://doi.org/10.1002/j.2161-1939.2014.00057.x

Dumaresque, R., Thornton, T., Glaser, D., & Lawrence, A. (2018). Politicized narrative therapy: A reckoning and a call to action. *Canadian Social Work Review, 35*(1), 109–129. https://doi.org/10.7202/1051105ar

Fitchett, G. (2017). Recent progress in chaplaincy-related research. *Journal of Pastoral Care and Counseling, 71*(3), 163–175. https://doi.org/10.1177/1542305017724811

Gadamer, H.-G. (2004). *Truth and method* (J. Weinsheimer & D. G. Marshall, Trans.) (2nd rev. Ed.). *Continuum*. (Original work published 1960).

Geertz, C. (1973). *The interpretation of cultures*. Basic Books.

Gendlin, E. T. (1981). *Focusing* (Rev. ed.). Bantam Books.

Glasner, T., Schuhmann, C., & Kruizinga, R. (2023). The future of chaplaincy in a secularized society: A mixed-methods survey from the Netherlands. *Journal of Health Care Chaplaincy, 29*(1), 132–144. https://doi.org/10.1080/08854726.2022.2040894

Gorski, P. C., & Goodman, R. D. (2015). Introduction: Toward a decolonized multicultural counseling and psychology. In R. D. Goodman & P. C. Gorski (Eds.), *Decolonizing "multicultural" counseling through social justice* (pp. 1–10). Springer.

Handzo, G. F., Cobb, M., Holmes, C., Kelly, E., & Sinclair, S. (2014). Outcomes for professional health care chaplaincy: An international call to action. *Journal of Health Care Chaplaincy, 20*(2), 43–53. https://doi.org/10.1080/08854726.2014.902713

Harbin, A. (2016). *Disorientation and moral life*. Oxford University Press.

Hughes, B. P., Massey, K., Bona, L., Barnes, L. J. D., Nash, P., & Hall, E. J. (2019). *The chaplaincy taxonomy: Standardizing spiritual care terminology*. taxonomy-for-chaplains.pdf (sdcoalition.org)

Jordan, J. V. (2017). Relational-cultural therapy. In M. Kopala & M. Keitel (Eds.), *Handbook of counseling women* (2nd ed., pp. 63–73). Sage.

Leget, C. (2012). *Ruimte om te sterven* [Space for dying]. Lannoo.

Leget, C. (2017). *Art of living, art of dying. Spiritual care for a good death*. Jessica Kingsley.

Leijssen, M. (2007a). Making space for the inner guide. *American Journal of Psychotherapy, 61*(3), 255–270. https://doi.org/10.1176/appi.psychotherapy.2007.61.3.255

Leijssen, M. (2007b). *Tijd voor de ziel* [Time for the soul]. Lannoo.

Lynch, G. (2002). *Pastoral care & counseling*. Sage.

Malet, P., Bioy, A., & Santarpia, A. (2022). Clinical perspectives on the notion of presence. *Frontiers in Psychology, 13*. https://doi.org/10.3389/fpsyg.2022.783417

Martín-Baró, I. (1994). *Writings for a liberation psychology* (A. Aron & S. Corne, Eds.). Harvard University Press.

McLeod, J. (2003). *An introduction to counselling* (3rd ed.). Open University Press.

Mearns, D., & Thorne, B. (2007). *Person-centred counselling in action* (3rd ed.). Sage.

Miller, J. B. (1976). *Toward a new psychology of women*. Beacon Press.

Mooren, J. H. (Ed.). (2013). *Bakens in de stroom* [Beacons in the stream]. De Graaff.

Nolan, S. (2015). Chaplain as "hopeful presence": Working with dying people. *Practical Theology, 4*(2), 165–179. https://doi.org/10.1558/prth.v4i2.165

Nolan, S. (2019). Lifting the lid on chaplaincy: A first look at findings from chaplains' case study research. *Journal of Health Care Chaplaincy, 27*(1), 1–23. https://doi.org/10.1080/08854726.2019.1603916

Nolan, S., & MacLaren, D. (2021). Religious, spiritual, pastoral … and secular? Where next for chaplaincy? *Health and Social Care Chaplaincy, 9*(1), 1–10. https://doi.org/10.1558/hscc.42735

Pargament, K. I. (2007). *Spiritually integrated psychotherapy*. The Guilford Press.

Payne, M. (2006). *Narrative therapy. An introduction for counsellors* (2nd ed.). Sage.

Schuhmann, C. (2015). Counselling and the humanist worldview. In A. Copson & A. C. Grayling (Eds.), *The Wiley Blackwell handbook of humanism* (pp. 173–193). Wiley Blackwell.

Schuhmann, C., & Damen, A. (2018). Representing the Good: Pastoral care in a secular age. *Pastoral Psychology, 67*, 405–417. https://doi.org/10.1007/s11089-018-0826-0

Singh, A. A., Appling, B., & Trepal, H. (2020). Using the multicultural and social justice counseling competencies to decolonize counseling practice: The important roles of theory, power, and action. *Journal of Counseling & Development, 98*, 261–271. https://doi.org/10.1002/jcad.12321

Smit, J. (2015). *Antwoord geven op het leven zelf* [Responding to life itself]. Eburon.

Stollberg, D. (1969). *Therapeutische Seelsorge* [Therapeutic care of the soul]. Kaiser.

van Deurzen, E. (2002). *Existential counselling & psychotherapy in practice* (2nd ed.). Sage.

van Praag, J. P. (1982). *Foundations of humanism*. Prometheus Books.

Westerhof, G. J., & Slatman, S. (2019). In search of the best evidence for life review therapy to reduce depressive symptoms in older adults: A meta-analysis of randomized controlled trials. *Clinical Psychology: Science and Practice*, *26*(4), 11. https://doi.org/10.1111/cpsp.12301

White, K. B., Murphy, P. E., Jeuland, J., & Fitchett, G. (2019). Distress and self-care among chaplains working in palliative care. *Palliative & Supportive Care*, *17*(5), 542–549. https://doi.org/10.1017/S1478951518001062

White, M., & Epston, D. (1990). *Narrative means to therapeutic ends*. Norton.

Woldemichael, M. T., Broesterhuizen, M., & Liègeois, A. (2013). Christian pastoral care and psychotherapy: A need for theoretical clarity. *Journal of Pastoral Care & Counseling*, *67*(4), 1–13. https://doi.org/10.1177/154230501306700406

Yalom, I. D. (1980). *Existential psychotherapy*. Basic Books.

Yalom, I. D. (1998). *The Yalom reader: Selections from the work of a master therapist and storyteller* (B. Yalom, Ed.). Basic Books.

Chapter 5

Humanist chaplaincy support groups

Annelieke Damen, Gaby Jacobs, and Eva Trapman

Box 5.1 Introduction to a chaplaincy support group in a penitentiary

The participants enter the hallway. After walking through a metal detection gate and handing in their pass to the hallway guard, they enter the meditation room. I shake hands with everyone and express that it is good that they are there. Oscar usually enters first and takes a seat next to the piano by the wall. Milo, Roger, Henry, Mohamad, and George follow. Milo, a man of almost explosive energy, takes a seat on a small bench on the other side of the piano. His legs are spread, his head bowed. He lets himself be carried away by the sounds of the piano, nodding to the beat with his eyes closed. When the song ends, he jumps up and exclaims with his arms wide open: "WOW! Thank you!" A beautiful start of the week, which came about so naturally.

Oscar and Milo then walk together to the tables, which are pushed together in a hexagon to form a circle. Today there are six participants, men at different stages of their detention and with different world-view backgrounds. I, the humanist chaplain, lead the group together with my colleague, Pastor Pieter. I pour everyone a cup of tea or coffee, or let them serve each other. It has become a familiar little group after three months of weekly meetings.

We welcome them, and light a candle, marking as it were, the introduction of a certain atmosphere. Then we start with a short check-in round in which every participant answers an introductory 'overview' question. Not "How are you?" but "How was your week?" or "How is your morning going?" Sometimes we ask them to pick a color to indicate their state of being. Such a question is especially welcomed in this group; they appreciate the unexpected. During the round we will not yet go into what is shared. The round is about

---

DOI: 10.4324/9781003428633-7

> *hearing everyone's voice. Not infrequently people tear up. Some are*
> *still on remand and are experiencing a lot of stress. That, too, gets a*
> *place in the check-in.*

Introduction

In Chapter 4 we have outlined the individual counseling which chaplains provide to support people in orientation in life. Besides working on an individual level, chaplains also facilitate groups. In Chapter 1 we defined orientation in life as a process of existential meaning making in which people on the one hand look for, figure out, and express what is of ultimate value to them, and on the other hand search for an experience of connectedness with themselves, others, and/or the sacred. Groups then are, like individual counseling, places where one can:

1. Express and explore experiences of disorientation.
2. Explicate and potentially revise visions of a good life.
3. Explore how to actually be close to or move towards (renewed or revised) visions of a good life.
4. Experience relational affirmation and empowerment.

However, groups also differ from individual counseling in several respects. In this chapter, we will look more closely at the facilitation of chaplaincy support groups. We will start with an introduction to the different kinds of chaplaincy support groups in the Netherlands. Then, we will introduce the rationale for organizing chaplaincy support groups, followed by a description of how the above goals can be realized within these groups. We will close the chapter with a short conclusion and take-home messages.

Chaplaincy support groups in the Netherlands

Chaplains in the Netherlands facilitate chaplaincy support groups in the contexts of health care, the military, penitentiaries, and in the outpatient context. Chaplains, for example, facilitate support groups for clients, staff, and executives in mental health hospitals, disability care, elderly care, military training programs, veteran care, and penitentiaries (see Boxes 5.1–5.7 with case descriptions), and in primary health and social care for citizens about abortion, climate change, or the last phase of life.

The chaplaincy support groups may take various forms. There are groups that mainly focus on *talking* about existential themes, these groups are the focus of this chapter. They are interactive and require active participation of the participants. There are also support groups that are highly *ritualized*, for example, for clients without strong verbal capabilities. A special variant of this kind is the contemplation meeting (*bezinningsbijeenkomst*), a ritualized meeting led by the chaplain. Here, it is the humanist chaplain who speaks the majority of the time, with the exception of a few moments of interaction. The rest of the time is filled with music, poetry, et cetera (see for an example Box 5.2). A third type of support group is the moral formation group, which is organized for uniformed professions such as the military and the police force. In this group, the emphasis is on the moral and ethical formation of service members, which includes thinking through the moral implications of their work from the perspective of their own worldview (Oosterhuis et al., 2023). Finally, chaplains work with groups around rituals (see Chapter 6), education and training (see Chapter 7), and moral deliberation (see Chapter 9). Of course, all possible intermediate variants of the above options exist. In the case descriptions in this chapter we can discern a mix of elements.

Box 5.2 Humanist contemplation meeting

Every humanist contemplation meeting starts with a ritual where the participants can choose to light a candle. They are seated on their chairs in a semi-circle. At the front of the room is a stand with dozens of tea lights in red casings. I ask them to become silent, and say:

> *"We start with a moment of rest, in which you can light a candle. During this candle ritual, take some time for yourself to land, turn inward, become silent. This is an hour in which nothing is expected of you. Where you can try to leave behind the hustle and bustle that you might be coming from outside the door of this space, and just be here, without having to do anything. See if you can observe what is going on inside with gentleness. You can listen to the music and pay attention to your breathing, whatever helps you. During these few minutes of peace and attention, you can choose to come forward and light a candle. You can light a candle for a loved one. Maybe someone you miss, someone close to you, someone dear to you. Or maybe for yourself."*

Then I read them a poem. After the poem they can stand up and walk to the candles, in silence, and light a candle one by one. They pass on the kindling candle, and when everyone is seated again, I thank the entire group and I go on with introducing this week's theme.

This little ritual is one of the differences between a support group and a contemplation meeting. In a support group, we sometimes light a candle, but then it is a short action; we take a candle and light it in front of us on the table in the circle. In the contemplation meeting it is a proper ritual and it takes 10 minutes. Sometimes accompanied by contemplative music or just silence. In a penitentiary, this atmosphere is very rare, and I know that to some men it is very important. Some men tell me during the week whom they lit the candle for. That is often the start of a meaningful conversation.

Chaplains, often together with their clients, prepare an existential theme for the (series of) group conversation(s). This theme is discussed in the group, or approached through a speech from the chaplain, music, poetry, or another artistic expression, followed by some conversation. Existential themes could be identity, freedom, transformation, wonder, belonging, peace, hope, wisdom (see for an example Box 5.3).

Box 5.3   Theme of a chaplaincy support group

After the check-in, we organically introduce this week's theme. Today we brought Nijhoff's poem 'Awater' with us (Colmer, 2018, p.8). We only read the first half, because it is not an easily accessible poem and it is a longer text than we usually pick. Participants take turns reading a paragraph. The poem speaks about a man without a name, we can give him all our names. The man is his father's and mother's son, known to his colleagues as Awater. His meagre body is clad in camel's hair, and nobody has ever understood what he is saying.

I ask the participants: what appeals to you in this poem, what touches you, what do you get out of it? Henry, the oldest participant, is the first to respond: "Not really anything, it went way too fast for me." Roger points out what touched him: "The man has no name, it says. But at the office his name is Awater. I recognize something in that: no one knows who the man is, not even he himself, it seems, but people in the office have a certain image of him. That is not who he is, that is one of his roles." About Roger, we know that he struggles with the image his wife has of him now that he is in prison. He prefers to be seen as the man he was before and has difficulty dealing with her anger about his crime. Through Roger's input we descend to the existential level. The group starts to exchange what different roles everyone has in life. Who are you when you are alone? Who are you when you are in a group? What groups are there in your life? Who are you with your parents, your friends, your children, as a detainee, a suspect, during the trial?

Rationale for chaplaincy support groups

The basic assumption in humanist chaplaincy is that people are, in essence, relational beings (Baker Miller & Stiver, 1997; Gergen, 2009). They function in connections with others, and they need these connections to exist and develop as agents in their own lives (Townsend & McWhirter, 2005). Experiences of disorientation often pertain breaches in the relational context, such as the loss of a loved one, relocation, or a divorce, leading to isolation, alienation, or questioning the meaning in life (see Chapter 1). Connectedness is a crucial existential need that can be met in humanist chaplaincy support groups. By sharing life experiences with others, expressing and exploring experiences of disorientation, chaplaincy support groups can initiate a process towards revised visions of a good life, i.e., reorientation in life.

Consequently, participating in a support group can lead to a renewed experience of relational affirmation and empowerment, conceptualized as the relational "capacity to produce a change" (Baker Miller, 1992, p. 241). Groups consist of different people, each with their own social and cultural backgrounds, worldviews, values, and preferences. Empowerment is fostered in the relationships that develop in the group, characterized by dialogue, i.e., a two-way communication in which a person "has a chance to get immersed in another's experiences, to become 'possessed' by their otherness" (Shotter, 2006, p. 132) and to learn from that. These so-called growth-enhancing relationships may lead to feeling recognized, valued, and connected; and to an increased ability to act in relationships with others (Jordan et al., 2004, p. 56). The difference here with therapeutic groups (e.g., led by psychotherapists) is that the primary focus of the group is not on learning to function better in relationships (Yalom & Leszcz, 2005) but on the exchange of how one experiences life. The social justice activist and group facilitator Maree Brown (2021) puts it beautifully: to "find our place in this complex existence, perhaps even making it simple to be complex together" (p. 10). An example of how creative methods, such as poetry, can help in finding this place is presented in the case in Box 5.4.

Box 5.4 Reorientation experience of a participant

A few days after the support group, Roger handed me a self-written poem. In the poem, he describes the many different roles, past and present, of his life. He writes he has been a baby, toddler, an impulsive

child. A loving boy, rebellious teenager, a parent. A son, brother, inde-
pendent, fat, victim, accuser, lifesaver, gardener, husband, big bad
wolf, critic, addict, psychotic, patient-worthy, criminal, an inmate. In
the poem, he asks the question if he is worth more than just one of
these roles. He wonders if all of them were to encounter each other,
would there be recognition? A line from the poem reads: "At best, I
think, they see each other as strangers who don't like each other. At
worst, as blind idiots who feel inclined to kill each other."

The poem ends with the following conclusion:
Being present, as it were, I would ask anyone
Not to ask how many times you live, but how many times can you die?
And from that become something different. Someone else.
In every moment, as a human being, of value.[1]

Empowerment may also happen in the group because personal orientation in life is linked to organizational and societal change, i.e., humanization (see Chapter 1). Support groups can be seen as narrative spaces or
sanctuaries within the often bureaucratic and objectifying institutions
chaplains work in. In these groups, stories are shared about experiences
and their attributed meanings, and through these, participants can become
aware of the organizational, social, and political factors that hinder their
reorientation in life and make them feel powerless and alienated from their
contexts. One could say that the presence of these sanctuaries in itself is a
humanizing factor (see Chapter 3). Moreover, chaplains can use the stories
on an aggregate level to advocate for changes within the organization and
society at large. The chaplain then becomes a spokesperson on behalf of
those that have less influence, a catalyst for dismantling (colonial) legacies
of oppression and supremacy (Maree Brown, 2021). In individual counseling, chaplains can work on systemic change. In groupwork, the opportunities are manifold.

Facilitating humanist chaplaincy support groups

While facilitating groups, many things happen at once. To somewhat structure this information, Geurts et al. (2015) propose to unravel the group
process into three dimensions:

- Content;
- Form;
- Climate.

The content of the conversation refers to any communication that is exchanged within the group. This not only includes verbal communication but also information that is hidden in the timing, the nonverbal, or the order of the communication. The content is not only about *what* is communicated (the topics that are addressed) but also about *how* it is communicated (which gives information about what the topic means to someone) (Geurts et al., 2015, p. 28). For example, in the case example in Box 5.3, what is communicated concerns the different roles the participants experience in their lives, expressed by Roger through how the poem touches him.

The form of the conversation refers to the containment and guidance of the interaction (Geurts et al., 2015). In short: the structuring of the conversation. Who is talking when? In the case description in Box 5.1, the check-in round structures the conversation in such a way that every participant can briefly say something. The form includes the type of facilitation the chaplain decides to exercise. The chaplain might let the conversation flow freely or intervene actively by steering the conversation towards a certain topic or giving someone the turn to talk.

The climate of the support group refers to the 'mood' of the conversation. The conversation may have a pleasant or less pleasant atmosphere; it is about how the group feels about the conversation and the group culture. The climate involves the emotional experience of the group, the group's dynamic processes, and unwritten rules that often occur below the surface (Geurts et al., 2015, p. 34). In Box 5.1, the chaplain, for example, speaks about a "familiar" group, lights a candle to evoke a calm and intimate atmosphere, and points out that people feel safe enough to tear up.

Generally, happenings in the group may relate to all dimensions. In Box 5.1, the chaplain greets the participants by expressing that it is good that they are there. This conveys the message that they are welcome, in the form of a handshake, and opens a climate of kindness to each other. As another example, a heated discussion encompasses a climate of tension, an antagonistic form of conversation, and a sensitive content. The chaplain can decide to intervene on one or more dimensions.

The dimensions of content, form, and climate are just empty vehicles – they need substance to realize the above goals. In the next paragraphs, we will therefore further discuss our main theoretical concepts of relational affirmation and empowerment with suggestions on how they can be facilitated on the above three dimensions.

Facilitating relational dynamics in chaplaincy support groups

---

Box 5.5   A moment of meeting

In the support group, a special connection has now been established between two participants: Milo and Oscar. They sit next to each other today. While discussing the poem, Milo's attention span is exhausted quite quickly. Out of the corner of my eye, I see that Oscar hands him a load of little wooden coffee stirrers when he notices that Milo's restlessness is increasing. "Here, go break them all," Oscar whispers. Then Oscar turns to me and asks: "Can Milo get a fidget spinner here?"

In the next 15 minutes, Milo breaks all the stirrers into very small pieces. He doesn't participate in the conversation, but he seems to be following it. At some point I feel that Milo is a bit calmer again. I glimpse in his direction and see that Oscar is tickling the back of Milo's neck with his hand. I have never seen this happen in my six years of chaplaincy work.

As stated earlier, we regard chaplaincy support groups as relational spaces that can lead to a renewed experience of relational affirmation and empowerment. How can a chaplain facilitate this space in such a way that participants experience change? For inspiration, we can look at relational constructionism (e.g., Gergen, 2009) and relational feminist therapy (The Stone Center for Developmental Studies at Wellesley College), where a lot of expertise is gathered on the relational dynamics in groupwork. Relational psychologist Shotter (2006) stresses the importance of dialogue and joint action in groupwork: participants do not act independently from each other. They co-act and co-construct meanings, guided by feelings that emerge in this relational process: "In this dialogue, a person participates wholly and throughout his whole life: with his eyes, lips, hands, soul, spirit, with his whole body and deeds" (Bahktin, 1984, p. 293; cited in Shotter, 2006, p. 68). At the same time, authors stress the difficulties in relational work: it is not something that can be fully controlled and steered towards certain outcomes because there are so many forces operating at the same time: "The path of connection is filled with disconnections, the vulnerability of seeking reconnection, and the tension around needing to move away, possibly to hide in protective inauthenticity" (Baker Miller & Stiver, 1997, p. 6). Along these lines, the Boston Stone Center has highlighted four relational paradoxes (Fedele, 2004):

1. The helping paradox: how to establish an equal human relationship within the context of an unequal professional helping relationship.
2. The connection paradox: participants are using strategies of disconnection, with the aim to stay connected (for example: not being open about one's thoughts or feelings because of fear that these may disrupt the relationship).
3. The diversity paradox: participants will experience a tension between commonality based on universal feelings and isolation and alienation because of differences. This implies a move between recognition and otherness.
4. The conflict paradox: conflicts may lead to breaches within a group, but sharing the experiences and meanings of the conflict may foster connection. It is also true that participants allow more diversity and conflict once they feel more connected.

The chaplain works with these relational paradoxes to try to invite 'moments of meeting' (Stern, 2004). Following the American psychiatrist Slater (1996), who gives us a view on the seeming hopelessness in working with people with a chronical psychiatric illness, we propose that it is in the small moments of connection that 'something meaningful happens' in the group, although after that it might seem lost again. Psychotherapist Stern (2004) calls these 'now-moments.' He is fascinated by the short, intense, and meaningful moments between persons in the here-and-now. These are often implicit but may be more effective than cognitively understood or verbalized happenings. In his theory, change happens through lived experience, stemming from feelings and actions in the present moment with real people. In now-moments: "there is an immediate sense that the existing intersubjective field is threatened, that an important change in the relationship is possible (for good or for ill), and that the preexisting nature of the relationship has been put on the table for renegotiation" (Stern, 2004, p. 167). Such moments can result in the experience of connection, felt by all participants in the situation – a 'moment of meeting.'

In the case example in Box 5.5, we have highlighted a moment of meeting: Oscar is helping Milo to feel at ease in the group, while the conversation about the poem is ongoing. The empathic gesture by Oscar demonstrates a climate of connection and inclusion. The case also shows the unpredictability of relational work, as the chaplain admits: "I have never seen this happen."

To facilitate relational paradoxes towards moments of meeting, the chaplain can do different things regarding the dimensions of content, form, and climate.

Content: Regarding content, the chaplain can facilitate towards moments of meeting by:

- An introduction in which everyone is welcomed with their full humanity.
- Content that speaks to the people of the group, such as an existential theme that occupies their minds, possibly chosen together with the participants. For example, one can discuss a poem to open a shared conversation or everybody introduces a song that is dear to them to get to know each other better, et cetera.
- Bringing the conversation towards the existential level: what does something mean to someone in their life? How does an experience connect to their worldview or overarching worldview stories (e.g., the Bible, the Koran, the Vedas, humanism, philosophical and artistic movements)?
- Creating space for the thoughts that are connected to bodies and emotions (Nussbaum, 2001): what are they telling you about what is important to you? What do they tell you about the relationships that you value?
- Appreciating aloud the connection, diversity, and conflict paradoxes: how does it feel to have shared this? Do you feel you are alone in this? What is the tension in the room about?

Form: In structuring the conversation towards moments of meeting, the chaplain can:

- State and guard the social contract of the group – e.g., listening to each other, what is said in the group stays in the group, diversity is invited – and aim of the group clearly, so the participants can help to collaborate together towards connection.
- Invite all the participants to shortly speak at the beginning of the group so every voice is heard and the hurdle to speak has been lowered (see the case in Box 5.1).
- Encourage participants to relate to each other's stories, the chaplain can stimulate the conversation between the participants: does someone recognize this feeling? Who would like to say something to [name of participant]? Do you hear what is valuable for [name of participant]?
- Sometimes groups might tend to 'interview' a participant. The chaplain has to safeguard that the conversation stays balanced by bringing the conversation back to the group and by letting different people speak.
- Split the group in subgroups if vulnerability in the big group is still too challenging.

- Work with diverse creative methods – music, writing, drawing, portraying something – to address different layers of life.
- If possible, invite participants to prepare something for the group, or take something with them.

Climate: To be able to facilitate the above, it is important to create a trusting environment in which it is ok to show feelings. The chaplain can foster this by:

- Small acts and interventions that allow participants to relate to each other. Think of:
  - The set-up of the room: a circle of chairs fosters an intimate atmosphere; coffee and tea makes people feel welcome.
  - The atmosphere of the room: flowers in the middle of the circle help people relax because there is something to focus attention on; not too bright lighting changes the ambience, as do artworks.
  - The values one embodies (non)verbally: curiosity in your gaze and questions, warmth in a smile, trustworthiness by doing what you are saying.
  - The happenings one wants to give attention to so a trusting climate grows: moments of vulnerability, emotion, reaching out.
- An attitude of listening to one's own body: what is it telling me about myself, the group, and the relationships within the group? Do I feel tension, and is that because I am nervous, or is everybody nervous? A clarifying question for the group can clear the air.

Facilitating power dynamics in chaplaincy support groups

Box 5.6   Empowerment

After much has been shared about the different roles we have, I will give an example of myself. It concerns role confusion that I had as a child and teenager when combining for instance parents with friends. Especially certain (loud) friends and my sensitive father. When they were together in one room, I struggled and wondered: who am I supposed to be? It made me slightly on guard. After my example there are sounds of recognition. I then ask how they balance their different roles. One of the participants responds: "I tried so hard to keep up an image outside. Yet I had a double life: my life with loved ones and acquaintances, and my criminal life online. Completely separate roles.

> *When my secret was discovered and I was arrested, everything I held dear fell apart, resulting in a lot of deep shame. Now that everything is already ruined, it is strangely enough easier to be myself. I no longer have to uphold myself; I no longer divide myself. As much as I'm ashamed, I'm more real now."*

A support group can be seen as a microcosmos (Yalom & Leszcz, 2005): a small society that is characterized by diversity and power relationships. Recognizing the power dynamics in groups is crucial in order not to reproduce or even strengthen the power dynamics. This is a double-sided process.

First, chaplains need to recognize the power dynamics in the existential themes that are brought forward in the stories, for example, in a migration story, a story of burnout, or the problematic relationship with the church. Disorientation is individually experienced but a relational and contextual phenomenon, as we have outlined in Chapter 1. There is an interwovenness of existential themes with political conditions, and these power dynamics should be part of the dialogue within the groups. In Box 5.6, for example, we can discern cultural narratives about what it means to be a good friend, daughter, husband, what one should feel ashamed of. These dominant narratives can be enforced in the group, as well as questioned.

Second, what happens in the group between participants should also be seen from a perspective of power. Participants, including the chaplain, may act and react unconsciously from their social-cultural positioning. Differences in for example social class, ethnicity, gender, worldview, social background, and age will influence the interaction. Intersectionality theory (e.g., Davis, 2008) stresses that people have multiple positionings, for example both belonging to a lower social class and an ethnic minority, which matter depending on the context and relationships one encounters. The aim of chaplaincy support groups is to become aware of and equalize the power hierarchies related to these axes of intersectionality.

Doehring (2015) distinguishes two kinds of power in chaplaincy relationships that are insightful for groupwork as well. Agential power refers to the active use of power by the chaplain or group members. It is the power of deliberately influencing the other person, for example, by interpreting what the other person said, giving practical support, or giving advice. Receptive power is the passive use of power, which is manifested, for example, in being present, in affirming the other person (verbally and nonverbally), and in the recognition of the other's uniqueness. Both kinds of power can be transformative, i.e., enhance empowerment, but they also involve risks: agential power may become too intrusive and thereby oppress the other's voice; receptive power may allow for a lot of space for the other but can fail to act for empowerment (de Lange & Jacobs, 2022).

Box 5.6 shows the use of self-disclosure by the chaplain in the support group and how it invites the participants to be open about their experiences and feelings as well. Self-disclosure in humanist chaplaincy is a fundamental act of human equality. On the human level, the chaplain and participant are equal. In their life circumstances and their social-cultural positioning, they differ. Self-disclosure is a means to explore the common universal existential themes while allowing for differences. It opens the possibility of discussing the power dynamics that influence the conditions of one's life.

The awareness of power dynamics and the aim of empowerment implies that chaplains employ different strategies regarding content, form, and climate within the support groups:

Content: Regarding the content of the conversation, the chaplain could:

- Express their shared humanity through self-disclosure, i.e., appear as a human being with life experiences and a social and cultural positioning wherever functional for the group process (see Box 5.6).
- Demystify groupwork by being open and giving information about what they do and why, including education about the existential theme if relevant.
- Prevent 'othering' in the group by focusing on the intersecting positions each participant holds and by asking 'the other question' (Davis & Lutz, 2023) when, for example, something sounds racist: who do you mean with 'we' or 'them'? How is gender involved in this?
- Invite multiplicity and ambivalence in stories, instead of trying to find consensus ('there exists not one truth'): who experiences this differently? Whose voice have we not heard yet? Which values are at play here?
- Bring attention to the systemic context of someone's story: what is limiting you to live the life you aspire to? Who are you limiting?
- Ask for stories about resilience: what did you do the last time you felt this way?
- Make sure everyone is hooked to the conversation and understands the content.

Form: In structuring the conversation, the chaplain could focus on:

- Decentralizing facilitation: such as drawing up the social contract together, shared agenda setting and decision-making regarding the content and form of the group, using a talking stick that participants can give to the next speaker.

- Employing self-involvement: not staying at a distance but participating in tasks or activities and making oneself vulnerable.
- Applying creative methods in order to include unheard voices (see also Box 5.7).

Climate: When it comes to an empowering climate, the chaplain should:

- Create a hospitable space where everyone's dignity is respected: help everyone arrive in ways that honor the cultures of the group (Maree Brown, 2021, p. 120).
- Allow for 'not knowing' (Anderson & Goolishian, 1992), the unheard, the difficult.
- Slow down the conversation to create space for depth, for example, by allowing moments of silence.
- Or, if needed, bring energy into the room: let us stand up and move our bodies!

Box 5.7   Closing the support group

I prefer to end each support group by listening to a song together, via a laptop connected to speakers. I like to do this to touch a different dimension than the cognitive and verbal. The function this listening together has differs from week to week: being silent together, making space for emotions, turning into oneself, singing along together. Sometimes it brings some light, airiness, or cheerfulness. In any case, it serves as a supplement to talking. Afterwards, I always shake hands with everyone, thanking them for their presence and wishing them a good week.

Conclusion

In this chapter we have given a brief overview of humanist chaplaincy support groups in the Netherlands. We have introduced the goals for the support groups, the different groups that exist, the rationale for organizing the groups, and pointers for facilitation. For chaplaincy support groups it is important to stress that the relational work in groups is not a means to an end but an end in itself. Through relationships, people feel recognized as human beings, and connected to others and the world. We see it as the task of the chaplain to create the conditions for relational affirmation in groups, in organizations, and in society at large. We hope this chapter offers inspiration for organizing your own groups.

Take-home messages

- Organizing (humanist) chaplaincy support groups is an important means to provide guidance in life orientation.
- A key goal of the group is fostering participants' experience of relational affirmation and empowerment.
- Compared to individual support, the added value of a group is that they can foster multiple growth-enhancing relationships.
- In facilitating relational affirmation and empowerment, the chaplain has attention for the group's content, form, and climate.

Note

1 *Op zijn best, denk ik, zien ze elkaar als vreemden die eenieder niet aanspreken.*
    In het ergste geval, als blinde idioten die zich geneigd voelen elkaar af te maken.
    Erbij aanwezig zijnde, als het ware, zou ik aan een ieder stellen.
    Niet te vragen daar je leeft maar één keer, echter hoe vaak kan je sterven.
    En daarvan uit iets anders worden. Iemand anders.
    In ieder moment, als mens, van waarde.

References

Anderson, H., & Goolishian, H. (1992). The client is the expert: A not-knowing approach to therapy. In S. McNamee & K. J. Gergen (Eds.), *Therapy as social construction* (pp. 25–39). Sage Publications, Inc.

Baker Miller, J. (1992). *Women and power: In rethinking power*. SUNY Press.

Baker Miller, J., & Stiver, I. (1997). *The healing connection: How women form relationships in therapy and in life*. Beacon Press.

Colmer, D. (2018). *Poetry from the Netherlands: The Enchanting Verses Literature Review*.

Davis, K. (2008). Intersectionality as buzzword: A sociology of science perspective on what makes a feminist theory successful. *Feminist Theory, 9*(1), 67–85. https://doi.org/10.1177/1464700108086364

Davis, K., & Lutz, H. (2023). *The Routledge international handbook of intersectionality studies*. Routledge International Handbooks.

de Lange, K., & Jacobs, G. (2022). Meaningful conversations. Reciprocity in power dynamics between humanistic spiritual carers and patients in Dutch hospitals. *Religions, 13*(2), 109. https://doi.org/10.3390/rel13020109

Doehring, C. (2015). *The practice of pastoral care: A postmodern approach*. Westminster John Knox Press.

Fedele, N. M. (2004). Relationships in groups: Connection, resonance, and paradox. In J. V. Jordan, M. Walker, & L. M. Hartling (Eds.), *The complexity of connection* (pp. 194–219). Guilford Press.

Gergen, K. (2009). *Relational being: Beyond self and community*. Oxford University Press.

Geurts, J., Müller, I., & Tenwolde, H. (2015). *Gespreksvoering in groepen* [Conversations in groups]. Coutinho.

Jordan, J. V., Walker, M., & Hartling, L. M. (Eds.). (2004). *The complexity of connection: Writings from the Stone Center's Jean Baker Miller Training Institute*. The Guilford Press.

Maree Brown, A. (2021). *Holding change. The way of emergent strategy facilitation and mediation*. AK Press.

Nussbaum, M. C. (2001). *Upheavals of thought*. Cambridge University Press.

Oosterhuis, T., Vos, P. H., & Olsman, E. (2023). Protestant theological perspectives on the contribution of military chaplains to moral formation. *International Journal of Public Theology, 17*(1), 5–23. https://doi.org/10.1163/15697320-20230075

Shotter, J. (2006). Understanding process from within: An argument for 'Withness'-Thinking. *Organization Studies, 27*(4), 585–604. https://doi.org/10.1177/0170840606062105

Slater, L. (1996). *Welcome to my country: A therapist's memoir of madness*. Anchor.

Stern, D. N. (2004). *The present moment: In psychotherapy and everyday life*. WW Norton & Company.

Townsend, K. C., & McWhirter, B. T. (2005). Connectedness: A review of the literature with implications for counseling, assessment, and research. *Journal of Counseling & Development, 83*(2), 191–201. https://doi.org/10.1002/j.1556-6678.2005.tb00596.x

Yalom, I. D., & Leszcz, M. (2005). *The theory and practice of group psychotherapy* (5th ed.). Basic Books/Hachette Book Group.

Chapter 6

Re-inventing rituals from humanistic perspectives

Joanna Wojtkowiak and Emy Spekschoor

The psychologist from a short-term revalidation care department where I work as a humanist chaplain requests my support for Nadia (pseudonym), a woman in her mid-forties of Surinamese origin who is suffering from the aftermath of severe COVID, is diagnosed with schizophrenia, and is dealing with loss whilst recovering from a delirium. She is not really religious but mentions some affinity with her Afro-Surinamese Winti background. It is clear she is still in mid-recovery, not all her sentences make sense and she alternates quickly between strong emotions. I sit with her for a while, we talk and listen to music she loves. Nadia tells me about her life, her family, and the loss of her mother who died when Nadia was in the hospital. She couldn't understand at that time what was happening. During our conversation, she repeatedly says: "I need to say goodbye before she leaves earth." Nadia declines to have a Winti priest but wants my help to say goodbye to her mother while receiving care herself, limiting the options.

Introduction

In this example, Nadia shares with Emy, the attending humanist chaplain, that she is struggling with her mother's death, as she could not say goodbye to her, and she expresses the wish to do so. Nadia is dealing with unresolved grief that is impacting her life and also her recovery. The chaplain identifies the 'need to say goodbye' as a 'ritual need' and suggests co-creating and performing a farewell with Nadia. The focus here is on rituals in chaplaincy and, more specifically, how humanist chaplains can further develop ritual sensitivity, competence, and repertoire.

In general, rituals such as prayer and service are central to the work of chaplains (Handzo et al., 2008) and lie at the heart of lived worldviews.

DOI: 10.4324/9781003428633-8

While "collective and individual rituals are activities that have notably increased, at least in the face of disasters and other deeply shaking experiences" (Danbolt & Stifoss-Hanssen, 2020, p. 37), nevertheless, rituals are often (understandably) still associated with traditional religion and belief systems and are less considered in secular or humanist contexts. Pinn (2017) argues that: "too often nontheists such as humanists insist that only theists need ritual – and that to entertain the development of humanist rituals is to open the door to theism" (p. 31). While humanism does not have a long history of ritual traditions or strict ritual rule books, there are, however, humanists across the world who have for decades been performing rituals from humanist worldviews, such as at birth, death, marriage, and initiation (e.g., in the UK, Australia, US, Belgium, but also in Poland, and Lithuania). In the Netherlands, for instance, humanist chaplains have been (re)creating and performing meaningful rituals for individual, organizational, and communal needs, such as remembrance rituals, seasonal celebrations, or rituals for individual needs (such as in the case of Nadia). In line with Pinn (2017), we, agree that the need for rituals does not represent a religious or theistic need, but instead "the human desire for community, for connection, for something greater than the individual" (p. 31). Religious studies scholar Grimes (2014) argues that rituals should be considered part of the cultural domain, similar to art and architecture, instead of strictly placing rituals into the domain of religions. However, rituals are embedded in cultural and philosophical worldviews, whether these are religious, secular, humanist, or pluralistic. Here, we will explicitly describe rituals that are created and performed from a humanist worldview. This chapter also critically reflects on the re-invention of rituals from different academic fields, aiming at a humanistic perspective (see Introduction).

In this chapter, we specifically focus on the notion of ritualizing, which refers to active, imaginative, and creative processes of ritual-making. Rituals are, on the one hand, legitimated by tradition, and on the other hand, re-invented creatively (Grimes, 2002). Grimes (2002) argues: "whereas rites depend on tradition and institutions, ritualizing, [...] appeals to intuition and imagination" (p. 29). 'Ritualizing' as a verb focuses more on the dynamic aspects of rituals.[1] In our view, ritualizing and ritual (re)design are important methods acquired by chaplains. Learning to re-invent and (re)introduce rituals is part of developing ritual competence, which is becoming increasingly important in post-secular and pluralist contexts. In this chapter, first, a short definition and description of ritual functions is given. Second, an introduction to the ritual work of humanist chaplains is given. Third, we describe a method for contemporary ritualizing and ritual (re) design to help humanist chaplains further develop ritual sensitivity and competence (Wojtkowiak, 2022).

What are rituals and what do they 'do'?

Rituals cannot be defined by causality, but rituals are meaningful. Rituals negotiate spirituality by creating symbolic spaces to connect with oneself, a greater community, and horizontal or relational transcendence. While spirituality refers to something that cannot be grasped (see also Chapter 2), rituals are also actively performed by people. Moreover, people report that rituals 'do' something, such as transform social and psychological statuses (Gordon-Lennox, 2017; Wojtkowiak, 2018). This leads us to understand that rituals influence people's bodies and minds (Schilbrack, 2004). What is more, liminality is addressed and performed and sometimes transformed in rituals (e.g., during the funeral the body is being ritually accompanied to the state of the dead). Liminality refers to an in-between state, outside of regular social structures and norms (Turner, 1979). For instance, when a person is dying or pregnant but also when a person is temporarily not living at home (e.g., being on a mission, staying in a hospital, being in prison). Liminality is an important concept in chaplaincy, as many clients are in states of liminality: "being-on-the-threshold" (Turner, 1979, p. 465). Rituals explore, negotiate, and canalize liminality, together with the accompanying feelings, ideas, and reflections. This means that in ritual it is more about exploring liminal states than explaining them. To understand the core elements of rituals, we will present a working definition.

While there are different definitions, views, and debates on what constitutes a ritual and rituals have different modes, from daily ritualization, celebrations, liturgy, or ceremony (Grimes, 2014), we will keep the working definition simple. Grimes' (2014) four family characteristics are found in all rituals, regardless of the context, and are described as "embodied, condensed, prescribed enactment" (p. 193). First, rituals are always embodied, they consist of 'bodies in action.' Ritual is not merely having an idea or thinking about something but actively doing it with one's body; it is put into action. Ritual is "one possible orientation of action, rather than a set of meanings" (Seligman et al., 2008, p. 6). Sitting in silence is also ritual action, as it asks for a different posture and mode of attention during the ritual. Second, rituals are condensed. Rituals ask for attention and intention and thus differ from autonomic responses in everyday life (though rituals can be integrated into one's everyday life, such as prayer, meditation, or contemplation, and can become habits). At the moment of the ritual, people are (or should be at least) attentive towards the ritual. This differs from a routine, where the cognitive load is generally low (Boyer & Liénard, 2006). Third, rituals always have one or more prescribed elements. The prescriptive character differs in ritual contexts (e.g., a birthday party or a military ceremony). Finally, rituals are enacted: put into action and performed. Rituals need to be performed in a specific way. This is also true for individually crafted and personalized rituals; while there might be room for personal input and spontaneity, rituals have specific orders, sequences, and structures that cannot be changed. Imagine starting a funeral with a fare-well at the coffin and then the speeches and welcome. Rituals follow a structured narrative, there is an emotional curve that the ritual unfolds. The goodbye at the coffin is often an emotionally intense moment, it is when ritual participants have a final interaction with the deceased body.

Ritual functions in society and chaplaincy

Rituals serve different functions in society, which are related to the work of chaplains. Humanists, as well as secular and religious people, face questions of meaning. Rituals contribute to social order, community, and transformation in moments of disorientation (Driver, 2006). They keep social order by defining 'who we are' as a community and by establishing social rules, roles, and structures, for instance, classic life-cycle rituals (e.g., birth, death, and marriage).

First, rituals are meaningful in the work of chaplains as they contribute to the community presence of chaplains. What we mean by that term is that chaplains can actively build a sense of community by being present for the community and by performing, for instance, rituals repetitively (e.g., weekly, monthly) or by bringing people together in moments of collective grief (see the last part of the case described in Chapter 10 for an example of a community ritual led by chaplains). An example from a religious context is a priest who spontaneously opened the church immediately after the shocking news of the murder of a couple by another member of the village. People could come together, light a candle, and share their emotions with others. We think this is an excellent example of community presence. Another example comes from Dutch penitentiaries, where humanist chaplains have been organizing weekly contemplation meetings every Friday (referred to as 'Humanist on Friday') that allow inmates to gather, contemplate on life themes (such as friendship, fatherhood, loss, and grief), and to celebrate events, such as New Years, together. Small rituals are introduced during the meetings, such as listening to music, writing wishes on cards, burning candles, and having coffee and tea with specific cookies at the end. The cookies have become an important ritual object for the inmates to be associated with the humanist contemplative meetings; without the cookies the ritual is incomplete. Here, liminality is enacted also: inmates are addressed as individuals during these meetings and can step out of the regular penitentiary environment (entering liminal space, within the liminal space of the penitentiary).

Second, rituals give structure to everyday life, such as the day or week, for instance, in care institutions where chaplains work with patients who receive temporary or long-term care or who are in their final stages of life. Rituals can help to give meaningful structure to life within (care) institutions, e.g., from starting the day or week together via contemplation to preparing one's last rites, as well as more monthly and yearly rituals, where seasonal celebrations (e.g., spring or winter) and memorials are part of an inclusive yearly ritual program. Military rituals serve to structure daily life and create and confirm identities but also to give some 'air' to the work, to give a more humane moment in everyday life which includes the use of weapons and being in a war zone. Here too, people step out of the daily environment of deployment into a liminal space where they are addressed as human beings with their musings, fears, and hopes. The humane aspect is also important in penitentiaries, where inmates can contemplate hopes, dreams, and moments of desperation. Research showed that military chaplains spend three hours a week on rituals, while hospital and penitentiary chaplains spend two hours a week, next to about nine hours on religious services including Eucharist (Kühle & Christensen, 2019). There are variations in work fields, for instance, military chaplains spend more time on religious services than pastoral care.

Third, rituals channel emotions within a safe space. What is meant by that is that through aesthetically and symbolically translating the experience (e.g. grief, loss, guilt, or shame) into symbolic, material form and ritually performing it, the emotions are felt but from a 'distanced' way. Putting aesthetic distance into a ritual narrative can lead to an emotional catharsis, e.g., first acknowledging the pain and grief and then finding a form to let it go (Wojtkowiak, 2018). What is more, rituals are emotionally ambiguous, which means they can evoke various emotions, due to their sensory, bodily, and material form. The symbolic translation leaves room for associations, not having to 'choose' clear, rational words to interpret one's narrative. The chaplain can use poems, literature, or lyrics from songs to create room for various emotions and associations. Hearing about difficult perspectives in the words of another person also helps to create *both* distance and identification with the topic.

Fourth, rituals express and shape the moral values and meanings that are shared within a group or community. In communal rituals, such as remembrance rituals or contemplative meetings (which we consider a part of ritual because they do fit into the working definition used before and make use of symbols and ritual actions), ethical and philosophical questions can be raised, and anxieties and uncertainties can be expressed through the use of symbols and symbolic language. But rituals "may do much more than mirror existing social arrangements and existing modes of thought. It can act to recognize them or even help to create them" (Moore & Myerhoff, 1977, p. 5). This means that rituals also create values and ways of thinking and acting and do not only express them. Therefore, rituals are embodied worldview practices.

In summary, rituals are found in many (semi-)secular contexts, and they change due to socio-cultural developments. Nevertheless, they serve many existential and spiritual needs, such as community, connection, attention, recognition, and contemplation. Rituals are embodied performances; they create space to act and share emotions in a collective setting. In the next paragraph, we discuss the specific role of rituals in humanist chaplaincy in more detail.

Ritualizing in humanist chaplaincy (and beyond)

What kind of rituals do chaplains conduct? From previous research in the New York area, it was revealed that the most reported ritual interventions by chaplains were prayer, blessing, and faith affirmation (Handzo et al., 2008). Interestingly, these were also reported by nonaffiliated chaplains and performed for nonaffiliated patients. Moreover, from a dataset collected among Dutch chaplains in the Netherlands (n = 433), it was shown that 39% of humanist chaplains report performing contemplative meetings regularly and 39% incidentally (Glasner et al., 2020). Besides, 50% of non-denominational chaplains report performing contemplative meetings regularly and 19% often. Another survey among Dutch humanist professionals revealed from 63 responses that 15% perform daily rituals, 14% weekly, 18% monthly, 28% a couple of times a year, 14% seldom, and 11% never do rituals, including contemplative meetings (Spekschoor, 2023). These numbers tell us at least two things. First, secular and humanist chaplains regularly perform all sorts of rituals in different contexts. Second, also secular (or semi-secular) people are interested in rituals. These rituals can be pluralistic, for instance, partially inspired by one's traditional background, and can also be performed by a humanist or nondenominational chaplain, such as with Nadia. Moreover, research from Denmark, a strongly secularized society, revealed that chaplains report a strong need for new rituals: 83% of chaplains working in health care, 73% in penitentiaries, and 85% in the military (Kühle & Christensen, 2019).

To give a more detailed overview, we collected different types of rituals that we know are performed by humanist chaplains in the Netherlands (see Table 6.1). The list is not exhaustive but a collection of the authors' knowledge. Rituals can be recurring (e.g., seasonal, monthly, weekly) or can be performed in specific (acute) situations (such as in Nadia's situation). The recurring rituals can be planned as a ritual year calendar (e.g., yearly, monthly seasons, celebrations, remembrance rituals). The second category, the specific (acute) rituals, is also part of the work of chaplains, and thus expected, but the individual rituals cannot be planned and occur spontaneously. Chaplains work together with chaplains from other denominations to perform some of these rituals, for instance, remembrance ceremonies or

Table 6.1 Overview of the ritual work of humanist chaplains[a]

Recurring rituals (yearly, monthly, weekly)

- Weekly service (e.g., contemplative meetings, Sunday ceremony).
- Memorials (e.g., monthly, yearly).
- Seasonal celebrations (often related to national holidays or seasonal changes).
- National celebrations or remembrance.
- Celebrating (special) birthdays or milestones.

Specific rituals (in acute situations)

- Individual rituals (e.g., personal achievements, moral injury, distress, disenfranchised grief).
- Transitional rituals (e.g., moving into a care home, hospice, revalidation center, or back home after recovery).
- Funeral rites (e.g., preparing and performing funeral speech and ritual, choosing personal symbol).
- 'Cleaning of cell' (in detention centers after the death of an inmate, together with religious chaplains).
- Ritual room cleansing (in nursing homes or psychiatric institutions when patients wish the room to be symbolically and spiritually cleaned).
- Rituals surrounding dying (e.g., final goodbye with family or without, euthanasia ceremony, moment of silence or "The Pause" after death, a hedge of people when the deceased is carried out).
- Crisis rituals (e.g., during and after acute and immediate situations, such as near-death in care settings and deployment, and also in a broader sense such as COVID, war, natural disasters, climate change).
- 'Stand-in' rituals: time-pressured or unexpected; when no other chaplain is available (e.g., 'emergency' baptism, final washing, blessings, weddings).
- Preparation rituals for future events (before surgery, deployment).
- Happenings for staff (new staff, leaving, retirement, having a baby).
- Soothing rituals for clients (e.g., singing, reading out loud, walking in circles/ spirals/ labyrinths, hand touching, braiding hair).
- Acknowledging or remembering rituals in perinatal loss (e.g., printing feet, lock of hair, writing name in the book, 'baby loss box,' et cetera.).

[a] The list is not exhaustive but offers an overview of the rituals that we know from humanist chaplains.

room cleansing. Moreover, the worldviews of the population within the institutions where chaplains work are increasingly pluralistic, as it reflects the Dutch population (CBS, 2022). As a result, chaplains not only work together but co-create a more inclusive style of rituals and ceremonies to include as many people as possible. An example is the 'service on Sunday' becoming an open, contemplative hour, led by either or both a religious and nonreligious chaplain, underlying the idea that chaplains are there for all, not just for one worldview. Sometimes they co-create new rituals together with clients, as per request or individual need.

Chaplains also perform 'stand-in' rituals in times of acute necessity or crisis, such as near-death, when a ritual is asked but a chaplain from a specific worldview is not present to do so. Other chaplains (such as humanists) are asked to perform a ritual that might not be from their worldview background (e.g., 'emergency' baptism for a dying baby or a final blessing for a dying patient). Humanist chaplains can be asked to follow a specific ritual protocol, without 'doing as if.' In the backstage of the ritual, in the preparation, it must be clear to the family that the performing chaplain is working from a humanist perspective, but they will perform the crisis ritual with dignity and care. The chaplain asks explicit permission to perform this ritual. For instance, with the emergency baptism, the Christian chaplain who is not present can be called, or the pastor involved, to give consent to the non-Christian chaplain to perform this ritual. It can be of great value to parents that this consent is given, which is why it can be part of the 'stand-in' protocol. Chaplains might feel discomfort performing rituals from different religious contexts. But in moments of acute necessity or crisis, openness, innovation, and creativity are asked, as well as protocols and guidelines on how to handle such situations.

Cadge and Sigalow (2013) found that chaplains working in interfaith contexts use two types of ritual language depending on the patient and the unique context. Sometimes chaplains neutralize their ritual language, by finding a universal connection with the patient who might be from a different worldview orientation, and in other cases they code-switch their one language and explain to the patient how they would approach a specific question within their faith. An example of neutralizing language was expressed by a chaplain: "It's the humanness that we share," he stated before telling his story.

> One man [patient], right away told me, said, "I'm an atheist." My first reaction was "So what?" … I said, "You're here sick, you're hurt. That is why I am here. I'm not here to bring you religion. I just want you to know that we care about you … you're not alone."
>
> (Cadge & Sigalow, 2013, p. 151)

In this example, the religious chaplain finds a common ground to connect with the patient from a caring attitude.

Ritualizing in practice: Identifying ritual needs

In the case illustration at the start of this chapter, a ritual need was identified. A patient who is struggling with unresolved grief, or any other life situation which cannot be changed but influences one's life or even health. Chaplains can introduce and co-create rituals to address the life situation.

Here, Emy, working as a humanist chaplain, translates Nadia's grief into ritual form and gives her the chance to say goodbye to her mother.

> *I design a small ceremony together with Nadia, to perform in her room. We take into account Nadia's affinity for Winti rituals. The ceremony is purposely held six weeks after her mother's funeral. In the weeks before, we carefully selected music and a poem. I gave Nadia a piece of clay that she could shape into a candle holder and imbue with wishes for her mother. After drying, Nadia painted it. On the day we start the ritual with music in her native language, Nadia sings and cries. Then I read a poem to her and put on another song. This time we dance together, celebrating and grieving her mother's life. After this, Nadia puts an electric candle in her candle holder, shaped like a star, and says her goodbye via this light. She cries and sings well-wishes while I hold her hand.*

Emy's ritual openness created the opportunity for Nadia to perform a last farewell. Klitzman et al. (2022) found that chaplains "create their own innovative, new kinds of rituals … that vary in both form and content, specifically in timing (e.g., in frequency), audience, size and formality, and in goals" (p. 3). In this particular research, ritualizing for hospital staff was studied, but new rituals were also created for and with patients and families. When new rituals are introduced, the question is: what kind of (implicit) needs does this ritual serve? These can be an individual, social, or societal need. Often a ritual need is not expressed explicitly ("I want a ritual"), but people might state that they want to 'do something' with a specific event or feeling. A ritual need has questions of meaning underlying it. The person might have missed something and would like to have the chance to do something, but the opportunity was not there (e.g., welcoming the birth of a child while in prison). Identifying a ritual need can take some time to get the narrative clearer and pinpoint underlying questions. For instance, how can I move on after this tragic life event? Who am I after doing something morally wrong? How can I learn to live with my disease?

How can I still enjoy and celebrate my life, even though I do not live in my home anymore? These existential questions are not solved quickly but need time and attention. Chaplains support this process, through (deep) listening, dialogue, being present, and (co)creating rituals. Rituals are a specific language of how existential questions can be addressed.

Speaking about a need is more a technical term for the ritual creator. In reality, this is not always verbalized explicitly. Identifying someone's ritual need is a particular skill, having ritual sensitivity. Recognition, demarcation, or reconciliation could be ritual needs. These needs can be as varied as individual narratives, but for chaplains, it might be interesting to consider ritual here due to its symbolic and active form. Rituals give time and space to intentionally, often in the presence of others ('witnesses'), perform underlying emotions and act on them. While in reality the event might lie in the past and there is nothing one can do about it, ritual creates symbolic space where an event can be re-lived, re-acted, and transformed. While the symbolic form of ritual is strong, ritual meanings are not merely symbolic. Rituals have performative power: by doing something, the ritual enacts and influences the world (Geertz, 1973). Emotions are expressed and transformed, and social identities are changed (e.g., from wife to widow). Moreover, the presence of other ritual participants is of importance here, it serves as a recognition of the emotions that have been hidden (sometimes for a long time). We believe it is important for humanist chaplains to develop a ritual sensitivity for ritual (re)design, in particular when in their work field rituals are not part of the repertoire yet.

Creative ritual-making and performing rituals

The actual ritual-making is a creative, intuitive process of finding symbols, symbolic acts, and a symbolic language that fit the unique context (see Wojtkowiak, 2022). A study from Denmark has revealed that "hospital chaplains reported the most frequent use of spontaneous rituals, and they mentioned actions such as lighting candles, singing, and praying together" (Kühle & Christensen, 2019, pp. 9–10). Ritual creativity and spontaneity are thus part of the work of chaplains. Still, it might not be obvious, especially in humanist worldviews, which traditionally have put the focus on rationality and science. Moreover, not every ritual context gives room for creativity (Driver, 2006; Grimes, 2002). Some ritual contexts are pregiven.

Ritual creativity can be maximized by working from the sensory and embodied dimensions: form has meaning. There is no abstract meaning to be explained, but the chosen ritual material carries meaning. A handy tool for ritual design can be checking Grimes' ritual elements: place, time, actors, actions, objects, languages, and groups (see Grimes, 2014, p. 286). These elements are the main ingredients in every ritual. But ritual is more than the sum of its parts (Grimes, 2014) and has an overall narrative that is coherent and expresses the ritual function or meaning (Wojtkowiak, 2022). The ritual performance is fluent and organic. Moreover, rituals address spirituality in the way that they leave room for interpretations, and they do not explain everything away. Rituals initiate something, without solving it. Although personal meanings and intentions of individual participants might vary (e.g., "I want to give my condolences, though I did not know this person well"; "This is the final thing I can do for my sister, to say goodbye"), there is an overall ritual theme or narrative that keeps the different ritual elements together and makes the ritual an organic whole, for instance, the narrative could be "embracing the light in dark times." Light is a symbol here and can be used in various elements (candles, texts, personal reflections). The chaplains think about the narrative or emotional curve that they want to tell in the ritual: what kind of movement is taking place in the ritual? Where do participants start and where do they end? These kinds of questions can help to create more coherence and structure in the ritual.

Finally, the ritual is going to be performed at a specific date and time. During the performance, the chaplain embodies the ritual, which means carrying the ritual via their presence. Now the planning and creating phase is over (at least when there is time for planning). The performance needs to be sincere and with authentic motives. If the celebrant or chaplain feels uncomfortable with certain aspects of the ritual or is insincere, the audience will feel this (Alexander, 2004; Wojtkowiak, 2018). In the backstage of the ritual (planning and creating), there can be room for critical remarks and doubts, but in the ritual's front stage, the actual performance, one needs to be sure of what one is doing and believe in the chosen ritual form. In the words of the Swiss secular celebrant Gordon-Lennox (2017): "Rituals […] are powerful when they are performed by and for the right people in the right context at the right time. They are confusing and disorienting when they are not" (p. 28).

The farewell ceremony for Nadia's mother is a meaningful experience, it opens up her grief.

> *Afterwards, Nadia shares with me that she felt her mother hug her and she told Nadia she would recover. Nadia felt her mother leave earth when she lit the candle. She thanked me for giving the gift of saying goodbye. I hold her hand and thank her too. I tell her she can light a candle in her self-made candleholder, as a remembrance or way to honor her mother.*
>
> *Later the psychologist tells me that Nadia held her candle holder often and never mentioned that she needed to say goodbye again. She recovered fully and was able to go home two weeks later.*

It creates a demarcated space for Nadia to step out of her daily recovery environment and into a liminal space where there is room for her unresolved feelings. Here she was not Nadia the patient, but Nadia the daughter, who was grieving the loss of her mother and a goodbye she did not get to have. During the ritual performance, as an embodied experience, the meaning of the ritual arises. This is something that cannot be planned beforehand but depends on the specific ritual context and performance.

Discussion

While ritualizing offers many new opportunities for communal and individual rituals in humanist chaplaincy and plural contexts, there are some challenges and potential problems that need to be mentioned here.

First, cultural appropriation arises when elements from an existing, oppressed cultural, and ritual repertoire are taken into another dominant cultural frame. Cultural appropriation emerges when there is a power relation (Rogers, 2006). For instance, members of a dominant culture use elements from a ritual tradition that has been oppressed in the past, often without any contextualization or acknowledgment (e.g., the use of elements from the traditional Navajo blessingway ceremony by secular Western people led to a discussion about cultural appropriation; see Wojtkowiak, 2022). Religious appropriation can have different layers, for instance, by using existing ritual names or carrying religious symbols out of solidarity but misusing these symbols from the perspectives of those who practice that religion (e.g., headscarves worn by secular women as a protest). While existing names can increase the recognition of the new ritual (e.g., baptism), it can also lead to confusion when the secular ritual is not an actual Christian baptism. An alternative name can be given, such as a welcome, naming ceremony, or mother's blessing. When clients have a specific religious or worldview background, the (humanist) chaplain can ask them to introduce elements from their own culture or religion but only if the chaplain feels comfortable working with these elements. Cultural and religious appropriation is a multilayered and complex issue; it touches on the question between ritual intentions and ritual meanings. While the intention might be to appreciate, celebrate, and advocate for a specific cultural or religious group or symbol, it can lead to confusion, misunderstanding, and harm. A humanist answer to this dilemma would be always to take on an attitude of not knowing in ritual design, especially when (re-) creating rituals from existing elements and forms. An attitude of not knowing comes from counseling psychology, where the patient is seen as the expert on their narrative (McLeod, 2013). It is hard to know what certain religious symbols or rituals mean to other people, therefore it is better to create your own ritual repertoire and use only the elements one knows and understands. There is not one golden rule or one-size-fits-all approach in ritual re-design, but the contextualization and co-creation is important, which is also a humanist principle. Critical, entangled, and inclusive humanism (see Chapter 2) also means that the ritualizing process is relational, inclusive, and critical. In the case description, the farewell ritual was co-created by the chaplain and client. The client could add her own religious and cultural background, and the chaplain was able to guide the ritual from her worldview perspective.

Another challenge lies in the creation of pluralistic rituals. When a collective ritual is created for various worldviews, it is challenging to choose a symbolic language that addresses different worldviews. Sometimes the choice is made for more neutral language (see also Cadge & Sigalow, 2013). An alternative to neutral language is to have a co-celebrant during the ritual from another worldview who can perform rituals that are important for this particular group. Multifaith remembrance ceremonies have been organized (e.g., in various cities in the Netherlands and in Belgium) with four or five ritual presiders. Choosing to represent different worldviews within one ritual can help in terms of cultural and religious diversity but can also lead to new questions, such as who is represented in the ritual and who is not? This needs to be closely considered with the question of who are the ritual participants? Who is the ritual for? Rituals therefore always carry certain power: who gets a voice and who does not?

Another point to note is that crisis rituals appear to have a special privilege. We refer to rituals performed in moments of crisis and acute time pressure, such as during the COVID-19 pandemic and when a patient is dying in the ICU (see Table 6.1). When facing such crises, it can be more important that someone receives the right ritual care before it is too late, rather than adhering to the normal ritual process. A 'stand-in' ritual can be performed. As an attending chaplain, one has to be open about one's possibilities and restrictions (backstage of ritual), but during performance one has to fully believe and perform the ritual with authenticity and sincere intention (front stage of ritual).

Conclusion

Rituals are powerful tools in times of disorientation as they translate difficult, ambiguous, hidden, or intense emotions into symbolic language and form. Rituals enact feelings and give structure and direction in times of disorientation. Humanist chaplains perform various rituals in different contexts, and they can furthermore develop ritual sensitivity and competence by performing and (re)designing rituals for individual and communal needs. Humanism as a worldview offers inspiration in the process of ritual-making, as well as the performance of values such as openness, curiosity, attitude of not knowing (see also Chapter 2). Humanist rituals pose existential questions and give room for contemplation and reflection, without giving all the answers. Rituals are a way to initiate something new in the world, to put something into action. Ritual (re)design from humanistic perspectives means understanding ritual theory and combining these insights with the unique context wherein the ritual is taking place.

Take-home messages

- Use rituals to create a community presence and a communal space to express, share, and exchange emotions.
- When crafting new rituals, identify the ritual need: why this ritual? For whom is the ritual and why?
- Consider who you need to speak to in order to have the insider's perspective for the ritual.
- In acute ritual situations (e.g., grief, loss, and disaster), be open to creating rituals with high time pressure, small gestures (e.g., open a ritual space where people can grieve) can have a big impact.
- Create a ritual calendar to structure the year.
- Use insights from ritual theory to combine them with the unique human context that the ritual is taking place in (hence a humanistic perspective on rituals).
- If you do not feel comfortable with specific ritual content, do not use it or ask someone else to present it.

Note

1 In contrast, the word 'rite' refers to the static, traditional nature of existing rites.

References

Alexander, J. (2004). Cultural pragmatics: Social performance between ritual and strategy. *Sociological Theory*, *22*(4), 527–573. https://doi.org/10.1111/j.0735-2751. 2004.00233.x

Boyer, P., & Liénard, P. (2006). Why ritualized behavior? Precaution systems and action parsing in developmental, pathological and cultural rituals. *Behavioral and Brain Science*, *29*. https://doi.org/10.1017/S0140525X06009332

Cadge, W., & Sigalow, E. (2013). Negotiating religious differences: The strategies of interfaith chaplains in healthcare. *Journal for the Scientific Study of Religion*, *52*(1), 146–158. https://doi.org/10.1111/jssr.12008

CBS (Centraal Bureau voor de Statistiek). (2022, December 22). *Almost 6 in 10 Dutch people do not have a religious affiliation*. www.cbs.nl/en-gb/news/2022/ 51/almost-6-in-10-dutch-people-do-not-have-a-religious-affiliation

Danbolt, L. J., & Stifoss-Hanssen, H. (2020). Health care chaplaincy in the Nordic countries: Transformations and perspectives. In E. Anron Zoder, P.-Y. Brandt, & I. Besson (Eds.), *Clinique du sens* (pp. 36–46). Editions des archives contemporaines.

Driver, T. F. (2006). *Liberating rites: Understanding the transformative power of ritual*. Booksurge.

Geertz, C. (1973). *The interpretation of cultures*. Basic Books.

Glasner, T., Schuhmann, C., van der Vaart, W., & Jacobs, G. (2020). Levensbeschouwing, samenwerking en profilering. Onderzoek naar de beroepsidentiteit van geestelijk verzorgers aangesloten bij de VGVZ [Worldview, collaboration, and profiling. A study into the professional identity of chaplains]. *Tijdschrift Geestelijke Verzorging, 23*(9), 10–20.

Gordon-Lennox, J. (2017). *Crafting secular ritual: A practical guide*. Jessica Kinglsey.

Grimes, R. L. (2002). *Deeply into the bone: Re-inventing rites of passage*. University of California Press.

Grimes, R. L. (2014). *The craft of ritual studies*. Oxford University Press.

Handzo, G. F., Flannelly, K. J., Kudler, T., Fogg, S. L., Harding, S. R., Hasan, I. Y. H., Ross, A. M., & Taylor, R. B. E. (2008). What do chaplains really do? II. Interventions in the New York Chaplaincy Study. *Journal of Health Care Chaplaincy, 14*(1), 39–56. https://doi.org/10.1080/08854720802053853

Klitzman, R., Al-Hashimi, J., Di Sapia Natarelli, G., Garbuzova, E., & Sinnappan, S. (2022). How hospital chaplains develop and use rituals to address medical staff distress. *SSM Qualitative Research in Health, 2*, 100087. https://doi.org/10.1016/j.ssmqr.2022.100087

Kühle, L., & Christensen, H. R. (2019). One to serve them all. The growth of chaplaincy in public institutions in Denmark. *Social Compass, 66*(2), 182–197. https://doi.org/10.1177/0037768619833310

McLeod, J. (2013). Developing pluralistic practice in counselling and psychotherapy: Using what the client knows. *The European Journal of Counselling Psychology, 2*(1), 51–64. https://doi.org/10.23668/psycharchives.1999

Moore, S. F., & Myerhoff, B. G. (1977). Introduction. Secular ritual: Forms and meanings. In S. F. Moore & B. G. Myerhoff (Eds.), *Secular Ritual* (pp. 3–24). Van Gorcum.

Pinn, A. (2017). *When colorblindness isn't the answer. Humanism and the challenge of race*. Pitchstone.

Rogers, R. A. (2006). From cultural exchange to transculturation: A review and reconceptualization of cultural appropriation. *Communication Theory, 16*(4), 474–503. https://doi.org/10.1111/j.1468-2885.2006.00277.x

Schilbrack, K. (2004). *Thinking through rituals: Philosophical perspectives*. Routledge.

Seligman, A. B., Weller, R. P., Puett, M. B., & Simon, B. (2008). *Ritual and its consequences. An essay on the limits of sincerity*. Oxford University Press.

Spekschoor, E. (2023). *Uitslag survey rituelen humanistische professionals* [Outcome survey rituals humanistic professionals]. (Internal publication by Dutch Humanist Association). https://humanistischverbond.sharepoint.com/

Turner, V. (1979). Frame, flow and reflection: Ritual and drama as public liminality. *Japanese Journal of Religious Studies, 6*(4), 465–499.

Wojtkowiak, J. (2018). Towards a psychology of ritual: A theoretical framework of ritual transformation in a globalising world. *Culture and Psychology, 24*(4), 460–476. https://doi.org/10.1177/1354067X18763797

Wojtkowiak, J. (2022). Ritual (re)design. Towards a framework for professional ritual making in postsecular contexts. *Yearbook for Ritual and Liturgical Studies, 38*, 108–123. https://doi.org/10.21827/YRLS.38.108-123

Chapter 7

The chaplain's educating role in spiritual care

Gaby Jacobs, Joanna Wojtkowiak, and Annemieke Kuin

In the cardiology department, in the span of a few weeks, nurses had to deal with many critically ill patients who would die in the short term. Although adept at providing palliative care, some nurses felt inadequate in meaningfully communicating with these patients and their loved ones. The team leader asked me and my intern if we could give the team a helping hand on their annual team training day. The team was divided in three groups and for each group 1.5 hours was available.

Introduction

Chaplains provide guidance to clients and patients in questions regarding orientation in life. Increasingly, they also educate other professionals and volunteers on how to provide spiritual care, since this is increasingly seen as a generic task for all health care providers (Puchalski et al., 2009; Balboni et al., 2014). Education therefore has become part of the training of chaplains in higher education in order to equip them for training other professionals, to coach students in their workplace learning, or give guest lectures at universities about specialized topics in the area of spiritual care. Education in chaplaincy includes the development of professionals' moral competency, which will be elaborated upon in Chapter 9. In this chapter, the focus is on spiritual care education of health care professionals and what this entails. Whereas spiritual care is aimed at supporting or guiding patients in existential issues, spiritual care education aims at developing knowledge, attitudes, and skills needed by professionals (or volunteers) for providing spiritual care to patients. Although chaplains can build on their competencies in spiritual care, educating is a different role for chaplains which requires additional competencies and has a different aim, i.e., professional development and learning. The chaplain needs to

DOI: 10.4324/9781003428633-9

cross boundaries between care and education in order to combine knowledge and skills in these two areas.

In this chapter, we will outline the relationship between spiritual care
and health care professions, and the state of the art of spiritual care education in the health care context. We will then discuss what chaplains need
in preparing for and conducting spiritual care education to health care
professionals. We will not elaborate upon the didactic skills needed by the
chaplain – such as the ability to constructively deal with group dynamics,
or to develop learning goals or assessment procedures – that are written
about in educational textbooks.

Spiritual care and the health care professions

In Chapters 1 and 3, we outlined our view on orientation in life as the
domain of chaplaincy. Orientation in life is an existential and relational
process, embedded in an embodied context and time that is characterized
by power hierarchies in worldviews and by structures that foster or hinder
this process. Chaplains themselves are educated in theology, religious studies, philosophy, or humanistic studies. In health care, they work with professionals who have a very different background, e.g., in medicine, nursing,
social work, or psychology, and who consequently employ a different perspective and approach.

Although spirituality became included in the World Health Organization's
view on health in 1984 (WHO, 1985), health care professionals have been
mainly educated in the biopsychosocial model of health. This means that
they are used to relate their work to either the biological/somatic dimension of health problems, the psychological dimension, and/or the social
dimension. In the last decades, palliative care proved that this model had
to be extended to include the spiritual dimension (Sulmasy, 2002). More
recently, this is also argued in other domains of health care, such as veteran
care (Carey & Hodgson, 2018).

A wide range of studies in health care indicate that spirituality is related
to quality of life, increased life satisfaction, resilience, and physical and
mental health (Jones et al., 2021). Additionally, several studies show that
patients expect health care providers to pay attention to spiritual needs
(Best et al., 2015; Mesquita et al., 2017) and to do so in a nonjudgmental
way and by showing interest in patients, thereby creating opportunities for
two-way communication (Yardley et al., 2009). However, health care professionals experience difficulties in providing spiritual care even if they are
willing to address spiritual needs. This includes a lack of knowledge, skills,
and – often following from this – confidence, and is the case for all kinds of
health care professions: general practitioners (Appleby et al., 2018;
Vermandere et al., 2011; Hvidt et al., 2016), nurses (Timmins et al., 2014;

Table 7.1 Educational needs

Knowledge about the concept of spirituality in general	Appleby et al., 2018; Smyth and Allen, 2011
Knowledge of spiritual needs of patient groups, and of different religions and worldviews and their perspectives and habits, e.g., on dying	Wesley et al., 2004; Timmins et al., 2014; Keall et al., 2014; Smyth and Allen, 2011; Hodge et al., 2021; Gardner, 2020
Knowledge and skills regarding how to act when the patient's values about medical treatment or care cause friction with one's own professional and personal values	Wesley et al., 2004; Gardner, 2020
Spiritual language and tools, e.g., assessment tools, genograms, rituals, life history	Appleby et al., 2018; Wesley et al., 2004; Timmins et al., 2014; Henoch et al., 2013; Keall et al., 2014; Smyth and Allen, 2011; O'Brien et al., 2019
The ability to deal with discomfort in going beyond the physical domain and to reflect on personal spiritual views or lack thereof	Balboni et al., 2014; Strang et al., 2014; O'Brien et al., 2019; Gardner, 2020
Knowledge and awareness of the spiritual care role of professionals and that of chaplains, and the possibility for referrals within the organization or neighborhood	Timmins et al., 2014; Balboni et al., 2014

Balboni et al., 2014; Henoch et al., 2013; Keall et al., 2014; Smyth & Allen, 2011; Strang et al., 2014; O'Brien et al., 2019), and social workers (Wesley et al., 2004; Hodge et al., 2021; Gardner, 2020). See Table 7.1 for an overview of educational needs in spiritual care.

Spiritual care education from a humanist perspective

The educational needs of health care professionals range from increasing knowledge and skills, to the more difficult to learn aspects, such as the ability to deal with ambivalence, discomfort, and differences in values and perspectives. Patients require attention for their spiritual needs, but professionals' insecurity in how to deal with them may withhold them from recognizing these needs. The challenge then, from our perspective, is to help professionals develop an attitude that does not focus on problem solving, but on orienting in life. Learning and developing a spiritual perspective and associated methods cannot take place in an instrumental way since the whole person of the professional is involved. This fits with education from a humanist perspective, in which learning involves the embodied and relational process of constructing and reconstructing meaning in relationship with others and the world.

The Brazilian educator Paulo Freire has been a source of inspiration for thinking about humanist education from a political perspective. In his educational method, learning is a three-step process of getting to know the self, the other, and the issue or situation at hand by sharing experiences, critical reflection, and action for change. This can be translated to professional learning about spiritual care in health care. Working with illiterate people, Freire argued that traditional pedagogy was oppressive and dehumanizing because it denied people agency and experience, which made them seem less fully human and diminished their moral worth (Freire, 1971). He posited the idea of 'problem-posing education' as a democratic and dialogical approach that presents the situation as a problem and affirms students as being in the process of becoming those who can transform themselves and their world. Interestingly, he softened the distinction between teachers and students, talking about teachers-as-students and students-as-teachers, to indicate reciprocity in education (Freire, 1974). Freire's ideas have inspired a view on humanist education in which the creation of spaces of hospitality and respect in which learners feel secure and welcome is central, and characterized by participation and dialogue (Wickett, 2005; Veugelers, 2011; Aloni, 2011). Transferring this to spiritual care education, educators then should be aware of how worldviews, existential questions, and moral values are embedded in both their own and the learners' professional practices, which requires a critical-reflective paradigm (Veugelers, 2011) and normative professionalism (see also Chapter 3).

Spiritual care education in practice

A systematic review by Jones et al. (2021) looked at spiritual care training to equip health care staff to deliver spiritual care. It shows that a wide range of content is taught to health care staff, including awareness of one's own spirituality, spiritual screening, ethics, self-care, and understanding spiritual needs. The methods used were also diverse: didactic teaching, role-plays, simulations with a professional actor, shadowing chaplains, direct contact with a patient, group reflection, as well as training to use specific tools or instruments, such as the FICA (Faith Importance Community Address) spiritual history tool. Outcomes were reported on almost all the educational needs mentioned in Table 7.1, except for the ability to deal with discomfort in going beyond the physical domain and to reflect on personal spiritual views or lack thereof. Not being willing to examine one's own existential themes was identified as a barrier to learning and professional development. This implies that educating health care professionals to provide spiritual care to their clients while they are trained in other disciplines or perspectives, does not mean simply adding some tools to their professional repertoire; it means changing the repertoire itself. Or as Paal et al. (2015) conclude in their review of spiritual care training: "It must be clear that, unlike many bodily concerns, spiritual concerns do not have a fix. Spiritual care is much more about attending the patient by being present and listening than 'delivering the message'" (p. 27). They found that spiritual care training needs three objectives: "firstly, developing trainees' sensitivity towards their own spirituality; secondly, clarifying the role of spirituality in health care; and thirdly, preparing trainees for spiritual encounters" (p. 26). Especially the first objective cannot be left out, the authors conclude: "The findings in this review make evident that without attending to one's own beliefs and needs, addressing spirituality in patients will not be forthcoming" (p. 27). This is in line with the Freirean approach to education and we now will turn to what this means for educational activities that chaplains may provide to health care professionals.

In the next paragraph, we will give some guidelines for how to prepare and how to conduct an educational activity (training, lesson, or workshop) on spiritual care as a chaplain in the role of educator. The focus will be on training that aims at the development of the spiritual competence of professionals by providing information on spirituality in health care, working with the experiences of the participants, and practicing new skills and attitudes. We discuss what educational steps, skills, and humanist values are required in preparing for and conducting the training. These aspects are illustrated by following up on the case introduced at the beginning of this chapter.

How to prepare spiritual care education for health care professionals?

Preparation of the educational activity allows for a well-designed educational session. In preparing, following loosely Freire's critical pedagogy, several steps are important that we will refer to as 'knowledge about self,' 'knowledge about the other,' and 'knowledge about the topic.'

> In addressing the wishes of the nurses of the cardiology department, the intern and I choose as the main topic: meaningful conversations with patients and loved ones by listening without judgment.
>
> We reflect together on what we think is of importance in training nurses. We recognize that we want to rely on the expertise of the nurses themselves, because there is a lot of knowledge in the group, and we want to offer them the opportunity to also learn from each

other. With regard to patient care, we feel it is also important to address the attitude, more than knowledge or skills, that is needed to have meaningful conversations with patients and loved ones.

At my request, the team leader asks the team for examples. Three nurses email a case they struggle with. The intern works a day with one of the nurses to gain insight into her daily challenges. She also asks the nurses where their hearts lie, what gives satisfaction, and what is experienced as frustrating. In this way, we discover that nurses:

- *Find it difficult to be empty-handed when it comes to patients in palliative care;*
- *Want to act meaningfully in their work;*
- *Find it difficult when dissonance occurs. For example, when the patient keeps fighting against the imminent death or if loved ones continue to insist on eating and treatment, while the patient no longer wants to or can no longer cope with it.*

In addition, I consult the Netherlands Quality Framework of Palliative Care (Boddaert et al., 2017) and the Guideline Spiritual Care at the End of Life (Integraal Kankercentrum Nederland, 2018). I also look into the competencies described in the Professional Profile of the Palliative Care Nurse. (Verpleegkundigen & Verzorgenden Nederland, 2022)

Knowledge about self

In preparing for an educational activity, reflection on the self of the chaplain in the role of educator is a first step. This includes several aspects (see also Table 7.2).

First of all, the chaplain should be able to reflect on their own vision on education and their teaching skills in their work as educators. What is your talent and what do you need to approve or which skills do you need to develop? How can you develop these skills?

Second, it is important to recognize what topics matter to oneself. This will help not only to choose a topic (see also 'Knowledge about the topic' below) one is familiar with and enthusiastic about but also to choose one that is of importance to the chaplain personally and professionally. Obviously, chaplains must be able to reflect on and work with their own existential themes and values, and how these influence who they are as professionals and persons (see also 'normative professionalism' in Chapter 3).

Table 7.2 Guidelines in preparing for educational activities

Knowledge about self (of the chaplain)

- Choose a topic or case that you as a chaplain find important and interesting or that makes you enthusiastic.
- Have a dialogue with self or others (colleagues) about this topic: what values do you bring to it; how is it related to existential themes in your personal life?
- Reflect on: What are your skills in education or training? What do you feel confident about, what do you feel to be your weak areas?

Knowledge about the other (the professionals that you will educate)

- Prepare specifically for the professionals you want to educate:
  - What are their work contexts and specific work conditions?
  - What are important underlying values in their work?
  - How are they confronted with existential questions?
  - What is the goal of their work and how is it related to meaning making?
  - What is their struggle with regard to spiritual care?
  - What are their educational needs?
- Explore what has already been taught on that topic to that specific group, what they found interesting to learn and also how they learn: what are their usual or preferred learning styles?

Knowledge about the topic (health care-related spirituality)

- Explore your own knowledge and experiences in health care and spiritual care and critically reflect on its socio-political context and developments.
- Dive into literature about the topic to determine the main perspectives of philosophies that you want to use (e.g., provide work definitions).
- Think about examples from your own work practice to clarify theory.
- Ask colleagues about theoretical frameworks, methods, and tools they employ when teaching about this topic.
- Find out about professional guidelines, protocols, and codes used by the group of professionals and how spiritual care is addressed/discussed in them.

Knowledge about the other

In preparing for an educational activity, first of all, chaplains need to obtain knowledge about the professionals they want to train. What motivates them, what is of importance, what gives pleasure and satisfaction in their work? But also: what are their struggles and frustrations? It is essential to explore what is important for the professionals to gain in relation to their own spirituality and meaning making. Also their interpretation of the concept of spirituality is essential: what meanings do participants give to 'spirituality'? This helps to identify their important underlying values and to accommodate the learning needs of the professionals.

Knowledge about the topic

In preparing for the educational activity, it is also necessary to have or collect the appropriate knowledge about the topic of education, e.g., moral injury or end-of-life care. Chaplains need to be aware of developments in their own field and should be able to link their practical and personal knowledge to (critical) philosophical perspectives and theoretical and practical knowledge about the topic. For the latter, chaplains sometimes will have to go back to their own education and what they learned about the topic. For practical knowledge, articles in professional journals are also relevant. Furthermore, they need to explore their own experiences with the topic in order to 'personalize' it, e.g., what are good examples from one's own practice in dealing with the topic? In addition, the chaplain needs to explore developments in the field of expertise of the professionals and clients (e.g., older persons, people with intellectual disabilities) and must learn about current professional guidelines and codes. From all this, the chaplain needs to decide what to offer the participants in terms of theory, information, and models regarding the topic, and what methods and tools help to bring across this knowledge so that participants can relate to it and critically reflect on it. The content of the training (see also the next paragraph) is thus closely related to the questions, dilemmas, and language of the group of professionals that are attending the course.

How to conduct spiritual care education to health care professionals?

In conducting an educational activity, a similar three-way division can be used as in the preparation, but now focused on the professionals (participants of the training) and referring to the actual teaching by the chaplain.

Based on the preparation, the intern and I formulate the goal as: how to communicate meaningfully with patients in the last phase of life and their loved ones, by reflecting on what is of value and importance to them. In line with the language of the nurses, we do not talk about spirituality but about 'meaning,' 'what really matters' and 'where your heart lies.'

- *We start the training with a small ritual by the lighting of three candles: one for the people in palliative care, one for their loved ones, and one for the people who take care of them.*

- *To open the conversation about their own experiences, we show a short animation about a patient in the last phase of life, including the nurse who encounters various dilemmas in taking care of her. My role in this is to make the nurses are aware of what skills they already have (attention, engaged curiosity, involvement, loving care) and to identify together what they struggle with.*
- *Furthermore, we challenge the nurses to think about what is meaningful to themselves. As a teaching method, we ask the nurses to write down on pieces of paper what is important to them. Subsequently, in order to relate to the impact of loss like their patients in palliative care, we ask them to feel what it is like to put these pieces of paper aside and what impact it has when fate determines this for them (the chaplain takes some pieces of paper at random). In the conversation about this exercise, the emphasis is on the dialogue about what is at stake for each of them and their differences in the experience of loss.*
- *Next, we transfer from the nurses' own experiences to the loss experiences of their patients and their loved ones. We start from the nurses' experiences about what is important in talking about their own loss and relate this to theory about grief as well as our experiences.*
- *From there on, we provide theory on how to enter a meaningful conversation (wanting to understand instead of advising; presence instead of intervention).*
- *Finally, we help the nurses to practice the new skills and attitude by using case studies.*
- *The training is concluded by ritually extinguishing the candles.*

We will outline the three aspects of conducting a training session or workshop (see also Table 7.3).

Knowledge about self

A key element of conducting a training session is to make sure that professionals' own personal narratives and questions are addressed, raising their awareness of their own life orientation and how it impacts their work, and how that might be translated to clients and patients. This means that the chaplain has to develop or choose methods that help the professionals that participate in the educational activity, to deepen knowledge about self. Most often, exercises and tools that help them to reflect on their own values

Table 7.3 Guidelines in conducting an educational activity

Knowledge about the self (professionals)

- Use methods and tools to enhance the critical reflection of participants to recognize their personal and professional values.
- Give room to discuss personal life orientation and spirituality, and profession-related struggles.
- Provide time and tools to professionals to reflect on existing skills related to spiritual care: strengths, values, and weaknesses.

Knowledge about the other (the persons/patients)

- Use participatory and dialogical methods and tools that help the professionals to recognize what is important (of value) for the people they care for.
- Provide the opportunity to discuss experiences/cases by professionals themselves.
- Show the skills and attitude that you want to teach the professionals, based on the humanist values of equality and respect, and let them practice to use these with their patients.
- Adapt to the learning styles of the participants, while staying within the humanist education paradigm.

Knowledge about the topic (spiritual care related to health care)

- Choose methods and tools to reflect on or discuss information/theoretical models and connect it with the experiences of the professionals.
- Explore existing associations and meanings of the topic, e.g., the terms of 'meaning making,' 'existential', 'spiritual,' or 'moral injury.'
- Use clear theoretical frames to clarify concepts that are central to the topic.
- Use examples from your own work practice to clarify the concepts.
- Use participatory and/or creative methods that help professionals to reflect on the topic in relation to themselves and their patients.
- Use methods and tools to position self, other, and the topic within its socio-political context.

Evaluation of the educational activity

- Make use of creative methods to collect their stories, short questionnaires, et cetera, and allow for dialogue on the learning process.
- Use personal reflections and notes on what the participants seemed to learn or do differently in the areas of self, other, and the topic.

and actions, can be used in enhancing knowledge about self for the professionals, too, e.g., the 'tree of life.'[1] In addition, giving space to reflect on existing skills related to spiritual care is important to help health care professionals see that they – in part – are already 'doing spiritual care.'

Knowledge about the other

The chaplain may need to include time to retrieve what the professionals already recognize in their daily care regarding spiritual needs of their patients. The chaplain can supplement this with what is known from literature and the experiences of the chaplain, preferably with the same patient group or work setting. A key part of the training session is then to help the professionals to relate to the 'other' (i.e., the patients) they work with in a different way than they may have been used to, based on the humanist values of recognition and equality. For health care professionals this may mean that they prefer to give attention to the person over the disease and start to relate from an attitude of attention and listening. Participatory and dialogical methods are very useful in establishing a learning culture based on these values; they foster skills of relating that are key in spiritual care. They will help the participants to recognize what is of value for the people they care for:

- What are spiritual topics or needs often related to disease or dependence on care?
- What struggles do the participants recognize with the patients?
- What struggles does the chaplain encounter in working with the patients?

Adaptation to the learning style of the professionals is important. For some, theory will have to be made transparent with concrete examples and assignments, while others need an insightful theoretical foundation or mostly need practical examples. Depending on the group, the chaplain can make use of experiences similar to inspiring a group during rituals, ceremonies, or contemplative meetings. For example: thinking about language versus imagination or images; methods that promote interaction and dialogue such as case discussions; or adding a ritual.

Knowledge about the topic

Education is also about content: knowledge about the topic. This knowledge is important to give words to experiences and to receive insight into, for example, the relationship between spirituality and health. This content can be drawn from diverse sources. The chaplain needs to include both clear theoretical or conceptual frames and hands-on examples and experiences from the work practice of the group of professionals and/or from chaplaincy. When discussing a concept, e.g., meaning making, the existing associations are as important as the use of concepts in the literature.

In learning about the topic, reflection methods and skills training make sure that the content will be processed in a personal and meaningful way.

A respectful approach towards commonalities and differences is modelled by the chaplain, and the sharing of differences is actively invited in order to link the discussions to the broader social-political context in which spirituality may be hindered by or is hidden behind policies and structures that try to control health care costs. This includes the recognition of power dynamics in society and the possibilities and limitations these give for finding orientation in life, for both patients and professionals alike. Establishing commonality within differences is important to see the bigger picture: "we have the same goal here (e.g., provide good care), but might have different views."

In conducting the training, it is very important that chaplains show the skills and attitude that they want to teach others, based on the humanist values of equality and respect:

• To listen, attune to the other and follow without judgment.
• To promote dialogue (instead of discussion) by collecting diverse perspectives and allowing differences to coexist.
• To demonstrate a change of perspective.
• To attend to underlying values and meaning frames.
• To support empowerment: providing space for learning and development.
• To adapt to what is at stake for the participants at the moment of training.

Turning discussion into dialogue

In the third group, a discussion ensued as to whether a nurse should tell a patient's loved one on the phone that her husband has just died. One nurse said with conviction that one should always do that, another interrupted her that this should never been done. I intervened by saying that it is interesting that they look at it so differently, and we explored which values are underlying the different opinions (e.g., honesty, safety).

Evaluation of the educational activity

Every educational activity requires an evaluation, however small. Evaluation is not only finding out the value of the activity for the professionals but also adds value to the activity because it is another moment of reflecting on the (hopefully) acquired new ways of being, knowing, and acting. It also provides information for improvement and fosters the learning of the chaplain as educator.

Evaluation can take different forms and should be congruent with the nature of the educational activity. In this chapter, we discussed educational activities that involve the self, the other, and the topic. The evaluation then should also cover these three areas. Possible evaluation methods are to ask professionals:

- To discuss what they learned in these three areas.
- To write this down, and then name the most important area and how/ when learning happened.
- To symbolize their learning in a short story, a poem, an image, et cetera.
- To fill in a short questionnaire, a few weeks after the educational activity.
- To indicate with an emoticon how they feel about the activity.

Of course, combinations of evaluation methods and tools are possible as well.

I evaluated the training by asking three questions: What appealed to you? What was lacking? What do you take with you? The participants could fill it in anonymously. Then I asked the group for tips on what to keep and what to improve for the next group. Reactions included:

- *I have learned that talking about meaning with patients and their loved ones is part of my job.*
- *I now understand the importance of listening without trying to solve anything.*
- *I do not feel like I am empty-handed anymore.*
- *I feel more confident in starting a meaningful conversation with a patient or family member.*

Conclusion

In line with the critical pedagogy of Paulo Freire, an educational activity should show a combination of knowledge about self (working with the values and experiences of the participants), other (in order to practice a spiritual care attitude and skills in relating to patients), and topic (theory and information to receive insight into the role and importance of spiritual care in health care and society). Not every chaplain will feel comfortable about educating other professionals, as most have their primary skills in spiritual care i.e., presence and counseling skills and attitude, but it is an important aspect of working in health care. Educational practice is aimed at professional learning and development. Although being an expert in spiritual care is a necessary requirement for educating on spiritual care, it is not sufficient. As we outlined in this chapter, preparing an educational activity is a planned and systematic effort that requires expertise in educational methods and knowledge about motivation, learning, and development. Chaplains who have not been taught this may have to learn this in continuing professional education.

In the introduction, we discussed that health care providers indicate that they mainly need knowledge on spirituality and religion. Whereas the people they care for, in regard to their spirituality and spiritual needs, mainly want to be seen and heard in what is meaningful to them and want to experience closeness in their grief and (existential) pain. Knowledge about the topic and learning techniques alone does not contribute to the integration of spiritual care within health care practices because it does not transform the professional's frame of reference and concomitant professional habits (Mezirow, 1991). The self and the other should be involved as well. The quest for knowledge and tools reflects the prevailing biomedical paradigm with its focus on solution-oriented work in health care and presents one of the big challenges in teaching spiritual care. The meaning-oriented and relational work of spiritual care will not seamlessly fit into this paradigm. A one-time educational activity will not make a big difference for the integration of spiritual care within health care practices, but it often brings to the surface what caregivers themselves recognize as important in addressing their patients' needs and can add to other initiatives in helping to evolve a health care system that fosters orienting in life.

Take-home messages

- Developing spiritual care knowledge, skills, and attitudes requires a humanist educational approach in which the creation of spaces of hospitality and respect is central, and in which learners feel secure and welcome.
- Do not start with the topic but with knowledge of the self and the other (the professionals or patients).
- Provide some working definitions of terms (meaning making, spirituality, et cetera).
- Use cases and concrete examples from the participants and yourself.
- Connections to personal narratives or biography are remembered and are transformative.
- Exemplify in the attitude you want to teach.
- If you do not feel competent in education, make sure you learn from a colleague or take a course.

Note

1 It is a visual metaphor and tool in which the tree represents human life and the various elements that make it up – past, present, and future; or the roots (values), the trunk (the professional working methods), the leaves (goals), and the fruits (outcomes).

References

Aloni, N. (2011). Humanistic education: from theory to practice. In W. Veugelers (Ed.), *Education and humanism: Linking autonomy and humanity* (pp. 35–46). SensePublishers.

Appleby, A., Swinton, J., Bradbury, I., & Wilson, P. (2018). GPs and spiritual care: Signed up or souled out? A quantitative analysis of GP trainers' understanding and application of the concept of spirituality. *Education for Primary Care, 29*(6), 367–375. https://doi.org/10.1080/14739879.2018.1531271

Balboni, M., Sullivan, A., Enzinger, A., Epstein-Peterson, Z. D., Tseng, Y. D., Mitchell, C., Niska, J., Zollfrank, A., VanderWeele, T. J., & Balboni, T. A. (2014). Nurse and physician barriers to spiritual care provision at the end of life. *Journal of Pain and Symptom Management, 48*(3), 400–410. http://doi.org/10.1016/j.jpainsymman.2013.09.020

Best, M., Butow, P., & Olver, I. (2015). Do patients want doctors to talk about spirituality? A systematic literature review. *Patient Education and Counseling, 98*(11), 1320–1328, https://doi.org/10.1016/j.pec.2015.04.017

Boddaert, M., Douma, J., Dijxhoorn, F., & Bijkerk, M. (2017). *Netherlands quality framework for palliative care.* IKNL/Palliactief. Retrieved from https://palliaweb.nl/getmedia/f553d851-c680-4782-aac2-2520632f2e8d/netherlands-quality-framework-for-palliative-care_2.pdf

Carey, L. B., & Hodgson, T. J. (2018). Chaplaincy, spiritual care and moral injury: Considerations regarding screening and treatment. *Frontiers of Psychiatry, 9,* 619. https://doi.org/10.3389/fpsyt.2018.00619

Freire, P. (1971). *Pedagogy of the oppressed.* Herder and Herder.

Freire, P. (1974). *Education for critical consciousness.* Continuum.

Gardner, F. (2020). Social work and spirituality: Reflecting on the last 20 years. *Journal for the Study of Spirituality, 10*(1), 72–83. https://doi.org/10.1080/20440243.2020.1726054

Henoch, I., Danielson, E., Strang, S., Browall, M., & Melin-Johansson, C. (2013). Training intervention for health care staff in the provision of existential support to patients with cancer: A randomized, controlled study. *Journal of pain and symptom management, 46*(6), 785–794. http://doi.org/10.1016/j.jpainsymman.2013.01.013

Hodge, D. R., Carpenter, B. M., Yepez, R. A., & Lietz, B. C. (2021). Spirituality and religion in leading social work journals: A 10-year content analysis. *Social Work Research, 45*(1), 43–50, https://doi.org/10.1093/swr/svaa026

Hvidt, E. A., Søndergaard, E., Ammentorp, J., Bjerrum, J., Gilså Hansen, L., Olesen, F., Pedersen, S. S., Timm, H., Timmermann, C., & Hvidt, N. C. (2016). The existential dimension in general practice: Identifying understandings and experiences of general practitioners in Denmark. *Scandinavian Journal of Primary Health Care, 34*(4), 385–393. https://doi.org/10.1080/02813432.2016.1249064

Integraal Kankercentrum Nederland. (2018). *Zingeving en spiritualiteit in de pallia-tieve fase* [Meaning in life and spirituality in the palliative phase]. IKNL. Retrieved from https://palliaweb.nl/getmedia/860b2dce-0074-4230-8347-a87dea48aa96/9120-Zingeving-en-spiritualiteit-20240624015210.pdf

Jones, K. F., Paal, P., Symons, X., & Best, M. C. (2021). The content, teaching meth-ods and effectiveness of spiritual care training for healthcare professionals: A mixed-methods systematic review. *Journal of Pain and Symptom Management, 62*(3), e261–e278. https://doi.org/10.1016/j.jpainsymman.2021.03.013

Keall, R., Clayton, J. M., & Butow, P. (2014). How do Australian palliative care nurses address existential and spiritual concerns? Facilitators, barriers and strate-gies. *Journal of Clinical Nursing, 23*(21–22), 3197–3205. https://doi.org/10.1111/jocn.12566

Mesquita, A. C., Chaves, É. C. L., & Barros, G. A. M. (2017). Spiritual needs of patients with cancer in palliative care: An integrative review. *Current Opinion on Supportive Palliative Care, 11*(4), 334–340. https://doi.org/10.1097/spc.0000000000000308

Mezirow, J. (1991). *Transformative dimensions of adult learning.* Jossey-Bass.

O'Brien, M. R., Kinloch, K., Groves, K. E., & Jack, B. A. (2019). Meeting patients' spiri-tual needs during end-of-life care: A qualitative study of nurses' and healthcare professionals' perceptions of spiritual care training. *Journal of Clinical Nursing, 28*(1–2), 182–189. https://doi.org/10.1111/jocn.14648

Paal, P., Helo, Y., & Frick, E. (2015). Spiritual care training provided to healthcare professionals: A systematic review. *Journal of Pastoral Care & Counseling, 69*(1), 19–30. https://doi.org/10.1177/1542305015572955

Puchalski, C. M., Ferrell, B., Virani, R., Otis-Green, S., Baird, P., Bull, J., Chochinov, H., Handzo, G., Nelson-Becker, H., Prince-Paul, M., Pugliese, K., & Sulmasy, D. (2009). Improving the quality of spiritual care as a dimension of palliative care: The report of the consensus conference. *Journal of Palliative Medicine, 12,* 885–904. https://doi.org/10.1089/jpm.2009.0142

Smyth, T., & Allen, S. (2011). Nurses' experiences assessing the spirituality of termi-nally ill patients in acute clinical practice. *International Journal of Palliative Nursing, 17*(7), 337–343. https://doi.org/10.12968/ijpn.2011.17.7.337

Strang, S., Henoch, I., Danielson, E., Browall, M., & Melin-Johansson, C. (2014). Communication about existential issues with patients close to death – nurses' reflections on content, process and meaning. *Psycho-Oncology, 23*(5), 562–568. https://doi.org/10.1002/pon.3456

Sulmasy, D. P. (2002). A biopsychosocial-spiritual model for the care of patients at the end of life. *Gerontologist, 42,* 24–33. https://doi.org/10.1093/geront/42.suppl_3.24

Timmins, F., Neill, F., Griffin, M. Q., Kelly, J., & De La Cruz, E. (2014). Spiritual dimensions of care: Developing an educational package for hospital nurses in the republic of Ireland. *Holistic Nursing Practice, 28*(2), 106–123. https://doi.org/10.1097/HNP.0000000000000015

Vermandere, M., De Lepeleire, J., Smeets, L., Hannes, K., Van Mechelen, W., Warmenhoven, F., van Rijswijk, E., & Aertgeerts, B. (2011). Spirituality in general practice: A qualitative evidence synthesis. *British Journal of General Practice, 61*(592), e749–e760. https://doi.org/10.3399/bjgp11X606663

Verpleegkundigen & Verzorgenden Nederland. (2022). *Profiel palliatieve zorg verpleegkundige* [Profile palliative care nurse]. V&VN. Retrieved from https://palvoor profs.nl/uploads/files/vvn_-profiel_palliatieve_zorg_-digitaal_lezen-_v2.pdf

Veugelers, W. (2011). A humanist perspective on moral development and citizenship education. In W. Veugelers (Ed.), *Education and humanism: Linking autonomy and humanity* (pp. 9–34). SensePublishers.

Wesley, C., Tunney, K., & Duncan, E. (2004). Educational needs of hospice social workers: Spiritual assessment and interventions with diverse populations. *American Journal of Hospice and Palliative Medicine, 21*(1), 40–46. https://doi.org/10.1177/104990910402100110

Wickett, R. E. Y. (2005). The spiritual and human learning. In P. Yarvis & S. Parker (Eds.), *Human learning: An holistic approach* (pp. 157–167). Routledge.

World Health Organization. (1985). *Handbook of resolutions and decisions of the World Health Assembly and the Executive Board, II*. World Health Organization.

Yardley, S., Walshe, C., & Parr, A. (2009). Improving training in spiritual care: A qualitative study exploring patient perceptions of professional educational requirements. *Palliative Medicine, 23*(7), 601–607. https://doi.org/10.1177/0269216309105726

Chapter 8

The chaplain as a researching professional

Annelieke Damen, Gaby Jacobs, and Niels den Toom

Box 8.1

Ruby, a thirty-year-old chaplain, has started working in a rehabilitation facility where people recover from strokes and brain injuries after car accidents. She is educated as a chaplain, and first started her professional career in a mental health care institution. After several years, she was looking for a new challenge, which she found in the area of rehabilitation. In the first months, she delves into rehabilitation literature, exploring the intricacies of strokes and brain injuries. Then, she specifically searches for literature on chaplaincy and spiritual care in the context of rehabilitation. The literature helps her to understand the client's experiences and to develop a new role as a chaplain. One of the major existential themes she encounters is the tension between becoming dependent on others and remaining autonomous. According to Ruby, this is the key challenge for many clients.

When searching on the internet on autonomy and dependency in rehabilitation, she notices a call for research participants around this theme. She becomes interested in the project and speaks to one of the principal researchers. She is convinced that the research might benefit the clients in her rehabilitation center, and she decides to cooperate with the study. She helps recruit the clients and is invited as one of the stakeholders to reflect on the findings at the end of the study. Participating in this study gives her new energy for her work. Ruby also feels that she can contribute to the study from her chaplaincy background.

During the following year, the idea emerges to study the rehabilitation process as a process of meaning making. First, she thinks of a small research project, but over time the idea of starting a PhD project becomes more attractive. Ruby seeks a supervisor who might be

---

DOI: 10.4324/9781003428633-10

interested in the project, and a university where her research might be well embedded. After some months, she finds a supervisor, and her employer grants her the opportunity to conduct the research partly in working hours. Ruby has now not only become a chaplain but also a researcher.

The context of chaplaincy research

When we talk about the growing role of research in the context of chaplaincy, often *empirical* research is meant. Since the 1990s, the idea of chaplaincy as an empirically research-informed profession has increasingly taken shape (VandeCreek, 2002; Fitchett, 2002). 'Should chaplaincy become more scientific?' was the fundamental question posed in a 2002 edition of the *Journal of Health Care Chaplaincy* (Weaver et al., 2008). However, before this empirical turn in chaplaincy studies, scholars were already engaged with chaplaincy research. These studies mainly drew on normative sources from theological or philosophical traditions to conceptualize chaplaincy, stemming from the humanities (*Geisteswissenschaft*) within academia. Think, for example, of the studies outlining the contours of chaplaincy (Boisen, 1936; Heitink, 1984; Mooren, 2008; Zock, 2007). Or, questions like what it means to be a human being, what 'caring' is about, how suffering can be understood, et cetera, that were studied. These studies were primarily internally oriented at professional chaplains to understand their profession and the clients they serve and less so described the added value of chaplaincy for others.

Until the empirical turn in the 1990s, empirical research was scarce in chaplaincy. Three developments led to the rise of empirical research in chaplaincy. First, the religious landscape in Western Europe, particularly in the Netherlands, became increasingly secular, as noted in the Introduction to the volume. Taylor (2007) speaks here about "a move from a society where belief in God is unchallenged and indeed, unproblematic, to one in which it is understood to be one option among others" (p. 3). The conceptualization and substantiation of chaplaincy based on specific worldview traditions was no longer naturally understood by others in that same society, so answering what chaplaincy is and on whose (religious) authority a chaplain works became a challenge. Second, within academic discourse, empirical research became increasingly common in humanistic and religious studies. The focus was not only on the history of ideas and philosophy but also on everyday experiences, practices, and embodied values. Third, within contemporary society, empirical research had become an important argument to substantiate the value of care practices when means are scarce.

Particularly in health care, a "growing emphasis on accountability and efficiency in recent decades, has demanded chaplains to demonstrate their expertise and their contribution to their clients' wellbeing, preferably in an evidence-based manner" (den Toom et al., 2023, p. 14). Empirical research was utilized as an answer to these changes.

Although many chaplains were at first ambivalent, or even opposed to chaplaincy becoming more empirical,[1] today there is a growing consensus that theoretical as well as empirical research should be an important part of the profession (Fitchett & Grossoehme, 2012). This becomes apparent in, for example, the addition of the competency of '(empirical) research literacy' to the competencies for professional chaplains by the Association of Professional Chaplains in 2009[2] (APC, 2017) or by the Dutch Association of Spiritual Caregivers in 2015[3] (Dutch Association of Spiritual Caregivers, 2015, p. 15).

Chaplains' rationales for becoming an empirically research-informed profession vary. They include internal and external motivations (Weaver et al., 2008). Internal motivations comprise arguments such as that research can strengthen chaplaincy by the professionalization of the practice (den Toom, 2022). Research on the outcomes of chaplaincy care might lead chaplains to use interventions that have greater impact rather than those that are their personal preference. Or research on clients' needs might enable chaplains to better attune to those needs. In other words, research can lead to the improvement of the quality of chaplaincy care (den Toom et al., 2024; Fitchett & Delaney, 2018). In the case above (see Box 8.1), Ruby turns to research to improve her knowledge about her clients' conditions and their prevalent existential themes *in order to* provide better chaplaincy care.

Furthermore, empirical research can confirm or question the importance of chaplains' ideological ideas. For example, in Chapter 3 of this volume, we pointed to the idea that every profession has a good it strives for: a "devotion to a transcendent value which infuses its specialization with a larger and putatively higher goal … Each body of professional knowledge and skill is attached to such a value" (Freidson, 2001, p. 122). For chaplains, we specified this goal in this volume as 'supporting people to have a sense of orientation in life.' Empirical research can help to systematically investigate if this is indeed a goal chaplains realize in their practice. Or, as another example, when chaplains argue that they follow Rogers' nondirective approach, empirical research can study whether that is really the case (de Vos & Braam, 2021). In other words, research may function as a mirror, revealing how chaplains' actual practice relates to their ideal practices. Finally, research can stimulate creativity, "an antidote for the boredom and burnout that accompanies a heavy pastoral care load" (VandeCreek, 1992, p. 67). With few further career opportunities for chaplains, it may also function as a new professional challenge, such as for Ruby.

The external motivations to participate in empirical research all have to do with the legitimization of the profession. Health care chaplains, for example, indicate that they function within the culture of evidence-based medicine, so they are required to demonstrate their added value through research or even to make chaplaincy an evidence-based profession itself (Handzo et al., 2014). These chaplains do not feel that they have much choice: 'research, or perish?,' as Hover (2002) suggested. Furthermore, chaplains argue that other professionals have been engaged in spirituality research, so chaplains should be cautious that their profession will not be taken over (O'Connor, 2002). Finally, on a more positive note, some point out that research increases the visibility of chaplaincy among colleagues and the public, and promotes interdisciplinary relationships (Fitchett, 2002).

We would like to put forward the perspective that both the internal and external motivations for becoming an empirically research-informed profession are important. As a profession, we do want to strive for quality improvement of our care, and we do not do this in a vacuum. The internal and external motivations for doing research lead to different research questions – such as 'How can I improve my care for rehabilitation clients?' or 'Is chaplaincy an important addition to the care team in rehabilitation facilities?' – and thereby to other research methodologies. Sometimes these methodologies might be at odds with important chaplaincy values; we will say more about this later.

In the above context, we have outlined how the role of research in chaplaincy has grown. In the next paragraphs, we will specify how a chaplain can start their research process.

The chaplain as a researching professional

As the case about Ruby exemplifies (see Box 8.1), research can be integrated into chaplaincy care in various ways. The first form of Ruby's engagement with research is that she searches for and reads research articles to get a better understanding of her clients. The second form is that Ruby becomes involved in a research project, which she helps facilitate and in which she contributes to the research project from her particular expertise as a chaplain. The third form is that Ruby conducts her own research as a PhD student. The three forms of engagement with research were described by the American Association of Professional Chaplains as three levels of research literacy: beginner, intermediate, and advanced (APC, 2015):

1. The beginner level: all chaplains inform their practice by the available evidence.
2. The intermediate level: some chaplains participate in research projects.
3. The advanced level: a few chaplains lead research projects.

This idea encompasses the perspective that not every chaplain should conduct research themselves, but that various forms of research engagement can, each in their own way, contribute to the chaplaincy profession. We will translate this suggestion into levels of participation (instead of levels of experience, e.g., an experienced researcher can also participate in another level) and extend the grouping on each level with some suggestions to participate (see Figure 8.1):

1. Research mindedness: all chaplains
    1.1. Inform their practice by the available evidence
    1.2. Support the conduct of research by other researchers in their practice
    1.3. Participate in research as a respondent
2. Active research practice: some chaplains
    2.1. Contribute by suggesting topics or questions for research
    2.2. Conduct research activities as a coresearcher
3. Leading on research: a few chaplains
    3.1. Are the primary researcher of research projects
    3.2. Write research proposals
    3.3. Raise funds for research
    3.4. Provide advice or participate in ethical research boards

Chaplains' participation in research: where to start?

To make the above levels of research participation more concrete, we will now give some examples with help of the case study (see Box 8.1). Ruby's first research steps in the rehabilitation center, the level of research mindedness, show that chaplains can get involved in research by for example reading about research in monthly newsletters, chaplaincy journals, and by

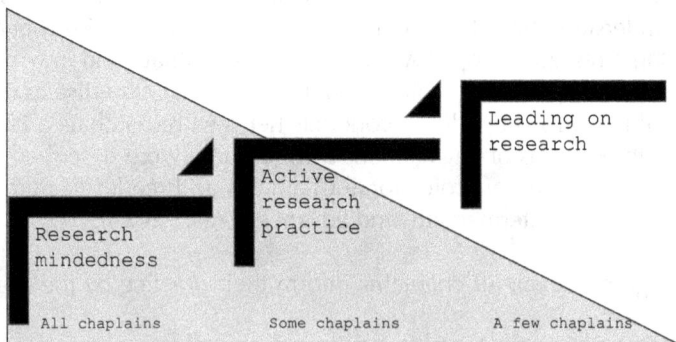

Figure 8.1 Participation levels in research.

following chaplaincy research webinars and summer schools. Per country the offer differs, so one might start at the website of the national professional chaplaincy organization or with an online search. For an international offer, one could have a look at the American website of Transforming Chaplaincy. Another good starting point is joining or founding a Chaplaincy Journal Club. See for an example of a Chaplaincy Journal Club the article by Fleenor et al. (2018). Research-minded chaplains will also support the conduct of research into their practice by other researchers, for example, by helping to recruit participants or providing information about the context to the researchers. A third way to participate at this level is to act as a respondent for research by other researchers, for example, by filling out a questionnaire or participating in an interview.

For the next step, if one wants to get more actively engaged in research, a place to start is a simpler theoretical, qualitative, and/or quantitative research project. Entry-level options are:

a. Joining an already ongoing study to add the perspective of the chaplain to the study team, that is, to provide chaplaincy expert opinion. See, for an example, Kestenbaum et al. (2015), which is an autoethnographic study of participating in an interdisciplinary research team.
b. Writing a case study, a detailed study of a specific subject. For example, see Drummond and Carey (2020).
c. Participating in an action research study. See, for example, Jacobs and de Cuba (2024) for a participatory action research project with the aim to enhance the collaboration between chaplains and mental health nurses in a general practice.
d. Conducting a small qualitative study. For example, see Olsman (2022) about chaplains as witnesses of hope in palliative care.
e. Conducting a small sized survey. For example, on the impact of chaplaincy in primary care (Snowden et al., 2019).
f. Writing a review of already existing knowledge on a subject. See, for example, Wolf and Feldbauer-Durstmüller (2018) on workplace chaplaincy.

In the case description (see Box 8.1), Ruby joins a research project as a co-researcher. One could look around in the organization where one is employed to see if research projects are carried out. Or one could join a project conducted by a knowledge institution such as a university or a national research project. The Case Study Project in the Netherlands is an example of a large collaborative project covering the different fields of chaplaincy, in which academic researchers and chaplains collaborated in building knowledge about chaplaincy, its goals and its approaches (Korver & Walton, 2017). Furthermore, chaplains can be involved in setting the research agenda, for example, within their institution or by participating in national committees or funding institutes.

Finally, for the 'leading on research' level, one would for example obtain a PhD, such as Ruby did, to acquire the necessary competencies to lead a research project, write research proposals to receive funding, and/or participate in an ethical research board. Since this is too far-reaching for this chapter, we will not discuss this further but refer chaplains to a university with a PhD program.

Positioning your research

When a chaplain considers becoming involved in a research project, it is good to start writing up one's presuppositions. Let us take Ruby's PhD project as an example. While the theme of her study is clear – the rehabilitation process as a process of meaning making – she can take various paths. She can, for example, investigate if the rehabilitation process can also be a process of empowerment. See, for example, Chapter 1, where empowerment is seen as an essential part of meaning making. Or, she can take an article about meaning making as a starting point and enrich this theoretical notion with her experiences of the rehabilitation process. Furthermore, Ruby could choose a more empirical method and explore rehabilitation clients' experiences of meaning making. Whatever choice Ruby may make for her research process, becoming aware of the purpose or desired outcome of her study, and the primary starting point, is important to determine what sort of research design she will formulate. In the following, we will describe a matrix with four ideal–typical poles, which can help to position one's research (den Toom, 2022).

In the introduction to this chapter, we wrote that chaplains have long been engaged in philosophical and theological research. Those studies were based on *ideas and values* and can thus be typified as ideological[4] research. Ruby's preoccupation with empowerment or enriching a theoretical notion may be regarded as such. Different from ideological research, empirical research is based on *observations, experiences, and measures*. Ruby's focus on her clients' experiences falls within this category. This leads to the first continuum of empiricism and ideals in Figure 8.2.

The continuum raises reflective questions for the chaplain–researcher. What is your research based on? Is *primacy* given to observations, experiences, and measurements, or to ideals and values? The question can be

Figure 8.2 Continuum of empiricism and ideals (den Toom, 2022, p. 131).

Figure 8.3 Continuum of practice and theory (den Toom, 2022, p. 133).

answered rather directly by typifying the study as an empirical study or a theoretical study. This does not mean that empirical studies do not contain any normative notions, or as is sometimes stated, are completely objective and value-free. In empirical studies, researchers also make normative choices. An example is Ruby, who in her empirical study would need to decide which definition of meaning making she may employ, e.g., the psychological definition of Park (2013), or a definition from a humanistic perspective as described in Chapter 1. Ideals may enrich our view on empirical reality, while empirical reality can confront or correct our ideals.

The second continuum we can distinguish is between practice and theory (see Figure 8.3). Is the research project mainly concerned with improving chaplaincy practice? In Ruby's case, this could be, for example, by interviewing rehabilitation clients about their meaning making in order to improve their care through a better understanding of their process. Or is the primary goal to contribute to the knowledge base about a certain topic (for example, Ruby's idea to enrich a theoretical notion of meaning making)?

Both continuums lead to the following matrix in Figure 8.4, in which chaplaincy research can be positioned. The model does not presuppose that research positioned in the center is the best kind of research. Rather, the model serves heuristically to reflect on your own presuppositions as a chaplain–researcher. If we were to attach a normative message to the model, it would be that chaplaincy research as a whole should include all four of the poles to keep its richness and variety.

Making your research perspective explicit

After having positioned one's research, the chaplain–researcher can even go a step further in explicating the *ontological* (what reality is), *epistemological* (what knowledge is and how it can be developed), and *axiological*

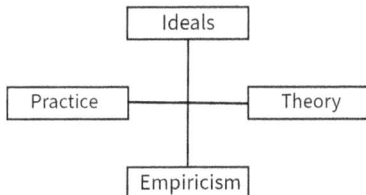

Figure 8.4 Matrix of research positions (den Toom, 2022, p. 133).

(what values are) assumptions behind the study. For Ruby, for instance, it is not only important to decide whether she wants to do theoretical or empirical research, or if she wants to benefit practice or theory. It is also important to know her philosophical scientific stance: what paradigm(s) (set of interrelated assumptions about the world) she relates to. In the literature, discussions on the research design are mostly narrowed down to the question of *what type of empirical research* (e.g., qualitative, quantitative, transformative) should be used but rarely about the ontological, epistemological, and axiological assumptions behind the study. The selected paradigm, however, guides the researcher in their further research path. In Table 8.1 we have outlined five paradigms in research with their ontological, epistemological, axiological, and methodological stances.

Ruby could position her research in the postpositivist paradigm, and decide to study meaning making by using questionnaires (e.g., the *Sources of Meaning and Meaning in Life Questionnaire (SoMe)* by Schnell & Becker, 2007). However, this will not provide her with data on the unique meaning-making experiences of individuals. She might reason that the uniqueness of each individual is an important chaplaincy value, so she decides to switch to the constructivist/interpretative paradigm and to use a qualitative method. Or, she realizes that she would like to follow the humanistic understanding that orientation in life takes place within a social and political context (see also Chapter 1), and that she would like to support the empowerment of persons and groups to change this context (Jacobs, 2002). This would put her in the critical/transformative paradigm. In her study she could recognize and value the lived experiences of people as an important source of knowledge and strength. Within a transformational view on knowledge, Ruby could collaborate with clients and other stakeholders in order to build knowledge that benefits the clients, improves practices, and adds to the knowledge on meaning making in rehabilitation. Fourth, Ruby could take a pragmatic stance and choose whatever method or combination of methods that are most appropriate for answering the research question. Finally, Ruby could decide she would like to focus on the meaning making of indigenous rehabilitation patients in order to decolonize rehabilitation practices. Of course, Ruby could also decide to do a *mixed methods* study and make use of various methods within a specific or multiple paradigms.

The above example of Ruby illustrates that chaplains, when they reason from their values, often feel more comfortable in the constructivist/interpretative, critical/transformative, or the indigenous paradigms. The positivist paradigm, which has been the dominant force in science for over 150 years (Ponterotto, 2005), and predominantly underlies the evidence-based paradigm in health care, many times does not fit with their research questions. In other words, particularly research methodologies that create a distance

Table 8.1 Five scientific paradigms

	Postpositivist paradigm: focus on explanation	Constructivist/ interpretative paradigm: focus on understanding (Verstehen)	Critical/transformative paradigm: focus on deconstruction and change (emancipation)	Pragmatic: focus on the research question	Indigenous paradigm: focus on local knowledge systems[5]
Ontology	Realistic: objects exist independently in the world and can be probabilistically known objectively	Relativist: reality as we know it, is a subjective construction	Historical–political: reality is formed by social, political, cultural, and economic forces and experienced as 'true' – this 'truth' is questioned critically	Realistic: unique individual interpretations of one reality	Relativist-relational: multiple, socially, and historically constructed realities, mutual reality-based on multitude of relationships, everything is part of an undivided whole
Epistemology	Representational: we can know parts of the world as it is and describe and explain it accurately Rule-based knowledge	Phenomenological: how we know the world, is deeply connected to how we understand ourselves, others, and the world In-depth knowledge from unique experiences and cases	Transactional: how we know the world is deeply connected to historical and cultural-political power relationships Value-based knowledge	Dependent on the particular research question of the study	Intersubjective experiential: we know the world through relationships, knowledge is collective and includes the entire cosmos Value-based knowledge

(Continued)

Table 8.1 (Continued)

	Postpositivist paradigm: focus on explanation	Constructivist/interpretative paradigm: focus on understanding (Verstehen)	Critical/transformative paradigm: focus on deconstruction and change (emancipation)	Pragmatic: focus on the research question	Indigenous paradigm: focus on local knowledge systems[5]
Axiology	Values excluded, influence denied	Values included, formative	Values included, formative Research as a means for social emancipation and solidarity with the oppressed	Dependent on the particular research question of the study	Values included, formative Research is guided by relational accountability that promotes respectful representation and reciprocity
Methodology[6]	Often quantitative methods (modified): experimental/ manipulative, questionnaire Falsification of hypotheses and causal relationships Researcher is at a distance from the research object, decontextualized	Often qualitative methods (hermeneutical/ dialectical): interviews, observations, and text analyses Researcher is close to the research object in order to give meaning to the phenomenon under study, contextualized	Often transformative methods (dialogic/ dialectical): informed by theories (e.g., feminist, postcolonial). Political, contextual, participatory such as action research, responsive evaluation Critically questioning the status quo and underlying assumptions, and fostering change Dialogue between researcher and participants	Dependent on the particular research question of the study: the approach matches the purpose of the study. Predominantly used in mixed methods	Often participatory, liberatory, and transformative methods: positioned in indigenous knowledge systems

between researcher and research 'objects' are criticized as not being compatible with chaplaincy values. For example, a randomized controlled trial (RCT) with highly standardized chaplaincy interventions could be antagonistic to a chaplaincy value such as recognition of the uniqueness of each person. Sometimes, however, the generation of knowledge within paradigms that feel further away from the chaplaincy profession might be asked for. Think of legitimizing the profession for insurance companies. Such study designs, however, do require extra attention from the researcher to ensure that they do not conflict with important chaplaincy values. This includes minimizing mechanistic ways of observing people and maximizing the individual experience of the participant. Scholl et al. (2014) argue that RCTs (and, more generally, quantitative methods) should not be written off as inevitably dehumanizing, and they give pointers on how to develop humane quantitative research.

On a general note, we would like to stress that research should be consistent with the values of the profession, although we understand that these values are not static and will change over time. Chaplaincy researchers who are developing research need to address the question how their current understanding of the values of chaplaincy relate to their study design. Addressing this question may prevent them from evaluating chaplaincy using values that are not consistent with chaplaincy values (Damen et al., 2020). For humanist chaplain–researchers, this could entail reflecting on how their study design aligns with humanist values such as outlined in Chapter 2.

Conclusion

In this chapter, we have focused on the chaplain as a researching professional to zoom in on the role of chaplains regarding research, as research is one of the competencies chaplains need to understand to strengthen their practice. We have touched upon several dimensions of chaplaincy research: the context and rationale for doing chaplaincy research; levels of chaplains' participation in research; some concrete research examples as a place to start; how a chaplain–researcher can position their research in terms of ideals, empiricism, theory, and practice; and the five paradigms of postpositivism, constructivist/interpretative, critical/transformative, pragmatic, and indigenous to help chaplain–researchers articulate their underlying research assumptions. We argued that not every chaplain needs to become an active researcher, but that we hope that every chaplain will cross the boundaries between the chaplaincy and research fields during their career path.

The participation of chaplains in research raises the following question: how much involvement, and in what way, is needed, possible, or desirable?

In some fields in the Netherlands, chaplains experience 'research fatigue' because their participation is requested in multiple projects at the same time. The fatigue appears to be strongest if chaplains are only asked to engage as informants for the project of academic researchers, for example, by filling out questionnaires or recruiting clients. Often they are not briefed on what will happen with the results and how these will improve their practice or clients' lives. To prevent this fatigue, it is important for (aspiring) chaplain–researchers to not always ask the same chaplains for research projects. Moreover, chaplain–researchers can work towards collaboration and co-ownership of the study with the study participants so an exchange is established between research and practice. This includes participating in the chaplaincy practice in which they conduct research, working together towards results (knowledge, interventions, and so on), and embedding these results collaboratively to enhance the practice.

Another pitfall of research is that results are not used in practice. The question of the implementation of knowledge to make impact is a major issue in all health care (and other) practices (see, for example, Wensing et al., 2015). There are at least two sides to this problem: the classic mindset of researchers to develop knowledge away from practice and the top-down organization of knowledge within a profession. The Dutch project The Knowledge Workplace on Spiritual Care in the Netherlands (Kenniswerkplaats Zingeving) aims to bring together several aspects of knowledge acquisition to create a spiral process that fosters the professionalization of chaplaincy: knowledge questions, knowledge building, knowledge sharing, knowledge utilization, and knowledge management. For this process, it was deemed essential to bring together researchers, chaplains, clients, educators, and policymakers to create impact, both societal and scientific. The Knowledge Workplace also makes the chaplaincy profession more visible within the broader political policy and research landscape. Each chaplain–researcher on their own or each single research project will not make a major difference; their combination and connection to a national research agenda on chaplaincy allows for a far stronger lobby for policymakers and funders.

Finally, it is important to emphasize that not all should be expected from academic knowledge. Ragsdale and Desjardins (2020) have argued that chaplains found it hard to connect their practices to academic and theoretical knowledge (cf. den Toom, 2022). Should we say that these chaplains' practices are not based on knowledge but merely on experience? Probably not, it rather requires from us to expand the definition of legitimate knowledge, as various forms of knowledge are at play here. Aristotle, for instance, already distinguished between episteme (scholarly knowledge), technè (craftmanship), and phronesis (practical wisdom). Reflecting on these various forms of knowledge, not all can be expected from theoretical knowledge (episteme). Moreover, chaplaincy is a profession *about* meaning and worldview but also *from* a worldview perspective (be it institutionally demarcated or not). Chaplains do not only respond to client-based generic theories about meaning, for instance, but also draw on their worldview traditions. The knowledge contained in these traditions can better be indicated by wisdom.[7] A wise chaplain knows that research adds to the professional care for clients, but also knows its limits when it comes to searching for meaning.

Take-home messages

- Chaplaincy is becoming a research-informed profession: research can improve the quality of chaplaincy care and support the legitimization of the profession.
- Chaplains can participate in research on various levels: research mindedness, active research practice, and leading on research. How are you going to participate?
- A good start of your research participation is to look up what your national chaplaincy organization is doing in terms of research.
- Once involved, to get a better understanding of the research process, it is helpful to position a study on the ideals-empiricism and theory-practice continuums.
- The same goes for the underlying assumptions: are they postpositivist, constructivist/interpretative, critical/transformative, pragmatic, or indigenous? How are the assumptions aligned with chaplaincy values?
- Finally, knowledge acquisition occurs at various levels. A study will make the most impact if these levels collaborate.

Notes

1 Concerns were raised that science was too reductionistic, unable to capture the transcendent dimension of chaplaincy, or that the standardization necessary for (some) research might "even distort the very nature of pastoral care itself" (McCurdy, 2012, p. 157, in Weaver et al., 2008; see also Damen et al., 2020 and den Toom, 2022).
2 The APC competency is formulated as: "Articulate how primary research and research literature inform the profession of chaplaincy and one's spiritual care practice.".
3 The Dutch Association of Spiritual Caregivers competency is formulated as: "Chaplains should be able to use results of research and participate in research.".
4 Ideological is not used in a pejorative sense but as referring to the world of ideas and ideals.
5 Adapted from Held (2019) and Walker (2015).
6 Often, specific methods are used within a certain paradigm. However, any of the paradigms could make use of any of the methodologies (McChesney & Aldridge, 2019).
7 For an elaboration on the issue of wisdom in chaplaincy, see den Toom (2022), section 0.

References

Association of Professional Chaplains. (2015). *Standards of practice for professional chaplains*. Retrieved from www.apchaplains.org/wp-content/uploads/2022/05/Standards-of-Practice-for-Professional-Chaplains-102215.pdf

Association of Professional Chaplains. (2017). *Common qualifications and competencies for professional chaplains*. Retrieved from www.apchaplains.org/wp-content/uploads/2022/05/2017-Common-Qualifications-and-Competencies-for-Professional-Chaplains.pdf

Boisen, A. T. (1936). *The exploration of the inner world. A study of mental disorder and religious experience*. University of Pennsylvania Press.

Damen, A., Schuhmann, C., Leget, C., & Fitchett, G. (2020). Can outcome research respect the integrity of chaplaincy? A review of outcome studies. *Journal of Health Care Chaplaincy, 26*(4), 131–158. https://doi.org/10.1080/08854726.2019.1599258

de Vos, J., & Braam, A. (2021). An empirical study on the nature of the verbal responses of humanist chaplains. *Religions, 12*(12), 1080. https://doi.org/10.3390/rel12121080

den Toom, J. N. (2022). *The chaplain–researcher: The perceived impact of participation in a Dutch research project on chaplains' professionalism* [Doctoral Thesis, Protestantse Theologische Universiteit]. Eburon.

den Toom, J. N., Kruizinga, R., Liefbroer, A. I., & Körver, J. (2023). The professionalization of chaplaincy: A comparison of 1997 and 2017 surveys in the Netherlands. *Journal of Health Care Chaplaincy 29*(1), 14–29. https://doi.org/10.1080/08854726.2021.1996810

den Toom, J. N., Visser, A., Körver, J., & Walton, M. N. (2024). The perceived impact of being a chaplain–researcher on professional practice. *Journal of Health Care Chaplaincy, 30*(1), 19–32. https://doi.org/10.1080/08854726.2022.2132036

Drummond, D. A., & Carey, L. B. (2020). Chaplaincy and spiritual care response to COVID-19: An Australian case study – The McKellar Centre. *Health and Social Care Chaplaincy, 8*(2), 165–179. https://doi.org/10.1558/hscc.41243

Dutch Association of Spiritual Caregivers. (2015). *Standards of practice*. Available online at Beroepsstandaard-2015.pdf (www.vgvz.nl).

Fitchett, G. (2002). Health care chaplaincy as a research-informed profession: How we get there. *Journal of Health Care Chaplaincy, 12*(1–2), 67–72. https://doi.org/10.1300/J080v12n01_07

Fitchett, G., & DeLaney, A. (2018). Opportunity for Catholic health care: The evidence-based spiritual care paradigm. *Health Progress, 99*(3), 12–16. www.chausa.org/publications/health-progress/archive/article/may-june-2018/the-evidence-based-spiritual-care-paradigm

Fitchett, G., & Grossoehme, D. H. (2012). Healthcare chaplaincy as a research-informed profession. In S. B. Roberts (Ed.), *Pofessional spiritual and pastoral care: A practical clergy and chaplain's handbook* (pp. 387–406). Skylight Paths.

Fleenor, D., Sharma, V., Hirschmann, J., & Swarts, H. (2018). Do journal clubs work? The effectiveness of journal clubs in a clinical pastoral education residency program. *Journal of Health Care Chaplaincy, 24*(2), 43–56. https://doi.org/10.1080/08854726.2017.1383646

Freidson, E. (2001). *Professionalism, the third logic: On the practice of knowledge.* University of Chicago Press.

Handzo, G. F., Cobb, M., Holmes, C., Kelly, E., & Sinclair, S. (2014). Outcomes for professional health care chaplaincy: An international call to action. *Journal of Health Care Chaplaincy, 20*(2), 43–53. https://doi.org/10.1080/08854726.2014.902713

Heitink, G. (1984). *Pastoraat als hulpverlening.* Kok.

Held, M. B. E. (2019). Decolonizing research paradigms in the context of settler colonialism: An unsettling, mutual, and collaborative effort. *International Journal of Qualitative Methods, 18.* https://doi.org/10.1177/1609406918821574

Hover, M. (2002). Research or perish? *Journal of Health Care Chaplaincy, 12*(1–2), 91–97. https://doi.org/10.1300/J080v12n01_10

Jacobs, G. C. (2002). *De paradox van kracht en kwetsbaarheid. Empowerment in feministische hulpverlening en humanistisch raadswerk.* [The paradox of strengt hand vulnerability. Empowerment in feminist assistance and humanist chaplaincy] SWP.

Jacobs, G., & de Cuba, S. (2024). 'A clear center but no clear boundaries.' The construction of professional identities in spiritual care through boundary work in participatory action research within health care. *Action Research, 22*(2), 179–195. https://doi.org/10.1177/1476750323119541

Kestenbaum, A., James, J., Morgan, S., Shields, M., Hocker, W., Rabow, M., & Dunn, L. B. (2015). "Taking your place at the table": an autoethnographic study of chaplains' participation on an interdisciplinary research team. *BMC Palliative Care, 14*(20), 1–10. https://doi.org/10.1186/s12904-015-0006-2

Korver, S., & Walton, M. N. (2017). Dutch case studies project in chaplaincy care: A description and theoretical explanation of the format and procedures. *Health and Social Care Chaplaincy, 5*(2), 257–280. https://doi.org/10.1558/hscc.34302

McChesney, K., & Aldridge, J. (2019). Weaving an interpretivist stance throughout mixed methods research. *International Journal of Research & Method in Education, 42*(3), 225–238. https://doi.org/10.1080/1743727X.2019.1590811

McCurdy, D. B. (2012). Chaplains, confidentiality and the chart. *Chaplaincy Today, 28*(2), 20–30. https://doi.org/10.1080/10999183.2012.10767458

Mooren, J. H. M. (2008). *Geestelijke verzorging en psychotherapie* [Chaplaincy and psychotherapy]. De Graaff.

O'Connor, T. S. J. (2002). The search for truth: The case for evidence based chaplaincy. *Journal of Health Care Chaplaincy, 13*(1), 185–194. https://doi.org/10.1300/J080v13n01_03

Olsman, E. (2022). Witnesses of hope in times of despair: Chaplains in palliative care. A qualitative study. *Journal of Health Care Chaplaincy, 28*(1), 29–40. https://doi.org/10.1080/08854726.2020.1727602

Park, C. L. (2013). The meaning making model: A framework for understanding meaning, spirituality, and stress related growth in health psychology. *European Health Psychologist, 15*(2), 40–47. www.ehps.net/ehp/index.php/contents/article/view/ehp.v15.i2.p40

Ponterotto, J. G. (2005). Qualitative research in counseling psychology: A primer on research paradigms and philosophy of science. *Journal of Counseling Psychology, 52*(2), 126–136. https://doi.org/10.1037/0022-0167.52.2.126

Ragsdale, J. R., & Desjardins, C. M. (2020). Proposing religiously informed, relationally skillful chaplaincy theory. *Journal of Health Care Chaplaincy, 28*(2), 239–254. https://doi.org/10.1080/08854726.2020.1861533

Schnell, T., & Becker, P. (2007). *Sources of Meaning and Meaning in Life Questionnaire (SoMe, LeBe)* [Database record]. APA PsycTests. https://doi.org/10.1037/t03408-000

Scholl, M. B., Ray, D., & Brady-Amoon, P. (2014). Process, outcomes, and research in humanistic counseling. *Journal of Humanistic Counseling, 53*, 218–239. https://doi.org/10.1002/j.2161-1939.2014.00058.x

Snowden, A., Gibbon, A., & Grant, R. (2019). What is the impact of chaplaincy in primary care? The GP perspective. *Health and Social Care Chaplaincy, 6*(2), 200–214. https://doi.org/10.1558/hscc.34709

Taylor, C. (2007). *A secular age.* Harvard University Press.

VandeCreek, L. (1992). Research in the pastoral care department. In L. A. Burton (Ed.), *Chaplaincy services in contemporary health care* (pp. 65–69). College of Chaplains, Inc.

VandeCreek, L. (2002). *Professional chaplaincy and clinical pastoral education should become more scientific: Yes and no* (1st ed.). Routledge. https://doi.org/10.4324/9780203050125

Walker, P. (2015). Indigenous paradigm research. In D. Bretherton & S. Law (Eds.), *Methodologies in peace psychology. Peace Psychology Book Series, vol 26* (pp. 159–175). Springer. https://doi.org/10.1007/978-3-319-18395-4_8

Weaver, A. J., Flannelly, K. J., & Liu, C. (2008). Chaplaincy research: Its value, its quality, and its future. *Journal of Health Care Chaplaincy, 14*(1), 3–19. https://doi.org/10.1080/08854720802053796

Wensing, M., Bal, R., & Friele, R. (2015). Knowledge implementation in healthcare practice: A view from the Netherlands. *BMJ Quality & Safety, 21*(5), 439–442. https://doi.org/10.1136/bmjqs-2011-000540

Wolf, T., & Feldbauer-Durstmüller, B. (2018). Workplace chaplaincy: A literature review. *Journal of Management, Spirituality & Religion, 15*(1), 38–63. https://doi.org/10.1080/14766086.2017.1385514

Zock, H. (2007). Spiritual caregivers and psychologists: Allies taking care of meaning-making. *Psychologie & Gezondheid, 35*(5), 243–250. https://hdl.handle.net/11370/5bd8186e-9333-483e-afd2-fa929992eb22

Chapter 9

Moral development of individuals, teams, and organizations

Gaby Jacobs and Vicky Hölsgens

"But I keep wondering if I did the right thing." I'm sitting with a nurse from the hospital I work at. A week earlier, during a shift, she tended to a family whose loved one had a stroke. The family had to make the decision to either continue treatment, knowing that the patient had severe brain damage, or to stop treatment, which would cause the patient to die. Together with the doctor, the nurse had a conversation with the family about these options. The family decided to opt out. They thanked the nurse for their support. Also, the doctor gave her compliments for her clear communication and empathic attitude. But here she was, a week later, sitting opposite me, with an agonizing feeling that she had not done the right thing.

I ask her if she has words for this feeling. Hesitantly she says that she might have pushed the family to make this decision. Because she herself would not want to live with such brain damage. "Maybe I projected my own feelings onto this family, leaving them with no choice but to stop the treatment, which caused him to die." To see if there is truth in this conviction, we run through the shift together, as detailed as possible. How was she feeling that day when she started the shift? When did she meet this patient and family? What was her role? What was her first feeling? What was the medical state of this patient, and how did it progress during the shift? How did she experience the contact with the family? How did the conversation go? Who said what, in what order? When and how did the family come to their decision? And when did that agonizing feeling start?

Interestingly, she got this feeling afterwards. During the shift, she had a good feeling about how she had handled it. "But maybe I had a blind spot for my own conviction." Therefore, we zoom in a little deeper into the conversation. Where did she leave space for the

DOI: 10.4324/9781003428633-11

family and where did she maybe direct the conversation? Although we conclude that she didn't have a very directive role in the conversation, I can tell by her body language that it still doesn't feel right for her. She still has a tense look and a frown on her face, shoulders raised. I ask her: "What if the family would have decided to choose the treatment?" Without hesitation she says: "Then we would have started the treatment." I can see her face relax and a smile appears: "I didn't push them! I would have been perfectly fine with their decision for treatment. I informed them and they made the decision."

Introduction

In this case description, we see a family facing a moral dilemma – to continue or to stop treatment of their beloved one – and a nurse who is informing them about the options and supporting them in making a decision. After the decision is made, the nurse herself starts to doubt the adequacy of her role, causing moral suffering. The hospital chaplain supports nurses, doctors, and other health care workers to be aware of and to deal with the moral questions and issues in their work. This we call the moral dimension of chaplaincy work.

Elly Hoogeveen was a Dutch humanist health care chaplain who was one of the first in the Netherlands to write a book (1991) in which she addressed the moral task of the chaplain. According to her, chaplains need to serve the interests of the patients and should be guardians of humanity within the institution. She formulated 11 principles that are key to this moral work, including: supporting the patient's choice; rejection of dehumanizing tendencies as a 'moral compass'; and presence in crisis situations to build authority within the organization. Building relationships with other professionals was very important as well, and characterized by asking questions, honest and open communication, and supporting them within the institution. Hoogeveen based her ideas on the work of the German philosopher Habermas; she discussed the systemic violence of hospitals and saw doctors and nurses (but especially doctors) as executors of this system who needed to become aware of the inhumane consequences of their actions. Her account dates from over three decades ago, and since then a lot has changed within health care institutions, but her key message remains topical: the moral task of the chaplain is to go beyond the support of individual patients to address situations that inhibit humanity within the organization. She also pointed to the need to connect with other professionals and to support them, as they encounter difficult questions and circumstances that cause moral distress in their work.

Organizations who do not care for professionals' signals of moral distress may show moral erosion: the slow disappearance of moral values that are part and parcel of professional organizations and that are needed to do 'good work' (Freidson, 2001). Chaplains work at the crossroads between humanizing and dehumanizing forces in organizations. They aim at normative professionalization (see Chapter 3) by being sparring partners for management and policymakers, thereby contributing to policy and vision development. This is important in order to express that moral questions and distress are not an individual's problem but emerge within institutional frameworks and processes that may cause moral damage and inhumanity. The moral work of chaplains even stretches beyond the organization, thereby contributing to interdisciplinary community programs through exhibits, art, or literary readings (see, e.g., Puniewska, 2015). Also, regarding complex societal issues such as loneliness and precarity within municipalities, chaplains may collaborate with social workers and other community-based professionals in supporting social involvement in streets and neighborhoods, thereby stressing the moral good of caring and compassionate communities.

In this chapter, we will explain what the 'moral dimension' of chaplaincy work entails when working with professionals within organizations. First of all, we will outline what we mean by the moral dimension. Then we will outline what chaplains do in order to try to enhance the moral competence within organizations, of teams, and of individuals. We conclude that chaplains have a crucial role in the moral dimension in organizations and communities and that they need to develop their own moral competence in order to facilitate this at their workplace.

The moral dimension: searching for humanity

In Chapter 1, we spoke about the centrality of 'visions of the good' in orientation in life. This is not different for the work that is done in public sector domains. Every profession strives for a higher good, such as well-being, social connectedness, autonomy, or social justice. For humanist chaplains, this higher good may be called 'humanity': recognizing each person as a valuable and equal human being. The moral dimension then refers to the dimension of values and norms that exist on personal, professional, community, organizational, institutional, and societal levels. Considering the moral dimension also means that we have to consider the contextual embeddedness of persons and their actions; how a 'vision of the good' is actually practiced.

Moral distress or moral suffering can occur when a professional as a moral agent is not able to act according to their own moral judgments because institutional or internal factors impede this (Rushton, 2023). Work in the fire service, penitentiaries, military, the police, health care, or other sectors raises moral and existential questions for the organizations and professionals involved, which require an orientation or reorientation in their work. Professionals and organizations are confronted with moral and existential questions due to the nature of the work, the policies, and procedures that need to be followed, or due to specific circumstances. For example, if they are faced with making decisions in life-and-death situations (Tunks et al., 2023); or have to make (ambiguous) choices in crisis situations, like in the COVID-19 pandemic when new procedures were in place almost every day (van der Geugten et al., 2022). Within health care, moral issues may include autonomy, power, scarce resources, guidelines, responsibility, and privacy (Bruun et al., 2018; Jacobs, 2019). Within the military, topics that cause moral tension are, for example, being a soldier but also a human, a culture of masculinity, being part of a group, uniformity, hierarchy, and privacy (van Baarle et al., 2015). In 1984, Jameton was the first to differentiate between forms of moral concerns, differentiating moral uncertainty, moral dilemmas, and moral distress (Campbell et al., 2018). Morley et al. (2022) have recently extended these with moral conflict, moral constraint, and moral tension all being forms of moral distress. This differentiation is important as it shows that moral issues do not only refer to the matters of life and death but also include the daily hassles and struggles professionals encounter (see also Jacobs, 2019). Not addressing the daily moral distress of professionals runs the risk of overlooking the continuous moral suffering that is triggered by witnessing or participating in actions that produce negative moral outcomes and will impact upon the vitality and zest of professionals.

How chaplains act in the light of moral issues can be understood by Walker's (2007) expressive–collaborative model of morality. In this model, moral work is based on communal experimenting and learning, allowing for sanctuaries to share stories about the good and imaging different ways of working, in order to be able to plan and implement them within a broader context. Walker argues that moral thinking and moral justification are narrative processes: stories bear essential knowledge on how practices seem and feel to the people acting in them. Therefore, it is essential to examine these different stories in order to hear factors or patterns that so far remained invisible and to transform morally damaging social practices. Moral work in essence then is narrative work, aligned to the specific context in which moral issues arise and adapted to the needs of those persons involved.

Different forms of moral work

Moral work can take different forms, and then has different aims. We will now discuss four forms of moral work conducted by chaplains: moral education, normative–professional reflection, organizational presence, and support in moral recovery.

The development of moral sensitivity through education

Ethics is to the average health care professional as water is to a fish: they are not aware of the morally charged environment they are working in, unless it has to do with the big moral dilemmas – to treat or not to treat? In other domains this may be different. In the military, for example, consideration for ethics is crucial because exercising violence, even if that is 'for a good cause,' leads to controversy within a democratic society. However, also in the military, the daily morality which can be found in care for each other, or the vulnerability one may feel beneath the strong appearance, can easily be overlooked. Consequently, it takes patience to build a culture wherein moral conversations are self-evident.

When a hospital department wants to invest in ethics or moral delibera-tion, moral education is a good start. Spekkink and Jacobs (2021) found three dimensions of moral sensitivity that are being addressed in nursing education – raising moral awareness, providing the ability to frame and name ethical issues, and improving reasoning ability. Their review is, how-ever, based on only a few available articles on this topic, which shows that so far there is not a lot of attention given to moral education of health care professionals.

In the military, moral education is a more structural part of the education of new personnel, in which chaplains have a key role (van Baarle et al., 2015). Gladwin (2013) points out in his Australian history text titled, 'Captains of the soul,' that chaplains have historically and regularly been involved in the education and character training of military personnel (dur-ing peace and war campaigns), thereby "helping to calibrate the moral compass of soldiers, who have been authorized to use lethal force in increasingly complex situations" (p. 32), a role which is receiving increas-ing recognition in the last years.

Moral education prepares military personnel to function in the complex moral world of the military, in which there is a continuing tension between personal values and following the orders and guidelines of the organization (van Baarle et al., 2015). Moral education aims at developing the moral competence and professional identity of professionals. Moral competence contains the following six elements (Karssing, 2000):

1. The awareness of one's own personal values and the values of others.
2. The recognition of the moral dimension of a situation and identification of which values are at stake or are at risk of violation.
3. The ability to adequately judge a moral question or dilemma.
4. The ability to communicate this judgment.
5. The willingness and ability to act in accordance with this judgment in a morally responsible manner.
6. The willingness and ability to be accountable to yourself and others.

This model can be criticized for being too cognitive and individualistic, but it still provides a framework to work with in chaplaincy practice. Intuition and emotion (Haidt, 2001), and dialogue and collaboration (Walker, 2007) should be included within this idea of moral competence. Also, these elements or dimensions do not need to be addressed in this particular order, although one should not try to work on the 'higher' three levels if moral sensitivity has not yet been established. A chaplain working in health care may, for example, first focus on the second element: making professionals aware of and sensitive to the moral issues they encounter in their daily practice. Through ethics education, professionals can become more sensitive to the 'smaller' ethical issues by sharing experiences or discussing examples from other locations. They can learn to recognize those moments when they feel a bodily sensation like a clenched throat or a knot in their stomach and a thought like: 'what to do?'

> "So basically, 'do I have to make a grilled cheese sandwich for a patient?' is a moral dilemma", one of the nurses in my ethics lesson concluded. "Because if one colleague makes them and I don't, we don't treat our patients equally. In my opinion, patients deserve the same treatment in equal cases. So, every patient who is allowed to eat, should get offered the same food."

As mentioned before, moral issues have a broader scope than patient care. They can also come up in interaction with colleagues or in organizational policies or procedures. Education then is a way to help professionals become aware of the moral environment they work in daily. One soldier participating in moral competence training, quoted in van Baarle et al. (2015), expressed: "You don't always have room to be your own person, you're always required to work in a system where your opinion doesn't really count" (p. 11).

However, education alone is not enough to create a culture wherein the moral dimension is self-evident. Another way to contribute to an ethical work culture is by creating spaces for normative–professional reflection.

Fostering normative–professional reflection

Structurally providing normative–professional reflection within teams is a desirable extension of moral education as presented above. Moral competence is a skillset that needs to be maintained during a professional career. A professional identity is based on a framework of norms and values (see also Chapter 3), often implicitly transferred upon professionals during their professional training and experiences in their career. The aim of normative–professional reflection is to make this framework more explicit, which also helps in developing moral competence, especially in becoming aware of your own personal values and the values of colleagues.

> The hospital chaplain explains: "Planning these moments [of normative–professional reflection] can be a challenge in the hospital setting, even more so at the emergency department. Schedules are tight, shifts unpredictable, and there are many topics and skills nurses and doctors must be trained in. Ideally it takes a group of four to ten professionals who have at least an hour wherein they won't get disturbed. Therefore, it is important that management sees the added value of these reflections and invests time (and thus money) to give their staff the opportunity to participate during worktime."

Various methods can be used for normative–professional reflection. Moral Case Deliberation (MCD), a methodically structured dialogue, is a form of ethics support that strengthens the moral competence of participants as described by Karssing (2000). It contributes to moral resilience, especially because MCD is action-oriented (Metselaar & Molewijk, 2023). In many Dutch health care organizations, MCDs are facilitated by chaplains. A moral case is needed to use this method and that is why moral sensitization through education is important before implementing MCD in a team. When professionals cannot recognize or experience moral concerns in their daily practice, it is difficult for them to participate (Metselaar & Molewijk, 2023).

There are different methods to guide an MCD, such as the dilemma method, Socratic dialogue, or CURA to name a few. At their core, they all follow the same structure (de Bree & Veening, 2016):

1. *Presentation of the case.* One group member presents a situation of moral distress (conflict, constraint, dilemma, et cetera) and asks a moral question, such as: how should I act?
2. *Clarification of the presented case.* The participants can ask factual questions about the case. The idea is that all participants can vividly picture the case – almost like a movie – and are able to take the perspective of the narrator who experienced the discomfort. They also ask themselves: what information would I need to answer the question myself?
3. *Joint moral inquiry.* The participants investigate who was involved and what perspectives, interests, and values play a role.

4. *Weighing values.* The participants answer for themselves the moral question that was asked in the beginning, based on the joint moral inquiry; and then share these answers with each other.

During an MCD, participants practice in reflective dialogue, which requires active listening, postponing initial judgments and conclusions, being open to new perspectives and learning from each other, and critically exploring their own convictions (Metselaar & Molewijk, 2023). It is a narrative space that allows for exploration and moral ambivalence, and in which answers are postponed until a later stage. When done regularly, participants take this attitude and these skills to their daily practice, which enriches the moral dimension beyond the MCD (de Snoo-Trimp, 2020).

Organizational presence, a relational approach

Moral education and normative–professional reflection contribute to a culture of moral sensitivity in organizations; they also help prepare professionals to deal with moral concerns. It is in the daily practice of their work that professionals need to deal with them when they are at hand. In addition, then, support and help is offered in case of incidental crises or trauma processing, e.g., the death of a colleague in a war situation, or during the COVID-19 pandemic, or encountering aggression from citizens. Joint reflection and guidance with moral and existential questions help professionals to tap into their own sources of strength and to support each other during difficult times. An example is the spiritual care provided by chaplains to ambulance personnel after a major trauma, natural disaster, terrorist incident, or death of a colleague (Tunks et al., 2023). This is characterized by a relational approach that facilitates trust, access, physical and emotional presence, and supportive conversations. It helps the ambulance personnel to focus on the difficult task at hand, and to reflect on it if necessary. This involves, first of all, proactive support: relation building so that if there is a crisis, the paramedics will approach the chaplain. This corresponds to one of the recommendations of the Dutch guideline *Psychosocial support for health care professionals* (ARQ Nationaal Psychotrauma Centrum, 2023), namely that support should be easily accessible and available for health care professionals, not only in moments of crisis.

During the COVID-19 pandemic, a psychosocial team was available for health care staff at the emergency department during the shift change. It did not appear to meet the needs of the staff. Looking back, professionals said things like: "I don't know them, so I don't feel comfortable talking to them about my vulnerabilities" and "When it has been a long and intense shift, that is not the moment to talk to someone who just drops in at that moment. I just want to go home then."

The management team did believe in support for their health care staff. With the experience of psychosocial support during the COVID-19 pandemic, they decided to recruit a chaplain for a couple of days at the emergency department (ED). After a year, the team evaluated the easy accessibility of support as the most successful: someone who knows the department and invests in relations with the staff. The barrier to ask for support can be high at the ED. A conversation about one's family or recent holiday lowers this barrier. It often happens that after such a conversation, a professional says: "now that we are talking, I was wondering if we could plan a moment to sit down and talk about …" It also works the other way around. As a chaplain, one gets to know the staff and their 'normal' way of being. When they suddenly show different behavior, the relationship you have built as a chaplain helps to address this without it being felt as a judgment.

Moral recovery

When professionals feel that deeply held moral beliefs and expectations are transgressed time and again, serious inner conflict can arise as to one's sense of goodness and humanity. This conflict causes deep wounds, i.e., moral injury, that are not easy to heal and that become manifest in a range of physical, mental, social, and spiritual symptoms. In a review study, Webb et al. (2024) discovered three higher order moral tensions that contributed to moral injury. These included the tension between 'profession and system,' 'relations with patients and relations with others,' and 'principles and practices.' These show that a wide range of experiences, e.g., incongruence in values, interprofessional conflict, or being witness to inadequate treatment of patients, can induce moral injury. Especially in the COVID-19 pandemic, the awareness of moral injury in health care staff increased (see e.g., Cartolovni et al., 2021; Roycroft et al., 2020; Riedel et al., 2022). However, it is in veteran care that the chaplain's role regarding moral injury is the most elaborated on so far. Walker (2006) uses the concept of 'moral repair' and defines it as "a process of moving from the situation of loss and damage to a situation where some degree of stability in moral relations is restored" (p. 6). Studies show that it is commonly agreed that chaplains are qualified to have a key role in the care and treatment of those professionals that suffer from moral injury (Carey et al., 2016; Nazarov et al., 2020), and that military personnel seems more likely to use chaplaincy compared to other mental health care services when they feel betrayed by their organization (Kopacz et al., 2019). This may be due to chaplains' visibility within the organization and their sanctuary role (Layson et al., 2022). Furthermore, spirituality is for many people a significant contributor to moral understandings, decisions, and behavior (Walker, 2007), which leads people to seek guidance from chaplains if they experience moral injury (Drescher et al., 2018). This guidance may take different forms, as is shown by the literature on this topic. A few authors present an overview of different methods:

- In a literature review, several methods are discussed that provide spiritual guidance in the case of moral injury (Carey et al., 2016). By utilizing the 'Spiritual Intervention Codings' (abbrev. 'SPICs') of the World Health Organization (WHO, 2017), and the 'Systematized Nomenclature of Medical and Clinical Terms' (see www.snomed.org/), chaplaincy roles and spiritual care were categorized according to one or more of the following interventions: spiritual (i) assessment, (ii) support, (iii) counseling, guidance, and/or education, and/or (iv) ritual activities.
- Drescher et al. (2018) provide an overview of different approaches, including presence, therapeutic exercises, promoting meaning making, and fostering internal and external resources (see Table 3 in Drescher et al., 2018).

In other publications, specific chaplaincy interventions for recovering from moral injury are reported. We highlight some of them:

- A structural intervention in which chaplains meet with veterans for twelve 50-minute sessions. Each session focuses on a specific domain of moral injury, such as guilt, betrayal, loss of trust, difficulty forgiving (Ames et al., 2021).
- An evidence-based, intercultural approach to spiritual care. This recognizes the complex and distinctive ways veterans' values and beliefs are influenced by diverse and interacting cultural systems, especially military training and cultures (Doehring, 2019).
- Another method is the Pastoral Narrative Disclosure (PND) rehabilitation intervention (Carey & Hodgson, 2018), designed specifically for use by chaplains for assisting veterans who may be suffering from moral injury. This method includes eight steps, including rapport, reflection, review, reconstruction, restoration, ritual, renewal, and reconnection.
- A particular contribution of chaplains revealed in the literature was that of retreats and extended seminars. McRae and Saunders (2014), for example, developed an eight-lesson program on 'moral injury and moral repair' for military personnel to help give soldiers insight as to 'what is

going on in their heart and head' and to help them develop the language needed to articulate their struggles and feelings (see Table 7 in McRae & Saunders, 2014).

Although in this chapter we focus on the chaplain's contribution to moral repair, the health needs of morally injured professionals will be best served when chaplains and health care professionals, such as psychologists, work collaboratively towards improved health outcomes (see also Drescher et al., 2018). In fact, latest research shows the value of chaplaincy–psychology collaborative models of care in fostering recovery from moral injury of veterans (Ames et al., 2021; Carey & Hodgson, 2018; Hodgson et al., 2021).

Conclusion

The moral dimension is about 'sustaining humanity,' cuts across different levels and domains, and includes not only the issues of life and death but also the everyday moral concerns and the small acts that belong to this. The chaplain's role is to address all experiences of moral damage: those seemingly small and daily ones, that nevertheless can have a big impact, as well as those that arise in extreme situations, such as war, political demonstrations, natural disasters, and fatal accidents. Even more importantly, it is their role to help build a culture in which visions of the good have a self-evident place. They can do this by providing moral education, creating space for normative–professional reflection, organizational presence, and facilitating moral recovery. These are often not large and earth-shattering interventions, but nevertheless make a difference for those involved.

However, this also raises the question how this moral work relates to the sanctuary role of humanist chaplaincy (see Chapter 3). Chaplains could easily play a role in building the moral resilience of professionals by the ethical practice they foster (Rushton, 2023), which is at odds with offering critique on organizational policies and procedures that hinder professionals in doing good work. Moral work then requires chaplains to be able to deal with this tension and to build their own resilience towards organizational pressures to conform. Creating chaplaincy learning communities may be one way of doing this.

Also, in a plural society, moral work includes diversity and intercultural issues within teams, between professionals and patients or clients, and within society. It is important that chaplains are well aware of their own sociocultural positioning in order to acknowledge different values and norms and deal with the tensions between them. They can take a participatory action research approach to collaborate with other professions and managers in transforming practices and routines within departments and organizations (Jacobs & De Cuba, 2024).

Take-home messages

- Moral work takes place on different levels, with different functions, and cuts across domains – e.g., health care, the military, penitentiaries – of chaplaincy work.
- It all starts with self-reflection and self-care, for example, by participating in supervision or learning communities with other chaplains.
- Do not try to develop moral judgment or action before moral sensitivity is developed by the professionals.
- Reflect on the moral functions your activity has: what are you aiming at? Are you aiming at building moral competence or recovering moral injury? And does your method fit this goal?
- Activities often run parallel: organizational presence along with educational activities or moral case deliberations.
- Build alliances with other chaplains and with other professionals in order to deal with the moral challenges and organizational pressure in this work.

References

Ames, D., Erickson, Z., Geise, C., Tiwari, S., Sakhno, S., Sones, A. C., Tyrrell, C. G., Mackay, R. B., Steele, W., Van Hoof, T., Weinreich, H., & Koenig, H. G. (2021). Treatment of moral injury in US veterans with PTSD using a structured chaplain intervention. *Journal of religion and health, 60*(5), 3052–3060. https://doi.org/10.1007/s10943-021-01312-8

ARQ Nationaal Psychotrauma Centrum. (2023). *Beleidsrichtlijn psychosociale ondersteuning zorgprofessionals. Een handreiking voor de praktijk bij ingrijpende gebeurtenissen* [Policy guideline psychosocial support for health care professionals. A practical guide for dealing with significant incidents]. https://arq.org/diensten/richtlijn-psychosociale-ondersteuning-zorgprofessionals

Bruun, H., Lystbaek, S. G., Stenager, E., Huniche, L., & Pedersen, R. (2018). Ethical challenges assessed in the clinical ethics Committee of Psychiatry in the region of Southern Denmark in 2010–2015: A qualitative content analyses. *BMC Medical Ethics, 19*, 62. https://doi.org/10.1186/s12910-018-0308-z

Campbell, S.M., Ulrich, C.M., Grady, C. (2018). A broader understanding of moral distress. In: Ulrich, C., Grady, C. (eds) *Moral distress in the health professions.* Springer. https://doi.org/10.1007/978-3-319-64626-8_4

Carey, L. B., & Hodgson, T. J. (2018). Chaplaincy, spiritual care and moral injury: Considerations regarding screening and treatment. *Frontiers of Psychiatry, 9*, 619. https://doi.org/10.3389/fpsyt.2018.00619

Carey, L. B., Hodgson, T. J., Krikheli, L., Soh, R. Y., Armour, A. R., Singh, T. K., & Impiombato, C. G. (2016). Moral injury, spiritual care and the role of chaplains: An exploratory scoping review of literature and resources. *Journal of Religion and Health, 55*, 1218–1245. https://doi.org/10.1007/s10943-016-0231-x

Čartolovni, A., Stolt, M., Scott, P. A., & Suhohen, R. (2021). Moral injury in health-care professionals: A scoping review and discussion. *Nursing Ethics, 28*(5), 590–602. https://doi.org/10.1177/0969733020966776

de Bree, M., & Veening, E. (2016). *Handleiding moreel beraad: Praktische gids voor zorgprofessionals* [Manual of moral deliberation: A practical guide for healthcare professionals]. Uitgeverij Koninklijke van Gorcum.

de Snoo-Trimp, J. C. (2020). *Outcomes of moral case deliberation: Using, testing and improving the Euro-MCD Instrument to evaluate clinical ethics support* [PhD thesis, Vrije Universiteit Amsterdam]. https://research.vu.nl/en/publications/outcomes-of-moral-case-deliberation-using-testing-and-improving-t

Doehring, C. (2019). Military moral injury: An evidence-based and intercultural approach to spiritual care. *Pastoral Psychology, 68*, 15–30. https://doi.org/10.1007/s11089-018-0813-5

Drescher, K. D., Currier, J. M., Nieuwsma, J. A., McCormick, W., Carroll, T. D., Sims, B. M., & Cauterucio, C. (2018). A qualitative examination of VA chaplains' understandings and interventions related to moral injury in military veterans. *Journal of Religion and Health, 57*(6), 2444–2460. https://doi.org/10.1007/s10943-018-0682-3

Freidson, E. (2001). *Professionalism, the third logic: On the practice of knowledge*. University of Chicago Press.

Gladwin, M. (2013). 'Captains of the soul': The historical context of Australian Army chaplaincy, 1913–2013. *Australian Army Chaplaincy Journal, 21*, 30–51. https://researchoutput.csu.edu.au/en/publications/captains-of-the-soul-the-historical-context-of-australian-army-ch

Haidt, J. (2001). The emotional dog and its rational tail: A social intuitionist approach to moral judgment. *Psychological Review, 108*, 814–834. https://doi.org/10.1037/0033-295X.108.4.814

Hodgson, T. J., Carey, L. B., & Koenig, H. G. (2021). Moral injury, Australian veterans and the role of chaplains: An exploratory qualitative study. *Journal of Religion and Health, 60*, 3061–3089. https://doi.org/10.1007/s10943-022-01572-y

Hoogeveen, E. (1991). *Eenvoud en strategie* [Simplicity and strategy]. Lemma.

Jacobs, G. (2019). Patient autonomy in home care: Nurses' relational practices of responsibility. *Nursing Ethics, 26*(6), 1638–1653. https://doi.org/10.1177/0969733018772070

Jacobs, G., & de Cuba, S. (2024). 'A clear center but no clear boundaries': The construction of professional identities in spiritual care through boundary work in participatory action research within health care. *Action Research, 22*(2), 179–195. https://doi.org/10.1177/14767503231195418

Karssing, E. (2000). *Morele competentie in organisaties* [Moral competence in organizations]. Van Gorcum.

Kopacz, M. S., Adams, M. S., Searle, R., Koenig, H. G., & Bryan, C. J. (2019). A preliminary study examining the prevalence and perceived intensity of morally injurious events in a veterans affairs chaplaincy spiritual injury support group. *Journal of Health Care Chaplaincy, 25*(2), 76–88. https://doi.org/10.1080/08854726.2018.1538655

Layson, M. D., Tunks Leach, K., Carey, L. B., & Best, M. C. (2022). Factors influencing military personnel utilizing chaplains: A literature scoping review. *Journal of Religion and Health, 61*(2), 1155–1182. https://doi.org/10.1007/s10943-021-01477-2

McRae, R., & Saunders, J. (2014). *Moral injury – moral repair: Retreat handbook.* Australian Regular Army 7th Brigade Chaplaincy.

Metselaar, S., & Molewijk, B. (2023). Fostering moral resilience through moral case deliberation. *Nursing Ethics, 30*(5), 730–745. https://doi.org/10.1177/09697330 231183085

Morley, G., Sankary, L.R., & Horsburgh, C. C. (2022). Mitigating moral distress through ethics consultation. *The American Journal of Bioethics, 22*(4), 61–63. https://doi.org/10.1080/15265161.2022.2044555

Nazarov, A., Fikretoglu, D., Liu, A., Richardson, J. D., & Thompson, M. (2020). Help-seeking for mental health issues in deployed Canadian Armed Forces personnel at risk for moral injury. *European Journal of Psychotraumatology, 11*(1). https://doi.org/10.1080/20008198.2020.1729032

Puniewska, M. (2015, July 3). Healing a wounded sense of morality. *The Atlantic.* www.theatlantic.com/health/archive/2015/07/healing-a-wounded-sense-of-morality/396770/

Riedel, P.-L., Kreh, A., Kulcar, V., Lieber, A., & Juen, B. (2022). A scoping review of moral stressors, moral distress and moral injury in healthcare workers during COVID-19. *International Journal of Environmental Research and Public Health, 19*(3), 1666. https://doi.org/10.3390/ijerph19031666

Roycroft, M., Wilkes, D., Pattani, S., Fleming, S., & Olsson-Brown, A. (2020). Limiting moral injury in healthcare professionals during the COVID-19 pandemic. *Occupational Medicine, 70*(5), 312–314. https://doi.org/10.1093/occmed/kqaa087

Rushton, C. H. (2023). Transforming moral suffering by cultivating moral resilience and ethical practice. *American Journal of Critical Care, 32*(4), 238–248. https://doi.org/10.4037/ajcc2023207

Spekkink, A., & Jacobs, G. (2021). The development of moral sensitivity of nursing students: A scoping review. *Nursing Ethics, 28*(5), 791–808. https://doi.org/10.1177/0969733020972450

Tunks Leach, K., Simpson, P., Lewis, J., & Levett-Jones, T. (2023). The role and value of chaplains in an Australian ambulance service: A comparative study of chaplain and paramedic perspectives. *Journal of Religion and Health, 62*(1), 98–116. https://doi.org/10.1007/s10943-022-01685-4

van Baarle, E., Bosch, J., Widdershoven, G. A. M., Verweij, D., & Molewijk, A. C. (2015). Moral dilemmas in a military context. A case study of a train the trainer course on military ethics. *Journal of Moral Education, 44*(4), 457–478. https://doi.org/10.1080/03057240.2015.1087389

van der Geugten, W., Jacobs, G., & Goossensen, A. (2022). The struggle for good care: Moral challenges during the COVID-19 lockdown of Dutch elderly care facilities. *International Journal of Care and Caring, 6*(1–2), 157–177. https://doi.org/10.1332/239788221X16311375958540

Walker, M. U. (2006). *Moral repair: Reconstructing moral relations after wrongdoing.* Cambridge University Press.

Walker, M. U. (2007). *Moral understandings: A feminist study in ethics.* Oxford University Press.

Webb, E. L., Ireland, J. L., Lewis, M., & Morris, D. (2024). Potential sources of moral injury for healthcare workers in forensic and psychiatric settings: A systematic review and meta-ethnography. *Trauma, Violence, & Abuse, 25*(2), 918–934. https://doi.org/10.1177/15248380231167390

WHO. (2017). *Tabular List of Interventions. The World Health Organisation International Statistical Classification of Diseases and Related Health Problems, Tenth Revision, Australian Modification (ICD-10-AM)*. WHO.

Chapter 10

Doing socio-political work in chaplaincy

Carmen Schuhmann, Tessa Heethaar, and
Marjo van Bergen

Introduction

In 1959, a large gas field was discovered in the most northern province of the Netherlands, Groningen. In a short period of time, the
Dutch government sought and found long-term partners in large
companies which started the exploitation of the gas field. Large infra-
structural and social projects in the Netherlands were financed from
the gas benefits.

In the 1980s, however, it became clear that, as a side effect of this
large-scale gas extraction, Groningen's soil had become unstable.
When in 2012 a heavy earthquake hit one of Groningen's small vil-
lages, inhabitants started legal procedures against the gas extraction
company in order to receive damage compensation, and to guarantee the safety of people and their homes in the context of an increasing number of earthquakes. The Dutch government, highly dependent
on the revenues from gas exploitation, did not stand up for the interests of the inhabitants of Groningen.

Initially, people in Groningen believed that they could count on
damage compensation. Over time, however, it turned out that this
was not the case, in part due to increasingly complex and tedious
procedures for determining damage and calculating risk. The deferral
and rejection of many compensation claims not only led to increasing
uncertainty but also to inequality among inhabitants as some cases
were processed faster than others. Destructive feelings like jealousy,
shame, guilt, resentment, sadness, hopelessness, and loss of self-
esteem found their way into communities. Stress and stress-related
(mental) health problems became part of people's everyday life.

In 2018, an initiative of the churches in Groningen led to the instal-
lation of GVA Groningen,[1] a chaplaincy organization employing

DOI: 10.4324/9781003428633-12

> chaplains to work in the earthquake area. Starting with two small part-time jobs, in 2024 GVA Groningen has grown into a team of eight chaplains. I work as a humanist chaplain in this team.

In light of current understandings of chaplaincy, it is not self-evident to perceive chaplaincy as comprising socio-political action in the public domain. Chaplaincy is generally associated with supporting people to deal with the inevitable – to come to terms with existential 'givens' that cannot be changed. It is often seen as a profession characterized by 'being' rather than 'doing' (Nolan, 2015). Furthermore, for chaplains, speaking out in public may seem to be at odds with the non-moralizing stance that they aim to take and their reticence to act as religious authorities. This reticence is reflected by a shift in the chaplaincy discourse which now revolves around spirituality rather than religion. The work that chaplains do has come to be understood in terms of addressing spiritual needs and supporting spiritual well-being. This adds to an individualized view of chaplaincy as focusing on suffering and healing at an individual level. Several authors, however, emphasize that doing political work in public space is an integral element of chaplaincy and should not be confused with taking a moralistic stance (Gärtner, 2011; Schuhmann & Damen, 2018). In relation to pastoral care, political action is often seen as originating from religious traditions of prophesy. Vandenhoeck (2011), for instance, writes that:

> prophetic pastoral counseling sees that the difference between the actual situation and the desired situation is never only the responsibility of the individual. Prophetic pastoral care aims to unmask the social situation which leads to the actual situation, becoming therefore a resistance potential for our times.
>
> (p. 8)

Throughout this volume, spiritual care is conceptualized in terms of caring for processes of orientation in life. These processes are entangled in socio-cultural contexts as systems, structures, and developments at a societal (macro)level may promote or hinder the capacity of individuals and groups to imagine, strive for, and live a good life (see Chapter 1). In Chapter 3 we therefore argued that chaplains, as professionals in the domain of processes of orientation in life, also have a humanizing task at a macrolevel, the level of communities and society. We refer to this task in terms of the (socio-)political dimension of chaplaincy. Here, we follow Mouffe's (2005) understanding of 'the political' as "a space of power, conflict and antagonism" (p. 9). In her view, given the plurality of perspectives and values in the social world, conflict is inherent in social life. In the domain of the political, order is created and consolidated through practices and institutions which also establish a particular configuration of power relations. While the dominant existing order is easily seen as the 'natural' order and taken for granted, it "is the result of sedimented practices; it is never the manifestation of a deeper objectivity exterior to the practices that bring it into being" (Mouffe, 2005, p. 14). Furthermore, no order represents "a 'rational,' i.e., a fully inclusive, consensus, without any exclusion" (Mouffe, 2005, p. 14). Any order excludes certain perspectives and values, pointing to the possibility of alternative orders. Political action may then be understood as action directed at exposing, questioning, or changing the dominant order – the macrosystems and -structures – that organizes human coexistence and power dynamics.

This chapter focuses on the humanizing role chaplains may play in society by exposing, questioning, or changing macrosystems and -structures. Taking up this role involves using power – something which is easily seen as conflicting with the basic attitude of chaplains. We follow Arendt's (1970) conception of power as "the human ability not just to act but to act in concert" (p. 44) to understand chaplains' use of power in public space. In this view, using power is directed at empowering communities to imagine and strive for shared, inclusive visions of the good.[2]

We start our explorations by looking into the existing literature about the political dimension of spiritual care. We mainly use literature from the domain of pastoral care, as here the question of how to provide spiritual care to communities and society has received more attention than in the domain of chaplaincy. Given the lack of empirical studies into the sociopolitical dimension of chaplaincy, we then turn to an explorative qualitative study of the subject by Heethaar (2022). In the study, ten politically engaged humanist professionals were interviewed about their experience of doing socio-political work. The study illustrates that there are different macrolevel influences which may impair people's attempts to live a good life; for instance, economic uncertainty, environmental issues, or different forms of discrimination, all of which call upon chaplains to not only take account of the brokenness in individual lives but also the brokenness of the world (see also Lee & Gibson, 2021). We then put the focus on political chaplaincy work in a specific context: the context of the earthquake area in the Netherlands (described at the beginning of this chapter). Here, the people suffering from systemic influences related to gas extraction on their lives live in a relatively concentrated area, and chaplains have been employed specifically to provide spiritual care to them. The chaplains working in the earthquake area are necessarily confronted with the crucial role of macrostructures and -systems in the lives of inhabitants. Addressing the impact of these structures and systems has thus become the primary task in their work. We describe the chaplaincy method for strengthening disrupted communities that was developed in this context. We think that chaplains working in other contexts, encountering other forms of systemic damage, may use (elements of) this method too.

In our explorations, ideas of Tronto (1993, 2013) about care as inherently comprising a political dimension serve as theoretical background. Tronto (2013) emphasizes that good care, apart from phases of *caring about* – noticing unmet care needs, *taking care of* – taking responsibility for meeting these needs, *care giving* – doing actual care work, and *care receiving* – assessing responses by care receivers, also involves a phase of *caring with* – embedding care practices in a public debate about how to meet care needs and assign care responsibilities in a way that is consistent with "democratic commitments to justice, equality, and freedom for all" (p. 23). Following this understanding of care, we may see chaplaincy as involving various phases of care. This includes a phase of 'spiritual caring with' in which chaplains, taking a perspective of inclusivity and social justice, contribute to public dialogues about how dominant visions of the good impact experiences of disorientation and the capacity of individuals and groups to (re)orient.

Providing spiritual care to communities and society

In the literature on spiritual and pastoral care, various authors argue that spiritual caregivers should not only provide spiritual care to individuals in spiritual need but also to communities and societies 'in spiritual need.' They point to situations in which individual suffering does, at least partially, arise from macrorealities that are beyond individual control. LaMothe (2014), for instance, writes that "human suffering arises from many sources, including dysfunctions within the community itself" (p. 9). In terms of processes of orientation in life, the claim is that negative experiences of disorientation may arise from macrodiscourses and macrostructures; for instance, those that lead to oppression and marginalization. Similarly, it was pointed out in Chapter 1 that understanding disorienting experiences of injustice and moral tension requires a political perspective, so that dehumanizing circumstances involved in these experiences – circumstances which can be changed – do not disappear from view. These disorienting experiences are contrasted with the disorienting experiences of tragedy and ontological insecurity, which arise from unavoidable life circumstances. However, in these cases, too, a political perspective is required when it comes to the question of how people may (re)orient in life. Due to existing macrostructures, certain people or groups may have less access to resources for (re) orientation than more privileged people or groups, no matter what kind of disorientation they are facing.

Various authors point to the dominant discourse of neoliberal capitalism in Western societies as a root source of people's spiritual suffering. In neoliberalism, the central beliefs of liberalism – individual freedom and rational self-interest – are interpreted in terms of economic freedom and economic self-interest. In a neoliberalist ideology, living a 'good' life is evaluated in economic terms, in terms of material gain: "neoliberalism produces entrepreneurial subjects" (LaMothe, 2019, p. 424). Given the hegemony of neoliberalism in Western societies, this ideology is easily taken for granted. Human suffering is then seen as individual failure, leading to a dynamic of self-accusation which underlies much of contemporary human suffering (Shin, 2021). In particular, in a neoliberal climate, human interdependence and vulnerability easily disappear from view, alienating people from each other and from communities (LaMothe, 2014). According to LaMothe (2019), people are also alienated from the natural world. He argues that neoliberal capitalism cannot be separated from what is often called the Anthropocene, the current age in which the climate is changing due to human activity. As those who profit from capitalism are not willing to give up on their privilege and wealth, the political and economic changes necessary to counter global warming are not made. Here too, the suffering resulting from climate change is usually individualized and depoliticized.

Religious traditions offer spiritual views of human beings that counter the neoliberal view of the entrepreneurial subject, while also countering dominant discourses that lead to oppression and marginalization. Central to these views are notions of transcendence, love, and social justice. The same is true of the humanist spiritual views that we described in Chapter 2. Chaplains seem therefore to be in the right position to offer a critical view of the ways in which people's suffering is individualized and depoliticized, and to uncover racism, colonialism, ageism, sexism, et cetera in dominant discourses. However, according to Rogers-Vaughn (2013), the fact that religious discourse is giving way to spiritual discourse in Western societies is in itself a consequence of the hegemony of neoliberalism and leads to an erosion of the social justice potential of chaplaincy. In his view,

> neoliberalism distributes to its isolated inhabitants a 'spirituality' tailor-made and marketed to their individual tastes – one which relieves them of the burden of the search for shared truth, the inconveniences of maintaining a common life, and the demands of social justice.
>
> (Rogers-Vaughn, 2013, p. 6)

Embracing a discourse of spirituality that is cut off from worldview traditions may lead to an individualized and depoliticized understanding of chaplaincy in which chaplains confirm the status quo rather than critically address systemic inequalities.

In the literature on pastoral care, we find several ideas about how to provide spiritual care at the level of communities and society. First, several authors emphasize that, in pastoral care, political work is rooted in careful pastoral listening (LaMothe, 2019; Sharp, 2019; Shin, 2021). It is only after identifying the impact of dehumanizing discourses in the stories that people tell them, that pastoral caregivers should aim for critical practices of resistance in which they publicly address the impact of these discourses. Sharp (2019) points out that it is crucial here that pastoral caregivers also reflect on and are accountable for their own involvement and potential complicity in dehumanizing discourses. Second, in response to community disasters, lamentation is proposed as a specific pastoral practice at the level of community (Graham, 2014). Third, pastoral caregivers may invest in hope by offering and strengthening visions of caring and just societies that support transformative processes in communities (Graham, 2014). Rogers-Vaughn (2016) stresses that this requires of pastoral caregivers to embrace a utopian, post-capitalist pastoral theology, so that they do not, however unintentionally, reproduce dominant neoliberal norms in these visions.

Results of a qualitative study of socio-political chaplaincy work

Given the paucity of literature about how to do socio-political work in chaplaincy, we draw from the results of an explorative qualitative study of the subject by Heethaar (2022). In this study, ten politically engaged humanist chaplains were interviewed about their motivation to do socio-political work, about what characterizes this work, and about the barriers they encounter. They worked in a variety of contexts like prisons, mental health care institutions, and homeless shelters. Their political engagement was focused on different societal issues; they were, for instance, engaged in climate activism, or supported queer communities. As most of the existing literature about the socio-political dimension of chaplaincy has a theological foundation, we think that presenting insights from humanist chaplains has added value when it comes to understanding how chaplains may provide spiritual care at the level of communities and society in (post) secular, plural contexts.

Motivation for and aim of doing socio-political work in chaplaincy

Not surprisingly, the humanist chaplains who were interviewed for the study by Heethaar (2022) all share a vision of chaplaincy as inherently comprising socio-political work. They explain that, as chaplains, they are the ones who embody a way of listening to people's stories which involves sensitivity to how existential issues are entangled with systemic injustice. They therefore know that processes of searching for meaning in life cannot be separated from the socio-political context – not only at a theoretical level but by witnessing how this actually happens in people's lives. As they time and again hear stories about systemic injustice, they feel that it is insufficient, and even misplaced, to only express support and understanding to individuals. In their view, not sharing more widely the knowledge they gain about the impact of systemic forces on individual lives would undermine their credibility as chaplains. They talk about this in terms of 'being called' to do something about the systemic injustice that comes to light at the microlevel of their work. This call is reinforced by the realization that, as chaplains, they are in a relatively privileged position. They are familiar with the various dominant discourses that circulate in society, they have a network, they have insight into systemic forces. When they speak out about something in public, this is more easily taken seriously by authorities than when the people they support speak out.

By doing socio-political work, the respondents aim to contribute to a better, more just, and caring society. Several respondents indicate that they are aware that they themselves will not live to see the better world they hope to bring about. This does not affect their motivation to work towards a better world, for instance, in order to serve the needs of future generations. Their motivation is rooted in their humanist worldview. One respondent, for instance, states: "I have my sources of inspiration to dare to make sacrifices when it comes to political activism. I feel that it is the right thing to do to courageously stand up for what you profoundly believe in." They want to contribute to a greater good, something that transcends themselves and their own lives, also when this implies that they need to make personal sacrifices.

Taking a worldview perspective in socio-political chaplaincy work

The respondents in Heethaar's (2022) study characterize the socio-political work they do as being grounded in what they call a 'worldview perspective.' They explain this first of all – referring to their humanist worldview – in terms of focusing on the actual attempts of actual human beings to live a good life instead of on abstract ideas about what it means to live a good life. One respondent explains this as follows: "human beings are my primary entry point for the rest of the world." This is in line with how, according to the literature about pastoral care that we referred to earlier, political work should only take place after careful pastoral listening. It requires thorough knowledge of how people's suffering is entangled in macrorealities to address these realities in public.

Second, according to the respondents, taking a worldview perspective in socio-political work means that this work is informed by visions of the good that include human vulnerability and fallibility in the picture. Addressing societal issues in public as a chaplain involves advocating for nuanced views, for a public dialogue in which all voices are included, and for the value of taking the time to search for answers and solutions together rather than aiming for quick fixes. Several respondents designate their socio-political work as 'soft activism': they do not proclaim a certain position as the right one but rather motivate people, in particular authorities, to keep questioning their fixed views and positions.

Third, the respondents indicate that grounding socio-political work in a worldview perspective requires of chaplains to engage in a continuous process of reflecting on their own deepest values and on the question of whether these may be realized within the existing macroreality. In this way, chaplains may clarify their personal involvement in the issues they address in their socio-political work. This allows them to nourish their motivation to do this work but also to critically question where this personal motivation colors their view of the struggles of the people they work with. The respondents indicate that this continuous reflection on their personal motivation in relation to their worldview has as a consequence that the issues they engage with in their political chaplaincy work and the extent to which they focus on the socio-political dimension of their work as a chaplain may fluctuate during their lives.

Finally, the respondents stress that taking a worldview perspective involves attuning to the specific situation at hand, so that there is not one predetermined way to do socio-political work in chaplaincy. They mention a variety of political activities that they engage in. They set up or join organizations, demonstrations, or events, they initiate conversations with authorities or the press, or they use social media or participate in research in order to expose the impact of macrosystems on human lives. They also see providing spiritual counseling to individuals or groups as a potential element of their socio-political work, for instance, when they support social activists, as in such cases the impact of counseling may be felt beyond the individual, in the public domain.

Impediments to doing socio-political work in chaplaincy

While the respondents in the study by Heethaar (2022) feel a strong drive to do socio-political work, they also point out different types of impediments. First, at a personal level, an impeding factor is the amount of energy and perseverance that it takes to aim for socio-political change. Respondents also mention feeling powerless when it comes to political engagement. The immense amount of injustice in the world may, at times, seem overpowering and have a paralyzing effect. Second, several barriers to doing socio-political work are related to the profession of chaplaincy itself. Respondents indicate that, as chaplains, they are trained to recognize and do justice to the moral complexity involved in all kinds of situations. Speaking out in public entails the danger of reducing this complexity. Also, the crucial task of chaplains to offer sanctuary to individuals is seen as a barrier to political engagement.[3] In principle, chaplains should not bring stories that were told to them in confidence out into the open. Third, respondents point to barriers related to working as a chaplain in an organization. Organizational rules may impede the possibility to go public with stories about struggles people face in the organization. Sometimes chaplains are requested not to speak out too explicitly and critically about politically sensitive issues. Furthermore, doing socio-political work may not be part of the task description of chaplains in an organization; the focus often is on individual spiritual care provision. Finally, respondents also speak about impediments related to the risks that are connected with doing socio-political work. Activist chaplains may, for instance, get arrested when they take part in demonstrations.

A chaplaincy method for strengthening disrupted communities

Let us now turn to the situation described at the beginning of this chapter – the earthquakes taking place in the north of the Netherlands due to gas extraction – and concentrate on the chaplaincy method which was developed by van Bergen (2023) while working as a chaplain here. The method is aimed at strengthening 'shattered communities' – communities which are disrupted due to challenging events or circumstances affecting all community members. It reflects a shift from an approach directed at individuals to an approach directed at the larger community and the relationships between community members. It consists of four interconnected elements.

Presence

The first element and starting point of the method is presence: immersing oneself in the lifeworld of people in the disrupted community.[4] Here, chaplains listen and learn. The goal is not to find people who need spiritual counseling but to try to get an understanding from the inside: what is going on here, in the lives of the people who experience the disruption of the community? What is the dynamic within the community? This involves learning about the different discourses and languages people use to describe disorienting experiences and circumstances in their lives. Usually, it is not clear beforehand what the best places are for being present in a shattered community. Presence therefore comprises an uncertain process of finding out where to go in order to get a broad picture of disorienting experiences across different groups in a shattered community.

> In the Dutch earthquake area, our chaplaincy team recognized the importance of presence as we tried to reach individuals in need of spiritual counseling. Groningen has a scattered population, consisting mostly of people who are not very talkative and keep to themselves. There was no obvious way to know beforehand which people were most in need of spiritual care. We therefore decided to find out what meetings were organized about the earthquake problem by institutions, local governments, and civilians organizing themselves, and to attend such meetings whenever possible. This allowed us to come into contact with many different people and gather numerous bits and pieces of understanding about how the earthquakes affected their lives.

Sharing community narratives

The second and central element of the method consists of collecting and sharing community narratives. In their presence work, chaplains meet with people from all layers of society and hear their stories. They analyze and reformulate these stories, highlighting the existential depth in what people tell. The idea is to arrive at 'community narratives': narratives which express shared existential concerns related to the events or circumstances disrupting the community, reflecting collective aspects of individual experiences.[5] The chaplains then share these narratives in the community, searching for and using channels by which members in a particular community may be reached. The goal of sharing community narratives is to offer language to community members for recognizing and verbalizing their existential struggles, and to empower communities to find ways to collectively handle existential damage.[6] This is in line with the three goals of chaplaincy at the macrolevel of communities and society which were formulated in Chapter 3. First, community narratives highlight shared existential concerns people struggle with, thus expressing a view of human beings as disorientable – as fallible and vulnerable. Second, community narratives may serve as input for dialogue among all parties in a shattered community as they represent different voices across the community, including those which are not easily heard in the public domain. Third, community narratives may feed into community projects in which people try new ways of healing the disrupted community.

When people in the Dutch earthquake area talk about the consequences of the earthquakes, they usually talk about material consequences. The existential dimension of these consequences is not so easily articulated. In our chaplaincy team, the stories we heard during presence work were shared, analyzed, and reworked into community narratives. These narratives are not primarily about cracks in houses but about cracks in lives, relationships, and the community. Shared existential concerns figuring in these narratives are, for instance, feeling that one's existence does not count, losing trust in people and in life, losing hope, not being able to work towards one's life goals, experiencing loneliness, feeling guilty and ashamed about not managing to be a good partner, parent, family member, or friend. We then shared these narratives during our presence work, when talking to people in the street or during meetings. We also used local media – radio, television, media websites, and written press – and developed our own social media channels. Furthermore, we participated in research about the consequences of the earthquakes. Our stories were then picked up by national media, confronting all inhabitants of the Netherlands, including those who felt that the earthquakes in the remote province of Groningen were none of their business, with stories about the existential damage experienced by inhabitants of the earthquake area, and with their own entanglement in these stories.

As van Bergen (2023) argues, chaplains, when collecting and sharing community narratives, need to emphatically stay out of the victim–perpetrator dynamic which is at play in disrupted communities. She refers to work by Ganzevoort (2017, 2018) who explains that people who are the victim of faceless systemic forces will attribute the role of perpetrator to (an) actual other(s) to be able to deal with emotions like anger, indignation, or resentment. So, people will assign the perpetrator role to certain people around them, who will in turn feel victimized and accuse the original victim of being a perpetrator or assign the perpetrator role to other people around them. In this way the disruption in the community keeps expanding and deepening. According to Ganzevoort, in order to counter this movement, chaplains need to consistently adopt the position of a bystander, refusing to identify as a victim or a perpetrator and resisting the call of others to appoint victims or perpetrators.

Adopting the position of a bystander allows chaplains to connect with everyone involved, whether they are seen as perpetrators or as victims, and embody the possibility of transcending the victim-perpetrator dynamic.

The chaplain is thus a committed bystander who invites community members, professionals, and politicians to recognize their involvement in this dynamic and look at each other beyond assigned victim-perpetrator roles. From the committed bystander position, chaplains may make a moral appeal to everyone involved to acknowledge their own contribution to the dynamic of expanding disruption and to accept responsibility for opposing the disruption and acting accordingly. They may thus initiate dialogues about experiences of suffering damage which are not framed in terms of pointing out who is a victim and who is a perpetrator, and which are directed at the question of how damaging and suffering in the community may be reduced. In this way, community narratives may be developed and renewed (van Bergen, 2023).

Forging structural partnerships

A third element of the chaplaincy method of strengthening shattered communities consists of forging partnerships with professionals, politicians, and organizations. Collaborating with people and organizations who also have an eye for the existential damage in a shattered community allows chaplains to increase their impact. This is a matter of mobilizing power in the sense of the ability to 'act in concert' (Arendt, 1970; see the introduction to this chapter). Forging structural partnerships involves actively connecting with professionals, politicians, and organizations during presence work. Chaplains may also build structural partnerships by retelling community stories: professionals, politicians, and all kinds of community-based organizations may thus be alerted to the work chaplains do and reach out to them for different kinds of support.

> When members of our chaplaincy team started to appear in local and national media, professionals dealing with psychological and social problems related to gas extraction, local and national politicians, and organizations established by inhabitants got to know what chaplaincy in the Dutch earthquake area is about. Between 2022 and 2024, the number of organizations that expressed interest in cooperation with us grew exponentially. More and more professionals refer people to our chaplaincy team when they struggle with existential issues. Furthermore, we train professionals to recognize existential damage, we help establish community projects, and we give workshops at conferences. We also regularly support local or national politicians and professionals or volunteers involved in the various organizations which have to do with gas extraction in weighing moral decisions.

Spiritual counseling

Even though the method represents a shift in focus from individuals to the community, spiritual counseling is still an inherent element of the method. Here, rather than being the central issue of chaplaincy work, it results from the other three elements of the method as a 'by-product.'

As the members of our chaplaincy team in the earthquake area in the Netherlands became familiar faces among inhabitants and professionals, people in need of spiritual counseling more easily came into contact with us. People either contacted us directly or were referred to us, both for long-term counseling and crisis counseling. As we started to recognize the perpetrator–victim dynamic in the community through which existential damage was transferred between members of the community, and also to family members, friends, professionals, and politicians outside of the community, we decided to exclude nobody beforehand from spiritual counseling. The primary focus was still on the inhabitants of the earthquake area, but everyone who was somehow involved and in need of spiritual support was welcome.

Finally, the temporal scope of this chaplaincy method extends beyond the period in which challenging events or circumstances occur. Community members and future generations may struggle with existential concerns long after the crisis is over, so that communities remain in need of renewing community narratives.

In 2023, the Dutch government adopted a law which forbade gas extraction in the Dutch earthquake area. This was a huge victory for the people in Groningen, the result of decades of activism. However, inhabitants also had mixed feelings: it will take over a decade to dismantle the installations; nobody knows when the earthquakes will stop after closing the installations; many houses still need reinforcement and new damage still occurs. It was clear that the impact of the earthquakes would be felt in the community for decades to come. When national politicians came to Groningen in 2023 to symbolically sign copies of the law, we chaplains, having attained a good working relationship with several of them, arranged that we were included in the program. We got the last time slot and thus the final word. In our contribution, we initiated a ritual involving a small apple tree which had germinated in the soil of Groningen. The tree will be touring through the province of Groningen and, eventually, will be planted in a symbolic spot where it can grow into a big tree, blossom, and bear fruit.

Conclusion

In this chapter, we explored the socio-political dimension of chaplaincy, which concerns the humanizing task that chaplains have at the level of communities and society. To summarize our findings, we describe political chaplaincy work in terms of the five phases of good care, distinguished by Tronto (1993, 2013): caring about, taking care of, care giving, care receiving, and caring with (see Table 10.1).

Political chaplaincy work starts with the phase of 'caring about' – noticing unmet care needs in chance encounters and planned meetings. This requires attentiveness to how existential struggles of people are interwoven with macrosystems and macrostructures. Chaplains need to be able to notice and clarify how dehumanization and systemic injustice resonate in personal stories about suffering. In the second phase of taking responsibility for meeting the needs that are noticed, 'taking care of,' the political work of chaplains starts with wondering what good chaplaincy consists of in this situation – whether listening is sufficient or whether systemic issues need to be addressed. This phase has to do with recognizing that it is not sufficient to be a 'compassionate witness' when it comes to suffering arising from systemic forces (LaMothe, 2019). The third phase of political

Table 10.1 Phases of socio-political chaplaincy work

Phase of care (Tronto, 2013)	Phase of socio-political work in chaplaincy
Caring about	Being attentive to how existential struggles of people are interwoven with macrosystems and macrostructures
Taking care of	Recognizing that it is not sufficient to be a 'compassionate witness' when it comes to suffering arising from systemic forces
Care giving	Initiating and performing activities in the public domain that are grounded in a worldview perspective, i.e., these activities need to: • Reflect actual struggles of actual human beings. • Advocate for nuanced views and inclusion of all voices in public dialogues. • Go hand in hand with reflection on the chaplain's motivation to do socio-political work.
Care receiving	Always again evaluating one's socio-political work with the people on whose behalf one addresses systemic issues
Caring with	Initiating public dialogue about the existential impact of politics with a view to fostering social connection and social justice

chaplaincy work consists of actually doing political work in the public domain. While this work may take a variety of forms, what characterizes socio-political work in chaplaincy is that it is grounded in a worldview perspective. This means that the political activities of chaplains (1) reflect issues that human beings actually struggle with; (2) promote nuanced views and inclusion of all voices in public dialogues; and (3) go hand in hand with reflection on the chaplain's motivation to do socio-political work. The fourth phase of good care – 'care receiving' – can be recognized in the method for strengthening disrupted communities described earlier. Here presence provides an opportunity for chaplains to always again evaluate how the community narratives that they distill from the many stories they hear in the community resonate with various community members, and whether these narratives are in need of revision. More generally, it seems crucial for chaplains doing socio-political work to always again evaluate their work with the people on whose behalf they speak and act. Finally, we saw how the fifth phase of good care – 'caring with' – may be practiced by chaplains in the method for strengthening disrupted communities by means of sharing community narratives. The aim here is to initiate and support public dialogue about the existential impact of macrorealities, thus fostering social connection and social justice.

Take-home messages

• Providing spiritual care to communities and society is an integral part of chaplaincy.
• Reflect on your own motivation to do socio-political work and on your own involvement in dominant and potentially dehumanizing discourses.
• Socio-political chaplaincy work needs to be grounded in presence and careful listening.
• In your socio-political work, take a positive view of power as "the human ability not just to act but to act in concert" (Arendt, 1970, p. 44).
• When speaking out about an issue in public, keep questioning whether your message reflects the actual struggles and stories of the people concerning the issue in question.
• Remain focused on the existential aspects of these struggles and stories.
• When working in disrupted communities, remain at all times a committed bystander who is not caught up in the existing victim-perpetrator dynamic.

Notes

1 Geestelijke Verzorging Aardbevingsgebied Groningen [Chaplaincy Earthquake area Groningen]. See: www.gvagroningen.nl.

2 This aim is in line with the chaplaincy goals at the macrolevel that were identified in Chapter 3.
3 See Chapter 3 for an explanation of the sanctuary function in chaplaincy.
4 See also Chapter 4, where presence was described in relation to one-on-one encounters.
5 The existential dynamic related to confrontation with systemic violence, which is usually at play in disrupted communities, has been elaborated on by van Bergen (2009, 2010, 2011).
6 The methodical element of sharing community narratives is theoretically grounded in the work of victimologist Pemberton (2018), who underscores the importance of developing community narratives for stitching back together shattered communities.

References

Arendt, H. (1970). On violence. Harcourt.
Ganzevoort, R. R. (2017). The drama triangle of religion and violence. In E. Aslan & M. Hermansen (Eds.), Religion and violence (pp. 17–30). Springer.
Ganzevoort, R. R. (2018). Trauma, geweld en religie [Trauma, violence, and religion]. KSGV.
Gärtner, S. (2011). Prophetic pastoral care. Resistance potential in late modernity? In A. Dillen & A. Vandenhoeck (Eds.), Prophetic witness in world Christianities: Rethinking pastoral care and counseling (pp. 23–30). LIT Verlag.
Graham, L. K. (2014). Political dimensions of pastoral care in community disaster responses. Pastoral Psychology, 63, 471–488. https://doi.org/10.1007/s11089-013-0571-3
Heethaar, T. (2022). In het moeras of op de barricades? Een exploratieve studie naar het politieke werk dat humanistisch geestelijk verzorgers te doen hebben op macrolevel [In the swamp or on the barricades? An explorative study into the political work of humanist chaplains at the macrolevel]. [Master's thesis, University of Humanistic Studies]. In het moeras of op de barricades? — University of Humanistic Studies Research Portal (www.uvh.nl)
LaMothe, R. (2014). Pastoral counseling in the 21st century: The centrality of community. Journal of Pastoral Care & Counseling, 68(2), 1–17. https://doi.org/10.1177/154230501406800206
LaMothe, R. (2019). Giving counsel in a neoliberal-Anthropocene age. Pastoral Psychology, 68, 421–436. https://doi.org/10.1007/s11089-019-00867-4
Lee, K. S., & Gibson, D. (2021). Justice matters: Spiritual care and pastoral theological imaginations in times of the COVID-19 pandemic. Journal of Pastoral Theology, 31(2–3), 81–88. https://doi.org/10.1080/10649867.2021.2010993
Mouffe, C. (2005). On the political. Routledge.
Nolan, S. (2015). The chaplain as a 'hopeful presence.' Jessica Kingsley.
Pemberton, A., Aarten, P. G. M., & Mulder, E. (2018). Stories as property: Narrative ownership as key concept in victims' experiences with criminal justice. Criminology & Criminal Justice, 19(4), 404–420. https://doi.org/10.1177/1748895818778320
Rogers-Vaughn, B. (2013). Best practices in pastoral counseling: Is theology necessary? Journal of Pastoral Theology, 23(1), 1–26. https://doi.org/10.1179/jpt.2013.23.1.002

Rogers-Vaughn, B. (2016). *Caring for souls in a neoliberal age.* Palgrave MacMillan.

Schuhmann, C., & Damen, A. (2018). Representing the Good: Pastoral care in a secular age. *Pastoral Psychology, 67,* 405–417. https://doi.org/10.1007/s11089-018-0826-0

Sharp, M. (2019). *Creating resistances: Pastoral care in a postcolonial world.* Brill.

Shin, H. U. (2021). Dangerous encounters and reconciling stories: Responding pastorally to the dominant stories of the capitalistic market economy. *Pastoral Psychology, 70,* 107–124. https://doi.org/10.1007/s11089-021-00941-w

Tronto, J. (1993). *Moral boundaries. A political argument for an ethic of care.* Routledge.

Tronto, J. (2013). *Caring democracy: Markets, equality, and justice.* New York University Press.

van Bergen, M. (2009). Een ja-zegger worden. Bestaansbevestiging en levensbeaming in geestelijke verzorging [Becoming a yes-sayer. Confirmation and affirmation of life in chaplaincy]. *Handelingen, 36*(4), 16–25.

van Bergen, M. (2010). Zelfdoding en levensbeaming in vreemdelingenbewaring [Suicide and affirmation of life in the context of immigration detention]. In J. H. Mooren (Ed.), *De moed om te zien. Humanistisch Raadswerk in justitiële instellingen* (pp. 69–87). de Graaff.

van Bergen, M. (2011). De beklemming blijft: Humanistisch raadwerk in de vreemdelingenbewaring [The feeling of tightness remains: Humanist chaplaincy in the context of immigration detention]. In P. Vlug & M. van Bergen (Eds.), *Humanisme en kwaad: Reflecties op het humanistisch raadswerk bij justitie* (pp. 27–45). SWP.

van Bergen, M. (2023). Rampen en crises als trage ontwrichting [Disasters and crises as slow disruption]. In W. Krikilion & A. Braam (Eds.), *Veerkracht in tijden van collectieve crisis* (pp. 63–88). KSGV.

Vandenhoeck, A. (2011). Introduction. In A. Dillen & A. Vandenhoeck (Eds.), *Prophetic witness in world Christianities: Rethinking pastoral care and counseling* (pp. 7–12). LIT Verlag.

Appendix
Vignettes

Marishelle Lieberwerth

Below are the six vignettes of humanist chaplaincy in the Netherlands, of which fragments are provided in the theoretical chapters (see Chapters 1, 2, and 3) to illustrate the theory. For each vignette, the perspectives of the chaplain and of the client are given.

VIGNETTE 1   Marriage rituals

Chaplain

Chris, a humanist chaplain and celebrant, is meeting with Noa and Robin. Noa and Robin want to have a humanist ceremony. "It is up to the couple whether they consider it a wedding or a different ceremony that celebrates love and expresses commitment. It can be a ceremony to celebrate a milestone in a relationship or a vow renewal, for example," Chris explains. It is Chris's second meeting with the couple. Chris is learning about who they are as individuals and as a couple, how they met, and what they find important. They are also planning the ceremony together: what texts, songs, and rituals would they like to incorporate, and what do these represent for the couple? During the ceremony, Chris will tell their love story. "But it is not just the ceremony that is important. Our time leading up to the ceremony is just as important. I am there to guide the couple during this time in their life when they look at the past, present, and future. It is about two people deciding together: how are we choosing to live our lives? By talking this through I hope to strengthen their sense of self and unity."

Chris aims to create an entirely bespoke ceremony. "The focus is on the couple and their community. Not on a higher power or on formalities. There are no predetermined structures or contents. It does not have to be anything other than what the couple wants it to be and wants it to mean," Chris stresses.

Humanism is not about strict rationality and atheism for Chris:
"Feelings and spirituality are important to my humanism and I under-
stand spirituality as a broad term. Spirituality can be anything that
makes someone feel connected in a transcendent way, to something
bigger, while still down-to-earth – or not. For example: if a couple wants
to honor their ancestors during the ceremony and either they feel like
their ancestors are watching over them or they feel this connection in
the sense of gratitude for what their ancestors have done to make their
current lives possible ... both can be examples of spirituality, if you ask
me. I adjust my ceremonies to be as spiritual or down-to-earth as the
couple wants. But there is also down-to-earth spirituality – connecting
with each other. That is important to my humanism."

"I draw from texts written by humanist thinkers, but also other
people who advocated for things that are of value in humanism.
Humanist values play a role in how I go about guiding couples. Most
importantly, reverence for humans as equal individuals but not just
individuals. We are social creatures, we need each other. Community is
everything. People want these ceremonies because they want to share
their story, they want to involve people in their story, they need others
to help them with their story. At the end of the ceremony, I ask if the
couple's loved ones promise to support the couple, and the guests say
'we do.' It is a fun and lovely moment."

Clients

It is Noa and Robin's wedding day. They are sat next to each other in a
circle with their guests. Across from them sits Chris, a humanist cele-
brant. Noa and Robin wanted a secular wedding. "A civil ceremony
with a civil servant seemed a bit dull and not personal enough. We
wanted something that allowed us to involve our loved ones more. Our
humanist celebrant had lots of ideas for this," Robin explains. "It is
amazing to be in love and make this commitment. It is also a lot to
wrap my head around. We really found each other and are taking this
step together, wow," Noa shares.

Their guests have sent in ribbons with wishes written on them, and
the ribbons have been braided together. The braided ribbons are
wrapped around Noa and Robin's hands. Chris explains that this sym-
bolizes how they are bound together and supported by their loved
ones. They exchange vows. The afternoon proceeds with speeches,
recitations, music, and dancing. There is also an empty canvas for
everyone to paint on throughout the afternoon. "With the humanist
celebrant, we designed a ceremony entirely suited to us. We had lots
of time for our guests to give speeches. Our humanist celebrant also
helped us by suggesting poems, readings, and music to use during

the ceremony. Touches like this were what made it more personal. From the beginning, leading up to the ceremony … Talking about our story, what we are promising each other, and how to celebrate – that helped us be more present during it all," Robin says at the end of the day.

"Throughout the process, Chris asked thoughtful questions that helped us think about what our relationship means to us and what kind of life we want to build together. We are not getting married because of God or simply because of legal and economic reasons, so what exactly does it mean for us to have this ceremony? Although we are both certain this is what we want, and it is wonderful and feels right, it can feel like a big step to merge lives and promise to do life together. How will we go about that, how will we maintain and grow who we are as individuals and as a couple? Taking the time to reflect on all this for ourselves and together has helped us understand where we are in our lives and what we are aiming for," Noa adds.

VIGNETTE 2   Elderly care

Chaplain

Nathan walks around the living room of the care home, stopping to greet the residents. The care home offers adult day care, housing care, and rehabilitation. Nathan is often asked what his job exactly entails. "The core of it is being present to talk about life, specifically a meaningful life, when people are in a care home. It is not always a pleasant place to be. Many of my clients miss home. They do not feel at home here, or struggle to still feel at home anywhere. They do not get to decide much and they cannot do much for themselves – permanently or temporarily. That is a difficult way to live: they are fragile, perhaps close to death, and at the same time they lack rooting. To deal with our fragility, we need to feel rooted in something. They do not feel very rooted here. Through our conversations, I hope to give them some sense of rooting. They are also often quite lonely. So I try to find connection where there is an excess of solitude. We talk about what they struggle with and what keeps them going, and we try to discover what a meaningful life can look like within these walls." One of his newer clients, Mrs. Smith, just moved in a month ago. Last time they talked about how she hated being in the care home but still preferred it over her daughter's caring for her. She preferred it because she does not want to be a burden to them, as she considers it her job to take care of them. Still, she feels somewhat abandoned here.

Many of Nathan's clients struggle to hold a conversation, let alone speak about the existential. With them, Nathan is happy to talk about their day or even a small detail, or to sit in silence. "The relation comes first – without it, we cannot explore the existential. The relational is valuable in itself," he says. One client, sitting by herself, tells him: "I won a prize." Nathan sits with her. "Oh wow! What did you win?" Nathan asks. "A pancake. We played bingo and I won a pancake. They are making it for me now," she explains. Nathan looks over at the kitchen. He sees no pancake batter, and it smells like fried fish. He looks back at the client and nods: "do you like sweet or savory pancakes?" The client unzips the toiletry bag she has been holding. "I am getting a pancake. My husband makes them with apple slices," she answers, rummaging through the toiletry bag. They continue talking, Nathan following her lead from the pancake to her husband to the items in her toiletry bag. Nathan does not know what this client was like before dementia and therefore just tries to join her where she is: "I think it is easier for me than for the family because I do not know exactly how she has changed." Other clients do not talk at all or are hard to understand: "Even when I have a hard time understanding them, I will keep trying my best to understand them. I want them to feel like they are worth listening to." Nathan also often connects with clients through music: "music contains slices of life that we can feel and recognize together. Listening together, sometimes holding hands, I see our shared human vulnerability. I might not know exactly what they feel or think then. But I know there is something known to both of us, intuitively, in that moment."

Recently, someone told Nathan they could not listen to old people all day. "Old or young ... Our shared human vulnerability and strength is a source of inspiration to me. From that place, I approach the person in front of me and I am reminded that there is a lot I can share with them. To me, it is about connecting with someone. Whether the client really grasps it or not. Humans need each other for the world to make sense, and they need more than management of their bodies because they are more than an old or sick body. My only goal is to help them feel rooted for a while – in their past, or in their present, or in our bond. It is not about a coherent story or new insights. It is about person-to-person finding something we can share."

Client

Mrs. Smith just moved into the care home a month ago. The move to a care home is a profound change. She could not take all her furniture and belongings. Her bed does not feel like hers. And where did her children leave all her items while unpacking? She has a hard time recognizing her new surroundings and all these new faces – it is making it harder for things to stick. If only they had let her stay home. Although she did start to feel scared at home by herself and kept having embarrassing accidents. If only they had let her unpack her own things. However, she does get so tired. She does not want to be here, making it all the more frustrating that she cannot seem to align for herself everything that is happening to her to find a path back to the way things were. Everything feels out of her grasp recently: her surroundings, her possessions, her thoughts, the people around her. If only she could do more, but she cannot and she does not want to burden her children. So she finally said yes to the move.

Mrs. Smith is sitting on the balcony when a man approaches her. "Good morning, Mrs. Smith. It's Nathan, the chaplain from last week. May I join you?" Nathan asks. Mrs. Smith seems a bit unsure – she has seen many new faces in a short time – but she nods. "Last week you told me about your move here and your three daughters. We talked about how it has been for you here," Nathan offers, as he sits down. Mrs. Smith's eyes widen, remembering now. Today, Mrs. Smith shares that she is having a hard time adjusting, and that she is unhappy about the bland meals: "I would not serve such meals to my guests!" she vents. "Is it important to you to host and cook for guests?" Nathan asks. Mrs. Smith talks about what she would serve her daughters and grandchildren and beams with pride as she tells him stories: "all the kitchen counters – covered in dishes!" She sighs and looks out the window. "But that is in the past. I guess I am just an old granny stuck in this place now," Mrs. Smith tells Nathan. "Is that how you feel, just an old granny stuck here?" Nathan asks. Mrs. Smith nods and shrugs, a sad look on her face. "I think you are much more than that. You carry everything from your past with you. That is not gone just because your life looks different now," Nathan suggests. Before Nathan leaves, they come up with the plan to send her children a recipe book so they can make a favorite dish of hers and bring it to the care home to enjoy together. Nathan does not confuse her as much as other people. Nor does he cut her stories short because she has already told him something and he is tired of hearing it. He does not tell her she is wrong about something. He does not seem to ask of her: "remember how we used to …?" When she worries about what is to come, how to deal with aging and this feeling of things being out of her grasp, talking to Nathan and sharing the things she holds onto, the things that brought her joy and pain and strength in her life, helps her feel more at ease.

VIGNETTE 3   Abortion

Chaplain

Kimberly has been working as a humanist chaplain for ten years. "I see my job as being a conversational partner in my clients' search for a meaningful life when confronted with questions about life. It is especially in times of difficulty that people may lose their foundations, their steady ground – for instance, when they experience a sudden loss. Or when they carry something around with them that makes them feel estranged from daily life, their body, and others – like abortion. I offer my clients space to feel and say what they might be holding back, in fear of offending, hurting, or scaring off others, or in fear of being misunderstood and judged." In her work, Kimberly is inspired by humanist values: she believes in and strives to nourish the power, potential, connectedness, dignity, and freedom of humans. A consequence of this is that she does not view herself as an expert with answers and solutions. Instead, she sees the client as her equal: while she is the expert on meaning in life in general, the client is the expert on what a meaningful life is to them.

It is the first group meeting for people who have had an abortion. "I would like for us to go around and introduce ourselves and please share: what brings you here today? My name is Kimberly. I am 35. My partner and I have a three-year-old son. I work as a humanist chaplain, meaning that I help guide reflection on life questions that we all encounter. I had an abortion six years ago. That is what brings me here today: guiding our reflection on abortion and all the questions and changes it brings about in us." In preparation, Kimberly has asked the participants to bring something that is meaningful to them regarding their abortion, for instance, an object, a song, or a poem. "Let us have a moment to silently reflect on the meaningful thing we brought today. Then we will go around and share. You do not have to share what you brought or what makes it meaningful to you if you are not ready to share." The first participant has brought a light blue gemstone: "my sister gave it to me afterwards. I hold it in my hands every now and then, to remember. Sometimes I do this when I am sad and wish things were different. At other times, I do this when I am happy in my life and it is like I want to tell them so they know I still think about them." The next participant has brought a picture of two positive pregnancy tests: "when I saw the test turn positive, it was like everything came crashing down on me. I had no idea if I could be a mother. I suddenly felt so

small and at other times I felt like I could do it. I still have not had children and I do not know how I will feel about having a child now."
Kimberly responds to their stories: *"abortion is a confrontation with our fragility and identity, many come to reconsider their view on the future and life."* Kimberly shares that she got a tattoo a few months after the abortion: *"it symbolizes my loss and transformation. Getting an abortion changed me. This tattoo makes that visible. That is something I missed: some visible mark that this happened to me. Though I do not always share exactly what the tattoo means if I do not feel like it. It just helps me feel in touch with what happened, when I look at it. Who would like to share something they have done that helped them?"* During the final meeting, Kimberly invites the group to write a letter to themselves and/or the child that could have been.

Outside of these group meetings, the participants have felt relief, grief, guilt, and more, but have often not found space in themselves or with others to speak about this. *"Abortion stories can also be stories of strength and agency,"* Kimberly states. Kimberly hopes that the participants feel a reconnection with themselves, their loss, and what they find meaningful, and that they can articulate what their choice and loss mean to them in their life story. One participant writes: *"abortion helped make me who I am today: successful and content in my career, a more conscious and grateful mother, and someone who understands the complexities of life better."*

Client

Anna, 26, decided to end a pregnancy when she was 20. Though Anna feels that she understood what she chose at the time, there was no way of knowing the full meaning of this decision. With time, her abortion experience changed with her. However, Anna would not speak much about the abortion after it happened, her experience remaining this unclear ball of feelings and thoughts she carried. She felt that she had to be silent about it, as others might be uncomfortable around the topic – like everyone should just silently move on. She felt that if she did speak about it, she could only do so either in an entirely certain and relieved manner or in an apologetic guilt-riddled way. On a bulletin board, she spotted a poster about an abortion group meeting guided by a humanist chaplain. She did not know what a humanist chaplain was, but the poster mentioned a safe space for joint reflection on abortion experiences and questions raised by this experience.

The humanist chaplain, Kimberly, had asked the participants to bring something meaningful in relation to their abortion to the group meeting. Anna selected a song. During the session, she shares: "I listened to this a lot while I was trying to make up my mind. It covers all the confusing things I felt at the time. I still listen to it sometimes, to allow myself to feel it again because sometimes I feel so simultaneously distant from it and affected by it." The chaplain asks: "when you listen to this song and the feelings come back to you, where do you feel it in your body?" Only then does Anna become explicitly aware of this, and she places a hand on her chest as the feeling grows inside her. Kimberly repeats the question for all group members: "where does everyone feel this in their body?" Some indicate feelings in their womb, some in their heart or chest, one participant describes a heaviness in her legs and a weakness in her arms. They all take a moment to sit with these feelings. Next, Kimberly asks the group to discuss in pairs: "reflecting on the meaningful things you brought to this session, what do you find meaningful in your life?" Anna shares that she finds her relationships meaningful, she sees it as her life's purpose to connect with people and make them feel heard. She finds it sad that not speaking about her abortion sometimes troubles this sense of connection which she finds so meaningful, as though she only ever tries to make others feel understood while she does not feel entirely understood herself.

Anna found the group meetings a positive experience that helped her look at her abortion experience with more clarity, recognizing more of the layers in her feelings and thoughts. The humanist chaplain's remarks about abortion being a life experience which asks for a reorientation in life that deals with impossibility and possibility, loss and life, fragility and empowerment, made Anna feel validated. Through sharing her experience of abortion, it went from cloaked in isolation, shame, and guilt, to something she had a better understanding of as a part of herself and her life. For example, it was helpful to her how the humanist chaplain repeated how the complexity of their abortion experiences did not need to be reduced to something one-dimensional and how she encouraged an exploration of the full experience. The humanist chaplain also helpfully put into words that abortion did not just have to make her stronger – it could make her stronger and simultaneously bring her more in touch with her fragility, pain, sadness, and uncertainty. What stayed with Anna was that everyone in the group felt that every group member was entitled to feel sad about the abortion, something which Anna had not always allowed herself to feel. Anna was happy to find that she could connect with others through their shared experiences and that she could help other group members feel understood.

VIGNETTE 4   Euthanasia

Chaplain

Lucas is on a home visit. "As a chaplain, I often come in when someone is facing something tragic – when things are out of control, cannot be solved, or there is no way out. I am with people in their loneliness, fears, and hopelessness. Although it is not just that. I am also with people in their happiness." Today, Lucas is visiting Jonas, who had his euthanasia request approved. The Netherlands allows requests for physician-assisted dying in cases of severe, unbearable suffering from a physical or psychiatric illness. "People who request physician-assisted dying often encounter people who want to fix the situation and encourage them to stay – through medication, treatment plans, peptalks, prayers, practical help. That is not what I do. I join them in that difficult place, I listen and ask. Then I watch what happens between the two of us."

Lucas has come in through the back door. Sometimes, when he arrives, Jonas is still asleep; at other times, Jonas sees him approach through the window. Lucas and Jonas usually start off the conversation by talking about how Jonas is feeling today. Today, Jonas quickly moves on to what is to be his last conversation with his sister-in-law. Jonas feels some pressure to get these last conversations right, and has asked Lucas to help him work out what he wants to say. Lucas asks him about his relationship with his sister-in-law. "I never had a sister, but I got to have a sister-in-law and that felt special to me," Jonas says. "Special?" Lucas asks. "Yes, she looked out for me, and she was not afraid to ask me serious, personal questions. And she let me look out for her, so I felt important to her too. And I do not have to worry about my brother as much. He gets all worked up about things. I know I can trust her to take care of him. Now that I am talking about it, I realize I appreciate the care she showed us all. I think I will tell her that."

Lucas and Jonas spend a lot of time exploring Jonas's life story. They cover the proudest, saddest, and also more mundane moments in his life; his hopes, fears, identity, and relationships. Lucas considers it a privilege to guide Jonas in these reflections. However, he does not always find it easy to do so: "It can be emotionally hard work. I have to be careful that I do not get stuck in the heavy, tragic feelings to a point where it gets too hard to guide reflection on life's big themes and questions. As a humanist, I support people's autonomy and thus the possibility of dying with dignity. I believe everyone has the right to choose for themselves how to live and die, and I believe that there are no ready-made answers to questions about life and death, only the answers we formulate and reformulate for ourselves. Human relationality is of immeasurable value, so when meeting with others, I focus on the connection between us and ask about meaningful connections to other humans and non-humans in their life. Amidst suffering, I want to give people some moments to experience the joy and beauty and connection in being human. I do not immediately move on to: 'so you want to die, alright.' We actually spend a lot of time talking about their life: who are you? That helps us look at how that individual wants to die with dignity, honoring their life and value as a human being."

Jonas is getting tired, nodding off in his chair. Lucas squeezes his hand and Jonas softly squeezes back. Lucas takes his mug to the kitchen, washes it, and places it back in the cupboard – careful not to wake Jonas. "I would not claim I have any solutions at all. I do not have an answer key or playbook. I cannot fix the situation. Sometimes that is difficult when I see so much suffering. All I hope to do is show people that they do not have to face this alone, and that together we can try to find words for what they are experiencing; so that they feel less stuck and alone in their muddled thoughts and feelings, without necessarily having to change those thoughts and feelings."

Client

Jonas is incurably ill, and these past months, every day has been harder than the day before. He no longer feels like himself and no longer looks like himself. "This is not me," he says over and over. Whatever sparks kept him going before, they cannot carry him further. "I felt myself get tighter, heavier, knotted, and weaker inside. I feel lost and powerless because my body is not mine anymore. It is hard to be here when I feel like this and I no longer know why I am here. This is not the life I want and I am not myself. I want to let go now."

Jonas has been talking to Lucas, a humanist chaplain, for the past few months. Lucas is not afraid to ask him questions about his wish to die, but never gives him the feeling that he questions whether Jonas really wants to die or should die this way. This is a relief to Jonas, who has felt like he had to convince people of his death wish. They also make jokes while talking. Jonas started by cautiously cracking some jokes about his approaching death with a slight smile. Seeing a smile appear on Lucas's face encouraged him to make more jokes, and their laughter grew bolder with time.

Jonas felt immensely relieved when his request for euthanasia was approved. He can see an end to his suffering now. "I was used to having control over my life. And then I worked on accepting that I do not have control over my illness. Now I want some control again. I do not *have the duty to stay alive, right? Knowing there is a foreseeable end to this, on my terms, gives me new space and strength to look at what I want in these last weeks." However, sometimes it does not just feel like relief. Jonas grew up Catholic and he sometimes worries that maybe he is doing something wrong. He thought he did not believe in God anymore and he did not think about afterlife much – until faced with death. His mother and extended family are all Catholic, and while they try to be as supportive as they can, they do struggle to fully understand his decision. All of this he discusses with Lucas. "Sometimes they say: 'but you had doubts about euthanasia!' Yes, but if I did not consider my doubts, it would not have been a well-considered choice, right? At the same time, it does not really feel like a choice," he says. "What would make it a choice to you?" Lucas asks. "I guess … If life and death felt like equal options, rather than life shutting me out and death chasing me. Then I would have more of a choice. But I am still choosing to go on my own terms, as much as possible. I worry that if I admit that it is all a bit muddled and that sometimes I feel a bit scared about dying, I will make it harder for everyone," Jonas replies, and exhales. Lucas remains calm and inquisitive. Sometimes, Lucas also expresses that he is moved by Jonas. It makes Jonas feel a bit lighter that all of this can be discussed openly.*

It gives Jonas peace of mind that he is taking time with Lucas to go over his memories, his regrets, his proudest moments, and what matters most to him. It helps him feel reconnected to himself – the self that was not so sick – and find out what his current self wants during these last weeks. "I have friends, family, and a chaplain who are on this final leg of my journey with me. Something good has come of this suffering: I am having some of the most valuable conversations of my life. Still, it does not make my suffering bearable. It is time for me to go." Jonas finds the courage to say things that he has never said out loud before. "Why have you felt like you could not share this with someone?" Lucas asks. Jonas ponders for a while, and they sit in silence. "Because I cared too much about what people would say. Now I do not mind so much anymore. I will be gone soon, and I do not want to spend much more time worrying," Jonas answers. "And if you told them now, what would that be like for you?" Lucas asks. "I think I will tell them these things. To be known for who I am, both the good and the bad parts, is better than to not be known at all. I feel like that is what it is all about. While I can … I would like to be known," Jonas shares. Lucas nods and asks: "And how would you like to be known? Who are you?" Jonas smiles: "I am someone who has a lot of love to give."

VIGNETTE 5   Ecogrief

Chaplain

In a lodge located in the woods, humanist chaplain Lilian is placing postcards on a table. The postcards depict somewhat surrealist landscapes and natural objects. Lilian offers a series of group meetings for climate activists who feel affected by the dire state of the planet. She aims to offer a sanctuary of solidarity and recognition for these people whose wellbeing is affected because of the ecological crisis. She explains: "there are no diagnostic tests or treatment plans involved. The participants' worries about climate change are entirely reasonable. This is about the participants entering into empathetic dialogue with each other, finding moments of rest, and getting their bearings for their continued coping and activism." In her work, Lilian is inspired by an ecohumanist perspective on life on this planet: she sees the value of all life forms, and sees human beings as a humble part of and connected to all life on earth. She also draws from indigenous views on land and water: "there is acknowledgment of what nature has to teach us and what it has done for us, showing a reciprocal and interdependent relationship with nature."

At the group's first meeting, Lilian invites the participants to pick a postcard in which they recognize some of their feelings and uncertainties about the ecological crisis, and to reflect on these feelings and uncertainties. She then invites them to share their reflections. One participant says: "I have always wanted children. I no longer think I can, knowing what kind of planetary devastation future generations will be affected by." Another participant shares: "I always saw myself as an optimistic person. Then I started watching documentaries on climate change that opened my eyes to the effects of climate change that are already visible today. Now things just feel meaningless. Why do I try? At the same time, I feel too anxious not to try and do my part for our planet." This exchange evokes many reactions in participants. Some sit upright, raise their voices, and chime in. One participant describes a heaviness coming over her which she often tries to keep at bay, but now she is comforted by how this heaviness is also carried by others, and she sits back as if to rest.

During the second meeting, Lilian invites the group for a walk outside. The participants are happy to enjoy nature together. During the walk, Lilian invites the group members to reflect together on the question: "what is a source of strength for you?" Through this question, Lilian focuses on what is meaningful for the participants while navigating life on this planet in crisis. This is Lilian's priority: helping participants to make sense of daily reality and find sources of strength, allowing space for the bewildering abundance of experiences that life brings forth. With the participants, she engages in an exploration of what is a meaningful life to them, how their sense of a meaningful life is in crisis, and what sources of meaning or ideas about living a good life can guide them in the face of grief and fears about the climate. Lilian considers it a successful group meeting when participants feel supported and can express in all its complexity and ambiguity what a meaningful life in the face of climate grief is to them.

Client

Robert feels powerless. Articles pointing to doom fill his digital feed. Droughts, fires, and floods fill his thoughts. Anger, fear, and doubt are pent up in his body – sometimes making him irritable. Robert cannot look away from the climate crisis. "Why do others not seem concerned? Why do some find this funny? Why do people look away?" he wonders. He turns to climate activism, and it offers him some purpose and solace. Still, he asks himself: "what am I doing this for? We are doing too little too late." Robert decides to attend four group meetings provided by a humanist chaplain, Lilian. He wants support for dealing with all the feelings he has about the climate crisis.

In the group, the participants explore what their activism is aimed at, and what it costs them. Robert shares: "others see fruit, I see estimates of the costs to the planet of out of season fruit. Every time I take out my trash, I feel a knot in my stomach." The other participants agree with him and share similar experiences.

The group goes for a walk in nature. Lilian invites group members to tune in to their body and to open themselves up to any feelings that come up. Soon, Robert allows himself to grieve. A participant expresses that she feels a connection, a pull towards their natural surroundings – "it is so special, how can we sit back and watch this be destroyed?" Robert and other participants recognize this connection, and they are moved by their moment of shared appreciation for nature.

Robert brings up his guilt: "I feel guilty about some of the things I have done that were bad for the environment before I realized all this. And it does not even make sense to feel so guilty because it is so much bigger than me and I am doing everything I can now. Some big players are destroying the planet, lives, and livelihoods, and they are getting away with it – it is wrong! Even though it never feels like I do enough, I try anyway and I feel bad. It does not make sense." Lilian asks the group. "Do others share this conflict between what you feel and what you do and what makes sense?" and various group members reply in the affirmative. After some reflection, the group comes to the insight that maybe they should not put so much pressure on themselves for all their feelings, thoughts, and actions to make sense – they are trying to do what is right and that is enough to ask of themselves. They reflect on how they can both believe in this fight and simultaneously feel that the situation is hopeless. Lilian offers reflective questions, invites various perspectives from group members, and encourages the group to continue their exploration. Lilian makes sure the group also pays attention to sources of encouragement by introducing the question what brings them joy, or pride, or contentment.

On the last day, Lilian asks the group: "what have these meetings meant to you?" Robert finds himself thinking: while he has given up a lot for this fight, which at times feels discouraging, he has also gained special connections to the planet and to like-minded people because of it. He deeply enjoys the moments where nature seems to envelop him, revealing something wondrous to him – and that inspires him to care for nature in return. His renewed focus on this helps him feel grounded amidst his worry and feelings of powerlessness. Through sharing both despair and hope, sadness and joy, anger and humor with others, Robert feels strengthened. In a world that will not slow down, with devastation physically nearby and digitally at his fingertips, surrounded by people numb to it all, Robert has found moments of respite amongst kindred spirits. Lilian and the group have helped Robert find sources of strength to continue.

VIGNETTE 6   Moral injury

Chaplain

Noor is a humanist military chaplain, often working at military barracks and bases, including during missions and exercises. Noor's job is to address spiritual needs of military personnel, through existential conversations and by holding celebrations and memorials, both individually and in groups. Noor describes her work as offering "a landing spot," somewhere to rest and reroute together. "I do not think my work is very different from the work of, say, a Christian chaplain. Obviously, we agree on things such as compassion and so on. And if I say I believe in the power and value of humans, a Christian chaplain will agree with me to some degree, except they will place God above it all and that I will not do. I do not care to define humanism very much; to me it is something I do rather than something I can define. Everything about my work is humanism in practice to me. I help the person in front of me figure out what they do, feel, choose, think as they search for the right path. I do not claim to know what path they should take. We are all humans trying to find our way, and instead of seeing a uniform, I ask about the person in the uniform that I encounter and try to offer a landing spot for them to rest and reroute. Humanist institutions, doctrines, and so on are of less interest to me than the very practice of humans showing genuine interest in each other: 'who are you, what matters to you, how can I help you along?'"

For Noor, being at the military barracks and bases with the soldiers, dressed in uniform, is crucial. "Sometimes, people around soldiers are hesitant to find out what happened in their lives and work, and they are scared to ask questions. Or the soldiers are uncomfortable about sharing. I am not scared to ask and I see it happen up close. So I ask them about their youth, their training, their present, their future. I ask what happened on their missions and I ask what got them through, the meaning of camaraderie, their values and beliefs. It is not something they are all always immediately open about, but usually they warm up to me and welcome me as an insider. And I see the complexity: soldiers are an instrument of the state, the military world contains levels and layers that make everything a single soldier does so much more complex than individual choices."

Today, Noor is visiting Wesley, a veteran, at home. They have been in contact for three years now. They discuss the pressing questions that Wesley struggles with, about guilt, shame, powerlessness, betrayal, uncertainty, and identity. Noor says: "soldiers and veterans cannot help but feel attached to their identity as a soldier. They have a hard time figuring out who they are apart from that. But the military identity is also connected with pain, physically and mentally. When soldiers leave the military, they are in no man's land in a way. They feel like they are neither soldiers nor civilians. By talking through their life, we search for who they are now – shaped by the past, but not fully determined by that past. For example, by discussing how the values of a mission compare to their personal values, we map who they are, where they have been and where they are going."

According to Noor the significance of her work lies in being a neutral insider party who does not serve anyone but the soldiers themselves, and does so unconditionally. "I am not focused on getting people back to work, I do not represent politics or superiors, I am not thinking about treatment steps, timelines and success rates. This is also a humanist principle – I have no end point in mind when I work with these soldiers and veterans. Dealing with the effects of military missions is not linear, it can be messy and tangled and circular. When veterans like Wesley feel like they are out of options, I want them to feel that I am still here to listen and support."

Client

Wesley retired from the military three years ago. "I still feel guilty sometimes, and ashamed. I go back and forth a lot. Why was I on that mission, what was it for? I was a pawn in some game. At the same time, I said yes. I wanted to make a difference and thought I could do that by doing as I was told. I did things and I do not know what they were for, ultimately. Even more so, I am ashamed because I was unable to do things I think I should have done. There were kids who needed my help and I could not or did not help them. The question whether in fact I could not help them or did not help them haunts me sometimes. I was trained and I was armed to be powerful, yet I never felt so powerless." Experiences like this are what have made him reach out for help. "Anxiety, feeling lost, flashes of what happened, and I still feel powerless and betrayed sometimes. My psychiatrist told me: 'there is nothing more we can do for you.' There were no more treatment options left. That only made me feel more alone and like a burden. I wish I was doing well, I wish I knew what it was for and who I really am," Wesley says. Since just before his retirement, he has been in contact with Noor.

In Wesley's trauma treatments, the focus was often on details of what happened during his mission. This was helpful for him, but now he feels that it is important to take a more all-encompassing approach. "With the chaplain, we talk about everything and anything that comes up. My past, my present, my future. The chaplain knows all about my youth and my family, about the new hobbies I am trying out. I guess the chaplain asks me questions to reflect, without this idea of what is a normal and an abnormal response to what happened, without talking about disorder, without focusing on fixing something. I used to think I could be 'fixed' and I would go back to the way things were. Now I am making peace with the idea that it is possible and worthwhile to let go of some things and hold onto new things. Our conversations usually give me hope: there is more to come still."

Moreover, the chaplain feels like a safe and understanding person to Wesley. "Civilians have their opinions on what I did or what they think I did. But they can never really understand what it is like, as they have not been there. The chaplain does not fully know either, but at least the chaplain knows the military and has heard a lot of similar stories and has been out there with us on missions. She asks me questions to help me understand myself and what happened to me, whereas other people give their opinions and want me to give them clear answers so they can understand."

"I feel less lonely when I talk to Noor. I do not have to make it sound better or worse than it was, I do not need to be able to explain. She listens, asks questions, remembers and repeats what I said, and sometimes offers her perspective on things. Sometimes she pieces together two things I have said on separate occasions, and it helps me realize something about how I look at the world and feel about things. And she is not there to talk me back into service or other work or say what I should be doing with my life. She lets me take the lead and sometimes suggests that I try taking a left or a right or looking back on things from where I am now. I feel relief every time after we have talked. It is as if the space within me to hold onto things that are valuable is bigger but also like I can let go a bit of some stuff."

Index

Pages in **bold** refer to tables, and pages followed by n refer to notes.

For Product Safety Concerns and Information please contact our EU
representative GPSR@taylorandfrancis.com
Taylor & Francis Verlag GmbH, Kaufingerstraße 24, 80331 München, Germany

www.ingramcontent.com/pod-product-compliance
Lightning Source LLC
Chambersburg PA
CBHW050647280326
41932CB00015B/2808